Va

C000283312

Adults Abused as Children

Adults Abused as Children

Experiences of Counselling and Psychotherapy

Peter Dale

SAGE Publications
London • Thousand Oaks • New Delhi

© Peter Dale 1999

First published 1999

All rights reserved. No part of this publication may be reproduced, stored in a retrieval system, transmitted or utilized in any form or by any means, electronic, mechanical, photocopying, recording or otherwise, without permission in writing from the Publishers.

SAGE Publications Ltd
6 Bonhill Street
London EC2A 4PU

SAGE Publications Inc
2455 Teller Road
Thousand Oaks, California 91320

SAGE Publications India Pvt Ltd
32, M-Block Market
Greater Kailash – I
New Delhi 110 048

British Library Cataloguing in Publication data

A catalogue record for this book is available from the British Library

ISBN 0 7619 5998 X
ISBN 0 7619 5999 8 (pbk)

Library of Congress catalog card number 98-61270

Typeset by Photoprint, Torquay, Devon
Printed in Great Britain by Biddles Ltd, Guildford, Surrey

Contents

Foreword

Adults Abused as Children makes an important contribution to our understanding of how children are abused and how the consequences can be
carried into adulthood. The needs of adults who have been abused as
children have been much neglected and there is a need for a wider
debate on how this shortfall can be met.

Recent years have seen a growing awareness of the needs of adults
who were abused as children. An analysis of over one thousand letters
received by the independent National Commission of Inquiry into the
Prevention of Child Abuse (set up by the NSPCC) from adults who were
abused as children, graphically described the lasting impact that child
abuse can have. With great courage, many wrote about their experiences
for the first time. Many had never received any help or support to deal
with the devastating effects of the abuse that had been perpetrated. I
shall forever remember the woman who commented to the Commission:
'Today I live with a rage and sadness that rules my life. I feel I shall
never be a whole human being. My mum used to say you shouldn't live
in the past. I don't. The past lives in me.' It is tragic that fewer than half
of those writing to the Commission had been able as children to tell
someone about the abuse they were experiencing. Many suffered for
years in frightening silence. For many this continues into adulthood. This
situation is unacceptable and cannot be allowed to continue.

A sad indictment of our society in the 1990s was that too few abused
children received treatment. Our society has a debt to these people. They
deserve to receive treatment. They should have a right to it. We have a
long way to go before this can be fulfilled. The NSPCC is committed to
campaigning for every child who wants it to receive treatment and
where others are not making provision, we will do so.

The National Commission identified that there is a desperate shortage
of treatment for adults abused as children. In large parts of the UK there
are no services at all. We have heard of many cases of adults being
passed from one agency to another and still finding no help or support.
Many informal groups provide a valuable service but prove to be very
transient because of the lack of formal funding. The NSPCC will use its

influence to press for more therapeutic services to be developed. For that reason we are pleased to support the establishment of a national UK group, the National Association for People Abused in Childhood, of which I am a patron. NAPAC is seeking to ensure that quality services are widely available and will act as a clearing house for information on provision.

A small number of NSPCC projects, including that managed by Peter Dale, provide therapeutic services for adults abused as children. We believe this work to be important for the prevention of child abuse, for a number of reasons. Firstly, we have a great deal to learn from adults abused as children – what would have made a difference to their situation as children? To whom do they feel they can turn for help? What helps create resilient children? We can apply these lessons to developing strategies for preventing cruelty today. Much more effort needs to go into stopping abuse before it happens and in this adults who were abused as children have a contribution to make, based on their experience.

Secondly, these adults can be powerful advocates for children. They do not want their experiences to be inflicted on today's children. Treatment can enable adults who were abused to channel their painful experiences into positive outcomes. Everyone should have a responsibility for preventing child abuse and speaking up for children. Many adults who were abused are good examples of how we can all act to protect children more effectively.

Thirdly, professionals and service providers have a great deal to learn from adults who were abused, particularly in terms of how we can create non-stigmatizing and supportive services. Time and again children who have been abused and their families tell us how the formal 'child protection system' and the criminal justice process, which is meant to be supportive of their needs, is often experienced as remote, impersonal, controlling, and blaming. Informal, community-based sources of help are often seen as being more beneficial. Professionals, service planners, and decision-makers need to listen to adults who were abused as children in order to better understand how appropriate and supportive services and systems can be established.

Finally, while by no means all, a significant number of adults who were abused as children harm their own children. This can be prevented through providing effective therapeutic interventions. A larger number of adults who were abused as children report relationship difficulties with their partners and with their own children. These difficulties can put considerable pressures on families and this can mean that children are less resilient and perhaps vulnerable to abuse.

Services for adults abused as children are crucially important. This work is grossly under-resourced and it is to be deplored that many adults who were abused as children have to pay for their own treatment, at great cost, or do without. As Peter Dale shows, treatment and therapeutic interventions can be very effective. I believe that *Adults*

Abused as Children is an important contribution to the body of knowledge and that the book deserves to be widely read. I hope it will influence both the development of practice and policy and also, importantly, the funding of services.

I also welcome this publication for one other reason. It is an example of practice and research coming together and of sharing experience. We need more practice-based research and crucially we need to learn from each other. Peter Dale has now been with the NSPCC for some eighteen years and has always combined his professional practice with a commitment to sharing his experience with others. His book *Dangerous Families* (1986) described the pioneering work and approach of the NSPCC Child Protection Team in Rochdale. That book was influential with many practitioners and I am sure that *Adults Abused as Children* will prove to have a similar impact. We consider ourselves fortunate to have Peter as a member of our staff.

Jim Harding
Director and Chief Executive
National Society for the Prevention of Cruelty to Children

Acknowledgements

I would like to acknowledge a great deal of professional and personal support received during the course of the PhD study upon which this book is based. However, first I express my appreciation to seventy-nine people who contributed to the research by being interviewed or providing written material. The diversity of experiences and opinions expressed by this large group means that the book cannot represent every view. I hope, however, that it reflects the predominant motivation of participants in the research – the wish to influence improvements in the provision and quality of therapeutic services for adults who were abused as children.

At the University of Brighton, Dr John Allen, my Director of Studies (latterly at City University, London, now retired) stimulated and encouraged my initial research interests and carefully piloted this project through safe waters. Dr Lynda Measor acted as my second supervisor and shared her experience and enthusiasm for qualitative research. It is too often said that research students suffer from inadequate supervision and support. I am very grateful to John and Lynda for a supervisory relationship which was consistently encouraging, stimulating and supportive.

The National Society for the Prevention of Cruelty to Children (NSPCC) played a fundamental facilitating and resourcing role in this research. Beverly Cohen (Regional Director, NSPCC Home Counties) was encouraging when the project was but a vague thought, and her support was instrumental in the step from ideas into action. Ron Lock (Regional Head of Child Protection, NSPCC Home Counties) maintained a close and consistent interest which was very motivating and supportive. I also wish to thank all staff, past and present, at the NSPCC Headley Library, who have assisted me for many years with a service which must be unsurpassed in the UK in its effectiveness and efficiency.

At a local level, I express my appreciation to all members of NSPCC East Sussex of which, I understand, I am the manager. Thank you all for your competence, maturity and humour during the periods of time when I have been absent or preoccupied. Particular thanks go to Ron

Fellows for sharing the depth of his knowledge and experience through many stimulating discussions, and for his critical and helpful comments on the themes contained in this book.

I also have a special thankyou for Dr Helen Westcott, Department of Psychology Open University (formerly Researcher, NSPCC National Centre). Helen's encouragement and critical yet supportive comments at several stages on many drafts have been invaluable.

I am sorry that my parents are not alive to take pride in the completion of this project. Many thanks go to my sister Sue Phillips for a lifetime of support; to my children Nathan, Rory and Rosanna; and Veronica Locke who has loved me throughout.

Material in Chapter 4 is expanded from Dale, Allen and Measor (1998). Material in Chapter 10 is expanded from Dale and Allen (1998).

Introduction

Over the past two decades there has been significant increase in public awareness, concern and also growing controversies about child abuse. Therapists of all persuasions have been faced with the challenge of applying their skills to explicit abuse issues.[1] People have increasingly sought help specifically for what they feel are the consequences of childhood abuse. Many others have felt more able to reveal this history in the course of therapy which began with a focus on other problems.

It is commonly alleged that, historically, mainstream therapy ignored or minimized the significance of childhood abuse. However, since the 1980s a large number of books have argued that abuse 'survivors' represent a special population of clients with special needs, and that 'special' therapy is necessary for their recovery. These publications gained a high profile and exerted much influence on public attitudes towards abuse and therapeutic practice. However, despite their prominence, the fact has been obscured that these rather prescriptive therapeutic models are almost completely unevaluated.

Surprisingly, despite the wealth of research in the fields of child abuse and psychotherapy, very little has been published about clients' and therapists' experiences in receiving and providing help for the effects of childhood abuse. In this book, the voices of adults who were abused as children will be heard directly in relation to their experiences of therapy. These experiences are for better – and unfortunately – for worse. We will pursue the question: Is there anything significantly different about effective therapy with adults who were abused as children in comparison with a non-abused client group that has experienced a wide range of other hurtful and harmful life events, losses and stresses?

An underlying premise is that clients are able to provide informed feedback about their experiences, and that therapists and the therapeutic process can only benefit from this.[2] Therapists will also be heard, including those who were themselves abused as children. This group has a unique dual perspective and a voice which has so far hardly been heard at all.

My interest in this area stems from a number of directions. Over a long career as a practitioner and supervisor (originally as a psychiatric social worker, latterly as a counsellor) I have worked with a wide range of client groups including substantial numbers of adults who were abused as children. Since 1980 I have worked as a practitioner and manager with the National Society for the Prevention of Cruelty to Children (NSPCC). The NSPCC is a national children's charity which provides a range of services to children and families. I have a particular interest in two of its many services: undertaking independent assessments following cases of serious child abuse, and providing therapeutic services for adults who were abused as children. Both of these have been major service areas of NSPCC East Sussex which I have managed since 1986.

My experience of independent assessment work over many years highlights the extent to which childhood abuse features in the personal histories of adults who seriously abuse their own children – approximately 70% of seriously abusing parents were abused themselves.[3] Working with so many parents who had caused great harm to their own children raised my interest in the potential for therapeutic services to help them overcome the continuing damaging effects of their own abuse – what is needed for them to be able to transform into non-abusive parents? These experiences also raise the question as to what extent therapeutic services for adults abused as children can act as a significant influence to prevent child abuse.

From these two motivations, at NSPCC East Sussex, a specific therapeutic service for adults who were abused as children was established in 1986. Referrals have increased steadily every year, indicating a huge community need.[4]

My role in the work reported in this book is of an experienced therapist and supervisor, turned researcher. From this perspective my starting point was (and is) one of confidence in the general value and benefits of various forms of therapy for people who experience a wide range of personal problems. My theoretical orientation has included humanistic, psychodynamic, systems, cognitive-behavioural and existential influences. While some may see this as a jumble, I dress it up as best I can toward respectability with the presumption that this is indicative of an integrative approach. I have also been a consumer of psychotherapy. My client career dates back many years and I have experienced four individual therapists of very different orientations, as well as group therapy. Given the focus of this book, it also seems important to acknowledge that (while family life was not always emotionally easy) I do not consider myself to have been abused as a child.

As a practitioner, supervisor and manager of therapeutic services, I have an interest in the outcome of this research having an impact on counselling and psychotherapy practice. This was also the major motive for the people who participated in the study. In addition to providing warnings about potentially harmful therapeutic practices, my hope is that the book will highlight the great benefits which can be derived from effective therapy and provide impetus for further development of therapeutic services for adults who were abused as children.[5]

Fifty-three in-depth interviews and additional written contributions provided a huge amount of data. This book presents description and analysis, some of it quite startling, about what participants felt was helpful and unhelpful in their episodes of therapy. The themes I have chosen to present are those which stand out for me as being particularly important to bring to the attention of the therapeutic community.[6]

A brief outline of the organization of the book is as follows. **Part One** sets the scene with a presentation of relevant theoretical and research issues. Counselling and psychotherapy with adults who were abused as children takes place in the context of two large literatures: child abuse (Chapter 1), and psychotherapy (Chapter 2). These two chapters focus on:

- the causes and effects of child abuse;
- theories of therapy;
- messages from psychotherapy research;
- review of previous research on therapy with adults who were abused as children.

Part Two presents an account of the methodology used in the study and detailed description and analysis of key issues from the research interviews.

Part Three focuses specifically on the current controversy regarding 'recovered memories' and 'false memory syndrome'. It concludes with a discussion of the implications for practice from the book as a whole.

Notes

1 There is no consistently agreed conceptual demarcation between psychotherapy and counselling (although many argue that there is or that there should be). Consequently, in this book I use the terms counsellor, psychotherapist, therapist and practitioner synonymously and interchangeably.

2 This is in contrast to a formal psychoanalytic belief that clients' feedback is so likely to be distorted by transference that its utility for therapists is negligible.

3 As will be discussed in Chapter 2, this does not mean that similar proportions of adults who were abused as children will abuse their own children. Discussion of independent assessments can be found in Dale et al. (1986a); Dale (1991); Tucci (1995); Dale and Fellows (1997); Dale and Fellows (in press).

4 Further research is currently in progress evaluating the NSPCC East Sussex client group. This sample is not discussed in this book.

5 In the UK, the government consultation document 'Working Together to Protect Children (Dept of Health 1998) has highlighted for the first time the importance of developing therapeutic services for adults who were abused as

children. This is also an important aspect of the Long-term Strategy for the Millennium of the NSPCC.

6 They are not therefore representative of the experiences of all of the participants. Because these themes have been selected (and many others not presented here) certain participants are quoted frequently and others less so or not at all.

PART ONE

THEORY AND RESEARCH BACKGROUND

1

Childhood Abuse:
Context, consequences and treatment approaches

In this chapter I will present a brief history of the concept of child abuse and review the major therapeutic approaches which have been used by therapists to help those who have sought help with abuse-related problems. This is a daunting task as the fields of child abuse and psycho-therapy/counselling contain huge theoretical and research literatures. Consequently my aim here is modest: to alert readers to key issues in child abuse and therapy that provide the context for the experiences which people describe in this book.

Identification and denial of child abuse

In the social history of child abuse, the story is often told of the scandal relating to a child called Mary Ellen in New York in 1874. Mary Ellen suffered serious ill-treatment by her adoptive parents who insisted that it was their parental right to do so. Laws existed to protect animals from cruelty, but not children. Consequently legal action to protect Mary Ellen was brought on the basis that she was 'a member of the animal kingdom'. The case was found proved and became a landmark in the legal assertion of child protection over parental rights. It also served as an impetus for the foundation of the New York Society for the Prevention of Cruelty to Children. This in turn set in motion the development of similar local societies in the UK, culminating in the establishment of the National Society for the Prevention of Cruelty to Children (NSPCC) in 1884.

It is remarkable at the end of the twentieth century that prominent disputes about child abuse mirror those occurring a century ago. These include: disagreement as to the nature and extent of abuse; the appropriateness of state intervention into family life; the reliability of memories of sexual abuse; and whether dominant influences in society work towards the suppression of knowledge of abuse. This discourse echoes that which surrounded the work of Sigmund Freud at the end of the last century, and which is still keenly debated. Although public awareness and concern about child sexual abuse was recorded in the century before Freud (Olafson et al. 1993), Freud's initial publications outlining the significance of child sexual abuse in the aetiology of 'hysteria' are often portrayed as the original 'discovery' of such abuse.

Disputes continue regarding the social influence of Freud's attitudes about childhood sexual abuse. There is little doubt that his views changed significantly during his career; a career during which, for the early part at least, child abuse was a matter of topical social concern with high profile child abuse trials reported in the Viennese press in 1889 (Wolff 1988). Freud is variously described as having abandoned, reversed, revised or refined his view about the sexual abuse origins of neurosis in his adult female patients. There are three main contrasting interpretations of Freud's views of the significance of childhood sexual abuse. The first holds that throughout his career he consistently believed in the reality and significance of such abuse, while increasingly coming to recognize the added complications contributed by phantasy elements, wish-fulfilment phenomena, and 'Oedipal' dynamics (Demause 1991; Robbins 1995). The second position asserts that Freud was correct in his identification of 'repressed' memories of childhood sexual abuse being the underlying cause of the symptoms in his adult patients (the 'seduction' theory); and that in response to social pressure Freud wrongly retracted this theory, substituting instead the 'Oedipal' theory which construed 'memories' of childhood sexual abuse as being wish-fulfilment phantasies (Masson 1985; Miller 1983; Summit 1988). The third view is that none of Freud's patients were likely to have been sexually abused as children. It was Freud's impulsive inductive belief that they had been and the authoritarian pressure of his techniques which led suggestible and vulnerable woman to comply and produce the 'memories' he expected (Crews 1995; Pendergrast 1995; Webster 1995).

In this context Freud has become both ammunition and target for polemical attacks from advocates of opposed positions in ongoing child abuse controversies. Many have indicted Freud with provoking social denial of the reality of childhood sexual abuse throughout the first three-quarters of the twentieth century (Dominelli 1989; Herman 1981; Masson 1985; Miller 1983; Summit 1988); while in contrast Pendergrast (1995) scathingly awarded Freud the accolade of being the first 'recovered memory' therapist on the basis that reports of childhood abuse related by his patients were in all likelihood a compliant response to pressure to produce such 'memories.'

Although charitable societies dedicated to the prevention of cruelty to children were developing momentum to protect them from gross physical abuse and neglect, for the first three-quarters of the twentieth century public awareness, social concern and research about sexual abuse of children was quiescent. This is reflected in Weinberg's (1955) psychiatric text which estimated the incidence of incest to be one girl in a million; and in the famous research by Kinsey and his associates on human adult sexuality during the same decade. The Kinsey research recorded a higher rate of adults' childhood sexual experiences, but this was not noted as being remarkable and received little public attention (Kinsey et al. 1953).

Child abuse again became a matter of significant social concern in the 1960s when advances in radiology led to a large increase in diagnoses of previously undetected non-accidental bone fractures in children and young babies. Motivated by these findings, Kempe et al. (1962) published the seminal 'Battered Child Syndrome' which intensified professional vigilance about the prevalence and dangers of physical abuse. According to Tzeng et al. (1991: 4), this marked 'the point at which the study of child abuse and neglect became a distinct academic subject'. Since then, physical abuse of children has rarely been out of public consciousness. In the UK this exploded further into controversy and concern following the official inquiry into the death of Maria Colwell in 1973. This case, and a sequence of similar inquiries into fatal child abuse which followed, highlighted concerns about the role of professionals and the operation of child protection systems (Reder et al. 1993). Unlike sexual abuse, because of the relative ease of identification and medical diagnosis, the actuality of serious physical abuse to children is not in itself particularly con-troversial (Finklehor 1984). Contentious issues surrounding physical abuse tend to be connected with professional practice relating to investi-gation, assessment and decision-making (Dale et al. 1986a; Parton 1985; Reder et al. 1993). The boundary between what is considered to be socially and legally acceptable parental chastisement and abuse also remains contentious, reflecting religious, cultural and ideological tensions (Tzeng et al. 1991).

The re-emergence of feminist thinking and the development of the 'women's movement' during the 1970s and 1980s promoted the re-instatement of social concern about the reality of child sexual abuse. Throughout this period there was large-scale pressure group activity by separate feminist and child protection lobbies. These challenged the denial and minimization of social establishments (especially the legal and psychiatric systems) about sexual abuse of children and pressed for improved child protection systems, treatment programmes and research (Finklehor 1984).

A new wave of research began to explore the prevalence of child sexual abuse in western societies. Most of the influential studies in the 1980s and early 1990s stemmed from the USA and Canada and explored retrospective reports of childhood sexual abuse within certain adult populations. Less research has taken place in relation to non-sexual forms of abuse. A problem in interpreting this research is that a wide range of definitions of abuse has been used. One of the difficulties in child abuse research is the absence of agreed standardized and oper- ationalized definitions of what child abuse, and its various types, actu- ally is. The concept of abuse is socially constructed and varies between cultures and over time; the lack of consistently agreed definitions makes comparisons of prevalence between eras and cultures problematic. This is compounded as methodological decisions about definitions of abuse to be used in studies have a biasing effect on results. 'Loose' definitions (for example, including non-contact incidents with strangers) produce high prevalence rates of abuse such as the 'one girl in every three' reports; while 'tight' definitions (for example, limited to penetrative contact with a blood relation) produce much lower rates.

Studies most commonly quoted are those by Finklehor (1979) which reported a childhood sexual abuse prevalence rate of 19% and 9% respectively for a sample of adult women and men; and Russell (1983) who reported a rate of 38% for adult women. In the UK, the most well- known study reported sexual abuse prevalence of 12% and 8% respect- ively for females and males (Baker and Duncan 1986). Reviewing these prevalence statistics across a number of studies, Peters et al. (1986) noted a range from 6–62% for females, and 3–31% for males. This is an enormous discrepancy, which results from incompatibility of research methods, the use of different definitions of abuse and confusion between categories of abusers.

Some have suggested that figures generated by such studies under- record the true prevalence of abuse as they do not include actual abuse not reported by people who have 'repressed' memories of abuse, or who are unwilling to disclose this history to researchers. Also, populations with known high rates of abuse (such as prisoners and psychiatric in- patients) are excluded from random survey samples. On this basis, one psychohistorian argued that figures from prevalence studies should be increased by 50% to correct for such sources of bias toward under- reporting (Demause 1991). In contrast, as the methodology of prevalence studies has become more sophisticated (for example, using behavioural indicators rather than conceptual definitions), two major reviews of retrospective prevalence studies of child sexual abuse concluded that rates of such abuse which occur within families is much lower than had been claimed in some of the literature of the 1980s (Lindsay and Read 1994; Wassil-Grimm 1995).

In the 1980s prevalence studies had enormous impact in generating public and professional debate about child sexual abuse, further research into the causes of abuse and action about preventive and treatment programmes. The high social profile of abuse enabled those affected to gain knowledge, often from media sources, that they were not alone in their experiences, to discuss these more openly and to seek the help they needed. This new level of social concern undoubtedly resulted in many abused children being protected, and abuse being prevented for unknown numbers of children.[1]

A constant professional and social tension exists in relation to the operation of child protection systems. While the goal of protection and prevention of child abuse is laudable, recent history has also shown that such systems have the potential capability to cause great harm to children and families in their own right (Dale 1998). For example, during an unfortunate era during the 1980s, in some localities inter-agency child protections systems appeared to develop almost paranoid beliefs about extensive undetected networks of ritualistic/satanic/sexual abuse. There were prominent cases in the UK and USA where groups of children were removed in dawn raids from their families in communities where police, social workers and paediatricians had become convinced that such abuse was taking place. Children were subject to intimate medical examinations and fervent interrogations by interviewers insistent on obtaining 'disclosures' about extensive and bizarre abuse. Incongruously, when children denied that they had been abused this was interpreted as a significant sign confirming abuse. The fact that little medical or other evidence was forthcoming to substantiate the suspicions only served to reinforce investigators' beliefs about the degree of cunning of the abusers. The place names of Orkney, Cleveland, Rochdale, Broxtowe and McMartin have become memorials to this dismal era of child protection practice (for example, DHSS 1988)

During the mid-1990s, in reaction to such highly publicized aberrations in child protection practice, there was a significant shift in public awareness and attitudes towards child abuse. To a large extent this resulted from the impact on the media of the highly effective activities of pressure groups such as Parents Against INjustice (PAIN) and the British False Memory Society (BFMS) in the UK; and Victims of Child Abuse Laws (VOCAL) and the False Memory Syndrome Foundation (FMSF) in the USA. These groups argued that the combined influence of a high cultural profile of abuse, the effects of social contagion, over-reaction by child protection systems, and certain forms of psychotherapy had led to a dramatic increase in false accusations of abuse. They stressed the danger in this context that unhappy suggestible adults may falsely come to believe that a history of abuse is responsible for current problems in their lives. Professionals who had become consumed by satanic and ritualistic child abuse beliefs and suspicions interpreted almost any feature of childhood behaviour as indicative of sexual abuse (Goodyear-Smith 1993).

In this emotive and complex area of child protection practice it is vital that risks of false allegations and unsubstantiated abuse must be carefully assessed in a consistent way. It is equally important that caution about such concerns does not leave children who are being abused unprotected and unhelped.

Consequences of child abuse

A great deal of research has been undertaken over the past twenty years to explore the consequences in adult life of childhood abuse. Consequences of abuse are reported in two literatures: in research studies exploring the prevalence of symptoms in specific populations; and in clinical accounts derived from the experiences of therapists. This research has provided an accumulation of evidence that significant lasting problems are more likely for those who were seriously, multipally and chronically abused over an extended period of time, beginning at an early age, and in the context of a significantly dysfunctional family.

Common categories of difficulties which may be experienced by adults who were abused as children include combinations of physical, emotional, cognitive, self/identity, relational, sexual and social problems (Beitchman et al. 1992; Briere and Runtz 1988; Browne and Finklehor 1986; Kendall-Tackett et al. 1993). Most of this research has focused predominantly on females who were sexually abused as children by men. However, more recently studies have widened to include abuse of males (Bolton et al. 1989; Etherington 1995; Hunter 1990; Mendel 1995); the role of women as sexual abusers (Elliot 1993; Finklehor and Russell 1984; Mayer 1992; Welldon 1988); and males as victims of women (Bolton et al. 1989; Hunter 1990; Mendel 1995).

Notwithstanding these studies, it remains unclear precisely how different types, severity or extent of abuse affects the development and progression of various symptoms and problems. There are also significant methodological difficulties in establishing that it is the abuse itself which actually causes the reported effects (Cahill et al. 1991b). Commonly reported consequences of abuse (for example, depression, sexual difficulties, problems in relationships, low self-esteem, poor self-image) are also combinations of problems which frequently affect people who have not been abused. One of the characteristics of the many clinical reports during the 1980s involved attempts to delineate a specific 'post sexual abuse syndrome' whereby constellations of adult symptoms, displayed in checklist form, could indicate a history of childhood abuse – even if the person had no conscious knowledge of it (Bass and Davis 1988; Blume 1990; Ellenson 1986). Despite becoming influential for a time, no such syndrome has been established which can reliably isolate child abuse as the specific cause of adult problems. Attempts to do so attracted fierce scientific criticism of the generic nature of the problems which purportedly indicated childhood abuse (Lindsay and Read 1994), as well as the ridicule of journalists (Pendergrast 1995).

A confusion between correlation and causation contributes to these misconceptions about the consequences of child abuse. The fact that certain symptoms and problems are commonly reported in retrospective surveys and clinical samples of adults who were abused as children does not mean that the symptoms are a result of the abuse (although they may be). In particular it does not necessarily mean that a person currently experiencing such symptoms has been a victim of child abuse.

In addition to uncertainty as to whether it is the abuse itself which causes the widely reported range of adult difficulties, the question also arises whether childhood abuse in itself necessarily has harmful short-term or long-term effects. The findings of many reputable studies query the inevitability of harm. In major research reviews, Browne and Finklehor (1986) concluded that approximately 40% of sexually abused children suffer consequences serious enough for them to need therapy in adulthood (and, therefore, that 60% do not). Kendall-Tackett et al. (1993) reported that many people do not appear to suffer long-term consequences. Research by Baker and Duncan (1986), Feinauer (1989), Ussher and Dewberry (1995) and Woods and Dean (1984) all indicated that certain proportions of victims do not consider their experience to have had long-term consequences, nor to have been damaging. In addition, studies consistently note small proportions of females and somewhat larger proportions of males who report that their abuse experiences had no negative effects – or even had positive consequences (Baker and Duncan 1986; Etherington 1995; Hunter 1990; Howitt 1995; Mendel 1995; Russell 1986; Woods and Dean 1984).

Feinauer (1989) made the important point that the literature on successful adjustment in life following childhood abuse is extremely limited. Sanford (1991) noted from research on concentration camp inmates that it is by no means automatic that lifelong emotional disability follows from early trauma. One simple factor is relevant here which is often overlooked: by definition, practitioners encounter abused children and adults who have suffered consequences severe enough to seek help. Such clinical samples include the most adversely affected people – but they are not typical of abused people as a whole. Generalizations from consequences of abuse seen in clinical samples need to be treated with considerable caution.

It follows from this discussion that to talk about 'child abuse' as a unitary phenomenon which is likely to have similar negative effects for those who experience it is over-simplistic. Indeed, the categorization of 'abuse' itself (and the subcategories 'physical', 'sexual' and 'emotional') force a supposed commonality of interpretation of experiences and perceptions which is not borne out phenomenologically: people (and different cultures) experience and define the same events and contexts in different ways, react in different ways and ultimately make sense of their experiences in different ways (Janoff-Bulman 1985, 1989).

Much of the abuse therapy literature of the 1980s presupposed some-what stereotypal responses from 'survivors', whatever the form, extent and context of the abuse experienced. However, as the material in this book makes clear, individual experiencing does not fit neatly into such predetermined topical (but transient) theoretical (and political) tem-plates. To think about the consequences of abuse and the therapeutic needs of abused people in a more sophisticated way, requires careful consideration of the interaction between various types of abuse and the individual characteristics of affected children. To anticipate the experi-ences of people in later chapters of this book, it is important to dis-tinguish between abuse which occurs in traumatic and non-traumatic contexts; between single and multiple incidents; and between single and multiple abusers. It is necessary to appreciate the context of – and the child's relationship with – the abuser(s); the characteristics (for example, gender/age) of the abuser(s); and the personality and previous life experiences of the child.

The experience of regular beatings and violent sexual assaults in a punitive family environment of high criticism and low warmth is very different from one where a child grows up feeling very loved and 'special' with an attentive and responsive parent who gradually sexual-izes frequent and enjoyed affectionate physical contact. The experience of an emotionally secure child who suffers a single serious sexual assault (say by a visiting relative) in the context of a loving and supportive family environment is very different from that of a neglected, lonely and emotionally deprived child who unwittingly regularly seeks attention and affection (which becomes sexualized) from adults with abusing proclivities.

While on one level these different scenarios (and there are many others) are all classifiable as 'child sexual abuse' – they reflect enor-mously contrasting experiences, have different consequences, and present different challenges in subsequent therapy.

Psychotherapy and counselling: therapeutic models

The terms psychotherapy and counselling are umbrella concepts which cover wide varieties of theory and practice. Although the origins of psychotherapy and counselling stem back to separate traditions, in practice it has consistently proved impossible to establish and maintain any generally accepted significant or practical differences between them (Gelso 1979). Consequently in this book the terms psychotherapy, therapy, counselling and practice are used interchangeably. Synthesis of decades of research in psychotherapy suggests that the theoretical orientations of therapists, and their use of favoured techniques, has rather less relevance and impact on the change process for most clients than therapists tend to believe (Bergin and Garfield 1994). For clients, the core of effective therapy is to be able to talk and experience honestly, in the context of a safe therapeutic relationship, where they feel understood and accepted; and can search for meanings in experience, self and relationships (Howe 1993).

The question arises as to whether this process should be any different for clients who were abused as children. Do people who have experienced some form of abuse require different and specific forms of therapy which depart from what is known to be effective with general populations of clients – many of which will have included people with abuse histories?

Many practitioners appear to believe that adults who were abused as children are a special population who require distinctive forms of therapy to aid them in their path to recovery. A large literature mushroomed throughout the 1980s and 1990s propounding models of therapy for abuse 'survivors' in what became a thriving, competitive and profitable marketplace. This literature generally ignored research knowledge about helpful and unhelpful factors in psychotherapy and counselling. Regrettably, the principles espoused in many 'therapeutic' and self-help publications about 'surviving' abuse have had major cultural impact over the past two decades without ever having been subject to basic evaluations of efficacy or ethical scrutiny. Certain features of 'survivor' models will be discussed later in this chapter. However, I will now provide a broader contextual overview of the range of therapeutic approaches which are influential in general psychotherapy practice.

Psychoanalytic/psychodynamic tradition

This theory for understanding the human condition and relationships is irrevocably associated with Sigmund Freud, the founding father of psychoanalysis. The theoretical transitions, conflicts and splintering which occurred between Freud and his analyst colleagues prefaced divisions which have continued for over a century in the psychoanalytic world. As a consequence, there is no one accepted school of psychoanalysis: there are many psychoanalytic theories with large differences and great rivalry (sometimes bitter) between them.

One of Freud's lasting achievements was to bring to general public and professional attention pre-existing knowledge of unconscious mental processes which influence thoughts, feelings and behaviour. His view of human nature was inherently pessimistic in that he construed the human condition as being a constant struggle to contain destructive unconscious sexual and aggressive instincts. The psyche is seen as a seething mass of unconscious dark instincts which challenge and threaten human development, behaviour and relationships.

The Freudian notion that awareness of unbearable instincts or traumatic experiences can be blocked out by being placed in an unconscious compartment of the mind, via a mechanism of 'repression', has had enormous influence on psychotherapy. This is particularly controversial in relation to the belief that extensive and severe sexual abuse is especially likely to be responded to by massive repression; and that 'repressed' memories need to be 'recovered' as part of the process of healing and 'recovery'.

Another significant unconscious process which stems from psychoanalytic theory is that of transference – a notion that has now been assimilated widely into many other non-psychodynamic theories, and indeed into common usage. Freud conceptualized transference as an inevitable phenomenon in the analytic relationship whereby aspects of the patient's relationship with significant others, especially early parent figures, become unconsciously built into the patient's perception of, and relationship with, the analyst. Although there are many debates about minute theoretical differences, in essence the concept of transference refers to the dynamic whereby the patient experiences the analyst as a representation of a significant other. Accordingly, whatever the patient experiences in relation to the analyst – be this intense love, hate, or indeed unmitigated boredom – this is seen as having little to do with the analyst but is instead the manifestation of unconscious feeling about others, usually parents.

One consequence of this view is that psychoanalytic therapists tend not to consider themselves to be personally present in the therapeutic relationship. The patient is seen as relating via fantasy to a representational figure who remains deliberately opaque, with the intention of promoting clients' awareness of feelings about significant others. As will be seen in later chapters, clients who were abused as children have strong feelings about the impact of this approach.

For anyone who has formed the impression that the origins of psychoanalytic theory were developed by a process of dispassionate intellectual discourse and rigorous scientific debate between Freud and his colleagues, psychohistorians and contemporaneous correspondence (for example, the Freud–Jung letters (McGuire 1991)) reveal a rather different and mundane picture. A fascinating account of psychoanalytic rivalry and politics can be found in *The Secret Ring* (Grosskurth 1991) and a devastating analysis of Freud's unscientific method in the generation of theory has been presented by Webster (1995). It is difficult to escape the conclusion that Freud was a bitter man, unable to tolerate difference in his protégés, many of whom he became estranged from or maintained enemy status with. Although some of his theoretical notions continue to have therapeutic relevance, Freud as a personality is far from a model of the postulated benefits of psychoanalytic awareness.

However, it would be inappropriate and unfair to reject the psychoanalytic paradigm on the basis of flaws apparent from the privileged position of a century's hindsight. Theory has continued to evolve throughout the post-Freudian era. An important development provided by post-Freudian thinkers has been to move the main focus away from the exploration of inner instinctual turmoil onto the impact of satisfactions and frustrations of needs in early and continuing relationships with significant others (so called 'object relations'). This amounts to a major revision of the classic analytic theory that relationship problems stem from unresolved inner instinctual conflicts. The work of attachment theorists (Bowlby 1969, 1988; Holmes 1993; Winnicott 1965) has been central to the conceptual development of psychotherapy as a reparative relationship in response to unsatisfactory childhood relationships. As a consequence, many psychoanalytic/psychodynamic therapists in recent decades have moved away from the traditional austere psychoanalytic position to adopt a more personally involved conversational style (Cashdan 1988; Hobson 1985; Lomas 1987, 1994; Mair 1989). Such therapists emphasize the importance of being both 'real' with the client, while also utilizing transference and countertransference dynamics which occur in the relationship.

In addition to this humanizing influence, an increasing tendency in abuse-related psychodynamic literature is the incorporation of features from models located in other paradigms including feminism, self-psychology, and trauma theory (Davies and Frawley 1994; Haaken and Schlaps 1991; McCann and Pearlman 1990; McElroy and McElroy 1991; Rose 1991). Eclectic analytic theorists construe child sexual abuse as a highly complex phenomenon involving the interplay between actual abuse and libidinal fantasies. This perspective incorporates concepts from trauma and object relations theories by acknowledging the significance of relational processes including abuse, attachment and loss; over and above the traditional analytic concerns with the mastery of instinctual drives.

One of the strengths of the psychodynamic paradigm is that it can recognize clients' feelings of attachment, ambivalence and loss regarding relationships where one aspect – but not necessarily all of it – was exploitative or abusive. Weaknesses are that the traditional rather formal, distant and emotionally abstinent stance within the therapeutic relationship can be experienced as cold and punishing by people who have histories of significant emotional deprivation. Also, because of the traditional inflexibility about 'boundaries' (for example, prohibition of contact between sessions and inflexibility in the arrangement of sessions), the approach is not generally effective in helping clients in post-trauma situations or those who are in crisis.

The humanistic tradition

A shared philosophical principle of the many diverse schools of humanistic therapy is an optimistic view of the growth and self-healing potential of the human organism. There is explicit rejection of medical 'sickness–cure' models: instead the philosophy of human development and change is essentially horticultural in that therapy provides the conditions to facilitate the client's growth towards fulfilment of potential.

Client-centred therapy (more recently known as person-centred) was developed by Carl Rogers in the 1950s and has been a central influence on the development of the humanistic tradition. An atmosphere involving warmth, genuineness, unconditional positive regard, empathy and congruence constitutes the 'core conditions' which are central to the therapeutic relationship and clients' development of positive self-concepts (Rogers 1957).

Therapeutic relationships involve clients and therapists attempting to establish authentic contact with each other as real people – commonly known, after Buber (1987) as an 'I–Thou' relationship. These relationships reflect person-to-person contact which is not alienated and distanced by the encouragement of transference distortions. Stemming from the real presence of the therapist-as-person in the relationship, the focus and course of therapy tends to be non-standardized, has few preconceived theoretical expectations or goals and is adaptable, creative and somewhat unpredictable. Flexibility is apparent in the timing, frequency and length of sessions. Humanistic therapists on the whole are much more willing than their psychoanalytic counterparts to be contactable outside sessions for support. The personal involvement of the therapist often leads to clients developing much greater levels of knowledge of the therapist's personal life than is typical in most other approaches; and therapists may facilitate this via deliberate self-disclosure.

Humanistic therapies have proliferated over the last thirty years and include a diverse collection of principles and techniques aimed at promoting the optimum conditions for personal development. Approaches such as gestalt and psychodrama use 'action techniques' to facilitate communication (for example, 'talking to the empty chair' and role play), and to express suppressed feelings (such as anger or grief) by beating cushions or being physically held and comforted by the therapist. Utilization of clients' creative inclinations and abilities (for example, through art and writing) is also characteristic.

There is little specific contribution to the child abuse literature from the humanistic perspective. This is understandable in view of the philosophical basis which considers each individual to be unique and has a traditional disinterest in diagnostic and classificatory systems. Humanistic approaches are not without risk for adults who were abused as children, as some of the examples given later in this book will highlight. In particular, the provision by a therapist of a liberal helping of the 'core conditions' with a new client can resemble processes of seduction in an uncanny way. This can be disorientating for emotionally deprived, unloved and lonely clients.

The principle of unconditional acceptance and non-judgemental listening (in the context of a disregard for psychological assessment) may also result in failure to help some clients to learn how to test the reality of some of their experiences. This can be disadvantageous and potentially dangerous for those who have a tendency to misperceive their environment. Similarly, therapeutic over-acceptance of the principle of client self-determination can have negative personal, family and social consequences. This was encapsulated in an old cartoon which showed a suicidal client poised to jump out of a high consulting room window, with an unanimated therapist responding: 'So you feel you're just about to jump out of the window'. While humanistic therapists believe that their approaches are based on non-authoritarian relationships, these therapies often produce the most domineering and charismatic gurus (Spinelli 1994).

The cognitive-behavioural tradition

There has been a tendency in recent years toward rapprochement between the originally separate cognitive and behavioural traditions. The cognitive element highlights the significance of learned thinking patterns and schemas by means of which experience is construed and meaning constructed (Fransella and Dalton 1990; Kelly 1955). From this perspective, problems arise when experience is misconstrued by learned distorted thinking patterns which filter perceptions and experiences, usually in a negative way. Negative affect, for example depression, is seen as a consequence of faulty cognitions and consequent misperception of self, others and the environment. As such, the therapeutic focus aims to 'restructure' thinking patterns to prevent experience from being routinely construed negatively, thus avoiding self-reinforcing adverse effects on mood and self-image (Beck 1976).

The behavioural component stems from the long history of applying principles of learning theory to specific observable human problems, and claims consistent success with clients who have problems associated with specific anxieties and aversions. In addition to cognitive restructuring, therapeutic techniques involve desensitization of clients to difficult situations (by graded encounters or over-exposure); forms of relaxation; and focusing on learning social and interpersonal skills. In the cognitive-behavioural paradigm, the therapeutic relationship tends to function in a friendly but rather technical way (somewhat analogous to an enthusiastic teacher and motivated pupil) in that it is the vehicle for collaboration between therapist and client in the application and review of specific verbal and active techniques. Unlike many other models, the therapeutic relationship in itself is not reflected upon as an element of therapy. Clients' transferential feelings are not elicited and explored, nor will the therapist offer any significant degree of personal involvement or self-disclosure.

For clients who experienced child abuse, cognitive-behavioural techniques are of great value in tackling many of the specific problems in living and relating which are typical consequences of abuse such as flashbacks, aversions, misperceptions of others and sexual problems (Jehu 1988). These approaches have been incorporated into the 'stabilization' phase of traumatic stress models.

Traumatic stress models

Traumatic stress models of therapy developed within the psychiatric tradition, predominantly influenced by research on the psychological effects on combatants in wars and survivors of other catastrophes (Horowitz 1986). Study of the psychological and emotional effects of involvement in warfare (such as the 'shellshock' of World War I and 'battle fatigue' of World War II), was significantly accelerated following pressure from veterans of the Vietnam war who lobbied for a new non-stigmatizing diagnosis which catered for their particular types of symptoms. This resulted in the development of the formal psychiatric category of 'Post-traumatic stress syndrome' which was introduced into the official international psychiatric classificatory system *Diagnostic and Statistical Manual of Mental Disorders* (DSM-111) (APA 1980). Post-traumatic Stress Disorder (PTSD), as revised in DSM-IV (APA 1994), highlights the three symptomatic criteria of:

- persistent re-experiencing of the traumatic event;
- persistent avoidance of stimuli associated with the trauma;
- persistent symptoms of increased arousal.

These responses follow (and last longer than one month) events which involve a threat to life or physical integrity, and which invoke a subjective response of fear, helplessness or horror.

Trauma theory provides a psychobiological paradigm for understanding human responses to extreme stress, including the conceptualization of symptoms as being normal adaptive responses to abnormal events. It is the tendency for reactions to persist for long periods subsequent to the traumatic events, when the person is again living in a non-traumatic environment, which constitutes the maladaptive element.

A great deal of research has been undertaken to explore the psychobiological effects of chronic and traumatic stress. Yehuda and Harvey (1997) provided a detailed review of the biological events that occur at the time of trauma and the different neurobiological responses between individuals who develop PTSD and those who do not. In contrast to what is sometimes believed, the development of PTSD is by no means an inevitable consequence of experiencing a major traumatic event – research indicates a prevalence range of 3–58% (APA 1994).

Traumatic stress treatment involves stages of stabilization, desensitization, cognitive restructuring and meaning attribution. This approach is of proven effectiveness for people in crisis and as such has relevance for many adults who were abused as children; especially in relation to dealing with emotional symptoms, intrusive recollections (for example, flashbacks) and numbing phenomena reported by many abused clients (Briere 1989, 1992; Lindberg and Distad 1985).

However, the PTSD model has limitations for understanding many other problems experienced by adults who were abused as children, especially those appertaining to self-constructs, interpersonal and sexual difficulties. This is hardly surprising as abuse which is chronic and takes place within ongoing family relationships is very different from experiences of military battles and natural catastrophes (Mendel 1995). The model does not accommodate the significance of variations of pre-traumatic personality or relationship factors affecting subsequent response to trauma. It does not recognize that not all abuse occurs in situations or relationships which are experienced as traumatic; that not all stresses promote disorder; and that stress, even traumatic stress, can induce personal growth.

Constructivist/self-psychology models

One of the main limitations of traumatic stress theories of abuse is the overemphasis on affective consequences and a lack of consideration of cognitive processes in the mediation of the effects of trauma on the individual (McCann and Pearlman 1990). The constructivist position emphasizes that experience does not exist unmediated by the perspectives, assumptions and beliefs of the individual (Mendel 1995). 'Reality' is therefore a subjective process, individually and uniquely experienced and constructed by each individual. Social constructivism posits the source of beliefs as being social inventions with meanings created and established through linguistic structures and dominant discourse (Berger and Luckman 1966; White and Epston 1989).

Constructivist models of the impact of trauma highlight that the personal meanings attributed to or derived from traumatic circumstances are crucial as intervening variables regarding negative, neutral or positive impacts of trauma (Janoff-Bulmann 1985, 1989; McCann and Pearlman 1990; Silver et al. 1983). Different people experience and construe the same events in different ways. However, while acknowledging the important influence of social constructs on individual ascription of meaning to experience, there is a need for caution about the possibility of negating the direct impact of reality (Speed 1991). Reality testing can be very important in therapy and it is important not to 'risk the logical nihilism that this constructivist road portends – the conclusion that all existence is a constructed illusion' (Beutler and Sandowicz 1994: 102).

Self-psychology is an associated developmental paradigm concerned with the interplay of maturational processes and social influences on the establishment (construction) of a consistent sense of personal identity; and the deleterious impact of a failure to achieve this. The establishment of a core identity (self) is seen as a major developmental task central to childhood, adolescence and periods of adult life (Erikson 1950). Of particular relevance here are the well-reported difficulties of many adults who were abused as children with regard to sense of identity. For Courtois (1988) and Briere (1992), following Winnicott (1965), it is the acquisition of adaptive 'false self' constructs as a consequence of child-hood abuse which therapy must tackle in search of the 'true self'. Failure to establish a core self and the consequent development of adaptive false 'selves' (following trauma and/or insufficiently consistently nurturing early environments) is seen as a more profound problem than transient existential uncertainty about identity which is experienced within a normal developmental process.

Severe disturbances in self-concept and identity range from a pro-nounced lack of sense of authentic self and depersonalization to the reported experience of numerous separate selves, each with their own characteristics. At the extreme end of this spectrum is the controversial diagnosis of 'Multiple Personality Disorder'. Adherents to the notion of Multiple Personality Disorder insist that this condition is caused in two ways:

1 As a creative and adaptive survival response to severe child abuse which has involved severe sadistic or ritualistic elements (Ross 1989).
2 As a result of extensive psychological 'programming' by secret cults (Noblitt and Perskin 1995).

In view of the increasingly controversial nature of this diagnosis, the deletion in 1994 of the term 'Multiple Personality Disorder' from DSM-IV (APA 1994) is an interesting development which may reflect height-ened concerns about iatrogenic and social contagion influences, and damage being caused to clients and their families by therapy based on this notion (Dale 1999). The essence of the condition is currently retained in the DSM-IV under the less dramatic label 'Dissociative Identity Disorder' (APA 1994: 477).

The existential tradition

Existential psychotherapy has historical roots within both the psycho-analytic and humanistic traditions. It emphasizes the importance of philosophical enquiry as the core element of therapy, reflected in an ongoing search for personal meaning in life and the acceptance by individuals of ultimate responsibility for their choices (Frankl 1946/1992; Laing 1967). In the search for the development of meaning, the focus has similarities with the constructivist and traumatic stress paradigms already discussed. According to van Deurzen-Smith, in existential ther-apy people explore:

> the basic concerns that human beings sooner or later are confronted with. These include death, isolation, loneliness, fate, time, illness and absurdity . . . the existential view is that it matters enormously to reflect on such issues and on one's ways of dealing with them. As an intrinsically philosophical approach existential therapy and counselling does not pretend to cure or change the person, but simply to assist in coming to terms with life and living. (van Deurzen-Smith 1996: 31)

Unlike many other models, existential approaches do not aim to suggest or impose favoured ways of developing meaning for life circumstances and experiences; rather they facilitate clients in finding their own personal meanings (Spinelli 1994; van Deurzen-Smith 1988). As will be seen in Chapter 8, the search for meaning behind histories of being abused in childhood can be a very poignant area of exploration which sometimes leads in unexpected directions.

Systemic models

In systemic approaches (developed from systems theory) the focus is less on the psychological functioning of individuals than on the operation of roles and dynamics between members of a group – particularly, in this context, family groups (Bott 1990; Hoffman 1981). In the child abuse field systemic influences have most prominently been reflected in family dysfunction models of abuse and interventions which were particularly influential in the 1970s and 1980s (Bentovim et al. 1988; Dale and Davies 1985; Gelinas 1983; Giarretto 1982a; Sgroi 1982). Interest is in the combined effect of individual motives and relationship processes within families which contribute to the occurrence and maintenance of child abuse.

Systemic perspectives highlight the mutual involvement, interaction and varying roles of both parents in generating, sustaining and repeating family relationships within which abuse occurs and continues over time. Typically, but not universally, predisposed fathers were seen to acquire the role of sexually abusing while mothers 'failed to protect' the abused child; and vice versa in relation to physical abuse. A systems perspective is often crucial for understanding abuse (both physical and sexual) which has occurred over a long period of time with the knowledge of a 'non-abusing' parent, who nevertheless has not taken effective action to protect the child.

In sexual abuse situations, rivalry between mothers and daughters can become a significant dynamic which reverberates throughout the family system. Therapeutic intervention is based on careful assessment of family dynamics with the aim of restructuring the family system (by strengthening the marital relationship and reinstating appropriate parent–child boundaries) to avoid individual adult needs being met directly or indirectly through the abuse or exploitation of children. This approach is particularly helpful when family members acknowledge that inappropriate events have taken place and where they wish to remain together as a family (Dale et al. 1986b; Furniss 1983; Gelinas 1983; Giarretto 1982a).

One criticism of the systemic model is the potential danger of underestimating the significance of intra-psychic/psychological factors in individuals' predispositions to abuse, resulting in a minimization of the personal responsibility of the abuser. This can place disproportionate onus onto other family members (especially children and mothers) to alter their behaviour to prevent the abuser from abusing again; an effect which has been characterized by feminist critics as both victim-blaming and mother-blaming (Hooper 1992; MacLeod and Saraga 1988).

Survivor models

As mentioned at the beginning of this chapter, survivor models quickly became very prominent in the 1980s and 1990s. A major influence was the feminist paradigm of that era which focused on high rates of reported sexual abuse of female children by men. This gave strength to the feminist theory that a primary cause of child abuse is power differentials between adults and children and between males and females (Herman 1981). These power differentials were seen to stem from the vested interests of patriarchal family and social systems which provide men (seen constitutionally as potential abusers) with the opportunity for the socially institutionalized dominance and exploitation of women and children (Miller 1983; Parton 1990).

This view of the aetiology of child sexual abuse underpinned treatment approaches based on self-help principles echoing the established 'twelve-step' recovery programme of Alcoholics Anonymous. Clients are seen as 'victims' whose path toward recovery involves transformation into 'survivors'. Therapeutic principles and practice derived from this perspective conceptualize the process of 'recovery' as following a largely predetermined pathway. Taken from prominent survivor publications (Bass and Davis 1988; Dinsmore 1991; Forward 1990; Frederickson 1992; Parkes 1990), specific stages and actions include:

- believing and accepting that one was abused;
- adopting a new identity as a survivor;
- joining and belonging to a survivor group (as a substitute family);
- 'reclaiming' or 'recovering' repressed memories of abuse;
- receiving therapist 'validation' of the truth of such memories;
- ventilation of cathartic anger in therapy;
- confronting the abuser;
- severing contact with family of origin;
- a great deal of 'reparenting' of the 'inner child'.

One of the reported strengths of survivor models is the solidarity and support generated by associated survivor peer groups. This is illustrated by testimonies of people in survivor publications who report that such fellowship has had profound impact upon their lives.

The theory and practice of certain aspects of this approach have become subject to increasing scrutiny and criticism from several directions. The underlying feminist theory which was influential in combating social denial of child sexual abuse in the 1970s and 1980s and in generating non-sexist treatment services for women, has itself faced, in more recent years, the need to review certain basic assumptions. In particular, feminist child abuse theory faces a challenge in conceptualizing the significantly increased reported rate of sexual abuse of children by females, which has promoted a revision of the belief that virtually all sexual abuse of children is perpetrated by males (Elliot 1993; Mendel 1995). Criticisms also stem from other theoretical perspectives in relation to the tendency for the survivor movement to underestimate the significance of other events not directly related to abuse, and in taking a simplistic view of therapeutic complexities (Davies and Frawley 1994; Haaken and Schlaps 1991).

Survivor models are also limited in that they are less congruent for people who were abused as children in the context of affectionate caretaking relationships; for those who experienced some degree of pleasurable sexual response to abuse; for those who feel a sense of loss in relation to the abuser; and for people who were sexually abused by women. These clients can feel deviant or inadequate in response to the expectations explicit in these models as to how stereotypical 'victims' are supposed to think, feel and behave.

The prominence of survivor models in the 1980s and early 1990s eventually led to a critical counter-reaction. This was led by parents who considered themselves to be falsely accused of child abuse (either by grown-up children or by child protection workers); and by concerned academics who felt that social concern about child abuse had grown out of control into a 'witch hunt'. Having in previous years given a great deal of prominence to child abuse in support of the survivor position, without any hint of embarrassment, the media switched sides. Stories began to portray being a 'victim' as a fashion statement:

Beware the Incest-Survivor Machine. (Carol Tavris, *New York Times*, 3 January 1993)

I have identified a new syndrome, abusorrhoea . . . it consists of wanting to talk to the media about how you were abused as a child and it particularly afflicts actresses who have a new film or play coming out. (Lynn Barber, *Independent on Sunday*, 10 November 1992)

Why are they making victims of us all? (Richard Gilliat, *The Independent*, 2 December 1991)

These views in turn, have been characterized as a 'backlash' drummed up by, at best, those who do not take child abuse seriously and, at worst, by denying abusers 'taking cover' within 'false memory' organizations. The dispute between these two perspectives (for example, as illustrated on the Internet discussion groups 'Witchhunt' and 'Dissociative Disorders') continues to reflect longstanding social conflicts about the nature of child abuse. The arguments remain polarized, driven by social, ideological, emotional and personal agendas which are always intense and sometimes venomous.

Eclectic-integrative paradigm

In postmodern philosophical culture there is a move away from the expectation that single grand theories can be sufficient to explain complex phenomena. This is reflected in the general psychotherapy world where, increasingly, the rigidity of traditional paradigms is being superseded by eclectic and integrative approaches which incorporate theoretical and technical flexibility (Bergin and Garfield 1994; Clarkson 1993; Clarkson and Pokorny 1994).

Notwithstanding the distraction of competing high social profiles of 'survivors' and 'witch hunters', most academically authoritative clinical publications discussing therapy with adults who were abused as children, have been located firmly within an eclectic-integrative paradigm. This highlights the importance of a flexible utilization of treatment approaches derived from varying models to address specific problems. Following from a recognition of the wide range of potential consequences of childhood abuse, emphasis in the eclectic-integrative paradigm has been placed on the importance of utilizing treatment approaches from across varying models to address specific issues. These involve a focus on therapeutic responses to combinations of:

- trauma (Blake-White and Kline 1985; Ochberg 1991);
- loss (Courtois 1988);
- cognitions (Jehu 1988; Salter 1995);
- affect (Cornell and Olio 1991; Gil 1988);
- self-psychology (Briere 1992; McCann and Pearlman 1990);
- unconscious processes (Briere 1989; Haaken and Schlaps 1991);
- object relations (Davies and Frawley 1994; Gardner 1990);
- family systems (Gelinas 1983; Giarretto 1982a and b);
- sexual (Maltz and Holman 1987);
- memory processes (Courtois 1992; Olio 1989; Sanderson 1990).

In this chapter we have covered important contextual issues relating to child abuse theory and research and a brief overview of major theories which inform therapeutic practice. In the next chapter we will consider important lessons from a significant history of psychotherapy research and a contrasting very small amount of research into therapy with adults who were abused as children. This material is particularly important as there is a culture in many counselling and psychotherapy training schemes virtually to ignore the body of psychotherapy research.

Note

1 The efficacy of prevention services is frustratingly difficult to prove – how to prove that something that did not happen would have happened without a specific intervention – when research ethics prohibit the necessary controlled experiments which could establish this.

2

What does Counselling and Psychotherapy Research Teach us?

Over the past fifty years a great deal of research has been concerned with the efficacy of therapeutic interventions, including the outcomes of therapy as well as the processes which generate beneficial effects. In this chapter we will consider key findings regarding helpful and unhelpful factors in psychotherapy and review the small numbers of studies which have focused specifically on therapy with adults who were abused as children.

Psychotherapy research paradigms

Before considering the relevant findings of psychotherapy research, it is important to locate this knowledge within a framework of the philosophy of science and methodology, since there are many debates and disputes as to what constitutes respectable or adequate research. Issues relating to ideology (belief systems) and epistemology (ways of knowing) inevitably colour the assumptions of researchers and promote the use of particular methodologies (Guba and Lincoln 1994; Howe 1989).

A longstanding distinction exists between positivist experimental research and naturalistic research. Experimental research is characterized by controlled experiments in standardized, artificial (laboratory) conditions; precise standardized measures; large samples and use of control groups. Typically, with two samples (experimental and control) tested and matched on relevant characteristics, the experimental sample is subject to carefully contrived additional influences. Subsequent changes in the experimental sample can then be statistically compared with the control group over periods of time. Research from this positivist paradigm is highly sophisticated and vitally effective. Few people would be happy to give their children medicines which had not been rigorously tested for effectiveness and side-effects by this form of research.

Naturalistic research, in contrast, seeks to describe and understand phenomena in naturally occurring settings. This perspective recognizes that the process of scientific observation and intervention can significantly affect the phenomena observed – especially social behaviour and individual subjective experiencing. A better understanding of how school children include and exclude peers within groups (which is helpful knowledge to prevent bullying) will be obtained by unobtrusive observations of playground behaviour rather than by some contrived experiment in an artificial setting. Similarly, honest descriptions of subjective experiencing and its impact on behaviour, such as socially deviant sexual fantasizing (which is helpful knowledge to develop treatment programmes for sexual offenders), is more likely to be obtained by in-depth interviews than by standardized questionnaires with limited response options.

Psychotherapy research has reflected both the traditional positivist and the more recent naturalistic paradigms. The distinction between these two philosophies has been described in many different ways:

- Science versus art (Eisner 1981; Hill 1982).
- Experimental (laboratory) versus clinical (practice) (Hill 1982, 1984; Garfield and Bergin 1978; Luborsky and Spence 1978; Neimeyer and Resnikoff 1982; Schein 1987).
- Individual versus group design (Butler and Strupp 1986; Garfield and Bergin 1978; Gelso 1979; Hill 1982; Tyson 1992).
- Deductive versus inductive (Garfield and Bergin 1978; Hoshmand 1989).
- Quantitative versus qualitative (Hill 1982; Mearns and McLeod 1984; Neimeyer and Resnikoff 1982).
- 'Rigor versus relevance' (Gelso 1979; Krumboltz and Mitchell 1979).

Positivist research designs in psychotherapy

Research of this nature stems from traditional methodology of the physical sciences. Experimental designs with control groups are utilized to isolate specific independent variables which may constitute the active components of effective psychotherapy. This approach involves studying:

- Micro-level therapeutic interventions (such as reflections, interpretations and silences) (Caskey et al. 1984; Elliot 1979, 1983; Friedlander et al. 1985; Hill 1989; Wiseman 1992).
- Therapists', clients' or independent raters' retrospective perceptions of the significant moments in therapy sessions (Elliot and Shapiro 1988; Llewelyn 1988).
- The relative effectiveness of different types of therapy with the same experimental client group, or matched experimental client groups (Cross et al. 1982; Llewelyn and Hume 1979; Shapiro and Firth 1987).

Research from the positivist paradigm has played an important role in the debate about the effectiveness of psychotherapy, and in the identification of 'helpful and unhelpful' factors. However, reservations exist about the authenticity of 'therapy' which takes place under such carefully contrived, controlled and observed conditions and the validity of measures of interventions and change.

Naturalistic research designs in psychotherapy

In this book I am particularly interested in clients' and therapists' perceptions of the therapeutic encounter. To gain access to such experiencing in depth requires research which is influenced by the naturalistic paradigm. Naturalistic studies of psychotherapy focus on the phenomenological experiences of therapists and clients of the process and outcome of therapy, including the nature of the relationship between the participants. The value of this approach has been increasingly highlighted (Elliot and James 1989; Elliot and Shapiro 1992; Hill 1982; McLeod 1990, 1994; Neimeyer and Resnikoff 1982; Oldfield 1983; Patton 1991; Rennie and Toukmanian 1992). Studies so far have adopted three main approaches:

1 In-depth interviewing by qualitatively orientated researchers (for example, Armsworth 1990; Dinnage 1988; Oldfield 1983; Park 1992).
2 Intensive case study analyses involving a combination of qualitative approaches with systematically contrived methods of data collection and analysis (for example, Hill 1989; Elliot and Shapiro 1992; Rennie 1992).
3 Reflective narrative accounts of experiences of psychotherapy written by therapists (for example, Dryden 1992, 1993; Fitts 1985; Hobson 1985; Mearns and Dryden 1990; Yalom 1989) and clients (Allen 1990; France 1988; Nin 1993; Spring 1987).

Naturalistic research emphasizes the importance of establishing safety, respect and trust in the relationship between the researcher and the researched (Hoshmand 1989; Mearns and McLeod 1984). By the use of in-depth qualitative interviews, access can be obtained into highly private areas of human thoughts, feelings, behaviour and relationships. Consequently, this approach is particularly fruitful when the research focus is on areas of human experience which are less researched, sensitive or traditionally private (Hoshmand 1989; Lee 1993).

A major principle of such research is to give a voice to the researched – in this context the clients and therapists themselves. The communication of this voice, with or without analysis by the researcher, provides material which is of direct clinical significance. Consequently, one advantage of naturalistic research in psychotherapy is the ecological validity (clinical relevance) of the findings of studies for practitioners. This overcomes the renowned difficulty in being relevant to practice (external validity) which has always been a major problem for positivist orientated research in psychotherapy (Gelso et al. 1988; Neimeyer and Resnikoff 1982); and which has contributed to the general lack of influence of research on practice in the field (Butler and Strupp 1986; Gelso et al. 1988; Greenberg and Pinsof 1986; McLeod 1994; Mahrer 1985; Sainsbury 1987; Tyson 1992).

The development of convergent methodology

The positivist paradigm has a long history and it is often claimed that this approach is scientifically 'hard' and therefore more respectable. Consequently, tensions between positivist (quantitative) and naturalistic (qualitative) paradigms, have been continually apparent. The effect of the absence of statistical analysis in qualitative research and the distortions of phenomena which can occur in quantitative research were encapsulated by one commentator: 'If you can't count it, it doesn't count; if you can count it, that ain't it' (Kiesler 1973).

The inadequacy of any single paradigm for understanding exceedingly complex phenomena was summed up succinctly in this way. Concerns about the validity of positivist studies question the inherent belief that experimental designs are neutral (that the research itself does not affect the behaviour of the participants); and whether they actually do produce 'objective' measurements of human behaviour and emotion. The 'context stripping' requirement of positivist experimental approaches (which have to simplify, reduce and quantify 'variables' in order to measure them) introduces a bias as it ignores the holistic and systemic complexity of the psychotherapeutic process and of human experience (Stiles 1995; Tyson 1992). It assumes a linear cause and effect model of action and response, rather than a systemic matrix of multidimensional influences.

Moreover, to reduce phenomena to forms which are quantifiably convenient can lead to the study of variables which can be clinically irrelevant and sometimes trivial (Neimeyer and Resnikoff 1982; Rowan 1992). This is partly the reason why, in general, much positivist psychotherapy research has had little influence on practice – it is seen as being too divorced and distant from real life therapy. Another reason involves the influence of the factors of time and context on previously accepted research findings. Research findings relating to psychotherapy are made in particular social–political–psychological contexts (for example, Rogers in 1950s America) and may not hold true in other places and eras. They also do not necessarily remain relevant for ever: as noted by Cronbach (1975: 122), 'generalizations decay'.

Compromises and trade-offs are necessary and inevitable in all research designs to obtain the most pragmatically available balance between factors of reliability and validity of studies (Gelso 1979; Hill 1982). Consequently, the history of psychotherapy research has involved 'swings of fads' between the major paradigms characterized by the 'flight to the laboratory' represented by experimental research and the 'return to the subjective and qualitative' (Dunnette 1966; Gelso 1979). The continuing oscillation between these perspectives supports Gelso's (1979: 8) view that 'there exist few, if any, clear resolutions to the complex problems of research methodology'.

Pondering on this, and inspired by the continued failure of one of his students to fix a plastic sticker on his car windscreen without an air bubble appearing somewhere or other, Gelso (1979) construed the paradigmatic problem in psychotherapy research as the 'bubble hypothesis': there is always some imperfection at some point or other in any paradigm. This state of affairs remains unchanged and vigorous debates continue regarding inadequacies in designs of psychotherapy studies (Barkham and Shapiro 1992; Eysenck 1992; Kline 1992).

An increasingly common conclusion is that ultimately no form of enquiry is truly objective, value or bias free (Hill 1984; Gelso et al. 1988; Guba and Lincoln 1994; McLeod 1994; Rowan 1992; Tyson 1992). This view is compatible with postmodernist perspectives on the multiple levels of reality and truth (Altheide and Johnson 1994; Howe 1994; Lincoln and Denzin 1994). Consequently the onus on researchers (especially in the field of psychotherapy) is to maximize awareness of and to make explicit the sources and impact of such influences upon their perceptions and the conclusions which they draw from their work.

In recent years many researchers commenting on the benefits and inadequacies of each perspective in its own right, have argued for convergent methodology or methodological pluralism which utilizes and respects the most valuable features of each perspective (Bergin and Garfield 1994). From this perspective, knowledge in the field is advanced by an accumulation of studies which reflect combinations of paradigms, attempts to integrate paradigms, or which use multiple paradigms (each with their own methodological shortcomings) to approach the subject simultaneously from different perspectives using different modes of enquiry. This produces a triangulation of theory, method and data source resulting in a rich composite of data which would not otherwise be accessible from a single approach (Hoshmand 1989).

Outcome studies: is psychotherapy effective?

From the late 1940s onwards one of the key research debates has been: 'Is psychotherapy effective?' A major challenge was presented by Eysenck's (1952, 1965) reviews of psychotherapy literature which concluded that the therapeutic effects of psychotherapy were small or non-existent in helping either disturbed children or neurotic adults. This assertion provoked an intensification of research activity into the effectiveness question. Truax and Carkhuff (1967) noted that a significant flaw in Eysenck's analysis was to treat psychotherapy as a unitary activity. In fact the 'psychotherapy' which he had addressed in his review included a wide variety of theoretical orientations, and disparities in the training and experience of its practitioners. Consequently, according to Truax and Carkhuff (1967: 18) to ask whether psychotherapy is effective is: 'very much like asking a pharmacologist "is chemotherapy effective" and then conducting research by randomly giving unknown kinds and quantities of drugs to one group of patients with various complaints, and no drugs to a similar "control" group'.

Truax and Carkhuff (1967) also pointed out that from the studies Eysenck had reviewed he had been essentially right to say that average psychotherapy as currently practised did not result in average client improvement. This had failed to take into account that some clients did benefit from psychotherapy while others got worse.

The last three decades have seen significant advances in research methodology and activity in this area. Others followed Eysenck in conducting meta-reviews of relevant research, including subsequent more sophisticated studies. By the 1970s, reviews of outcome studies of psychotherapy were regularly concluding that the question regarding the effectiveness of psychotherapy had been conclusively resolved in favour of psychotherapy (Bergin 1971; Bergin and Lambert 1978; Garfield 1992; Garfield and Bergin 1978, 1986; Gelso 1979; Lambert et al. 1986; Lambert and Bergin 1992; Luborsky et al. 1975; Smith et al. 1980). However, despite the continuing general acknowledgement in the literature about the overall effectiveness of psychotherapy, the controversy continues to resurface from time to time (Dryden and Feltham 1992; Eysenck 1992; Garfield 1992; Masson 1992).

An associated area of research has explored the question whether certain forms, or models, of psychotherapy are more effective than others. In a frequently quoted conclusion to their meta-review of studies exploring this question, Luborsky et al. (1975) echoed the view of the Dodo bird in *Alice in Wonderland* (Carroll 1993 [1865]) that 'everyone has won and all must have prizes'. Following this, the view that different schools of psychotherapy produce similar outcomes has been labelled the 'Dodo bird hypothesis' (Gelso 1979). On this question, Gelso concluded: 'The most recent analyses of approaches by theoretical "schools" do support the Dodo bird. On the whole, all theoretical approaches produce about equally positive results, although some approaches do emerge as superior for certain problem types' (Gelso 1979: 16).

Over the last decade the Dodo bird hypothesis has continued to be explored and the results of various studies vigorously debated (Mair 1992; Orlinsky and Howard 1986; Shapiro and Shapiro 1982; Rowan 1983, 1992).

Process studies

Process research explores which components of therapy lead to positive change – the 'who, what, when, and where' questions (Gelso 1979). A great deal of such research has been undertaken over the past twenty-five years and meta-analyses have been presented by Elliot and James (1989); Greenberg and Pinsof (1986); Orlinsky et al. (1994). Carl Rogers is often credited as having been in the vanguard of therapists keen to open up the therapeutic process to scientific observation. Much of the early exploratory process research focused upon analysis of taperecordings of Rogers and his colleagues' client-centred therapy (Rice 1992). Rogers was keen to establish from micro-analysis of therapy sessions what were the active contributions of therapists which led to positive client change. This led him into the conceptually challenging position of developing positivist laboratory research designs for humanistic client-centred therapy.

Rogers concluded that there were three 'necessary and sufficient conditions' for effective therapy (Rogers 1957). The fact that these conditions (accurate empathy, non-possessive warmth and genuineness) were attributes of therapists, rather than therapeutic techniques or theoretical orientation, provoked a flurry of further research. Truax and Carkhuff, anticipating the 'who, what, where, when' questions, extended the chemotherapy metaphor, pointing the way for psychotherapy process researchers during the 1970s, 1980s and 1990s: 'The psychotherapy researcher should be asking in effect, "*what* dosage level of *what* drug produces the therapeutic effects?" ' (Truax and Carkhuff 1967: 22).

Commenting on the limited overall success of process research, Stiles (1988: 27) noted that in general 'research on linking observable process components . . . to outcomes . . . has been disappointing'. Partly as a reaction to such disappointments, Hill (1989) noted that current process research tends toward a convergent methodology exploring the relative contributions of:

- therapists' characteristics;
- clients' characteristics;
- the therapeutic relationship;
- therapeutic techniques;
- the impact of factors external to therapy.

Client perspectives in psychotherapy research

It is surprising how little research overall has sought to describe the experiences and perspectives of those who receive and provide therapy. If the client studies which are not strictly to do with psychotherapy are excluded,[1] the comment of McLeod (1990: 1) is particularly apt: 'Hardly anyone has ever asked clients what they think about the counselling or psychotherapy they are receiving.' In the few studies that have looked specifically at individual counselling and psychotherapy, clients' perspectives have been directly included in two main ways: in process research as reviewers or raters of the therapy they have experienced (Hill 1989; Rennie 1992); and descriptively in a small number of qualitative studies (Armsworth 1990; Oldfield 1983).

There is also a valuable developing literature of narratives written by clients giving accounts of their experiences of psychotherapy and its effects (for example, Allen 1990; Grierson 1990; Nin 1993; Rippere and Williams 1985; Spring 1987). France (1988) provided a particularly compelling detailed review of her experiences with three psychotherapists over a period of eight years, from the position of a client having considerable theoretical knowledge of psychotherapy. France's impressive (and clinically very insightful) book introduces the perspective of the sophisticated and theoretically well-informed client reflecting in detail on helpful and unhelpful experiences of therapy. This perspective is developed further in this book via the equally well-informed and articulate participants in the study.

In addition to narratives from clients, a number of therapists have also reflected on personal experiences of their practices (Casement 1985; Clarkson 1984; Fitts 1985; Hobson 1985; Lomas 1987, 1994; Mearns 1990; Storr 1979; Yalom 1989).

Key findings regarding outcome and helpful and unhelpful factors in psychotherapy

Many of the studies which have sought the opinions of the consumers of counselling and psychotherapy have reported high rates of satisfaction with the outcome. This is typical of consumer surveys (Canter 1989) and may involve a degree of bias in favour of positive comments in that less satisfied consumers may not be inclined to respond in a critical fashion, or at all. Table 2.1 illustrates results from some of the key studies where some form of satisfaction outcome figure was presented (data obtained by use of questionnaires, tests or combinations of these).

A range of other studies have reported quantitative findings relating to clients' evaluations of other forms of help such as social work, marital therapy, mental health services and family therapy. Table 2.2 illustrates equivalent results for several of these studies.

Other researchers have provided comments rather than figures to illustrate levels of satisfaction, as shown in Table 2.3.

Overall, this research (especially that relating specifically to psychotherapy and counselling) shows a consistently high rate of expressed client satisfaction with the help received. The striking exception is the qualitative study by Howe (1989) which revealed almost unanimous and

Table 2.1 *Client satisfaction rates from psychotherapy*

Study	Client expressed satisfaction rate %	Sample size
Lipkin (1948)	71	(N = 35)
Feifel and Eells (1963)	90	(N = 63)
Strupp et al. (1964)	93	(N = 44)
Strupp et al. (1969)	87	(N = 122)
Heinemann and Yudin (1974)	80	(N = 50 approx.)[1]
Persons et al. (1974)	100	(N = 93)
Werman et al. (1976)	82	(N = 80)
Sloane et al. (1977)	80	(N = 50)
Kaschak (1978)	100	(N = 75)
Llewelyn and Hume (1979)	97	(N = 37)
Cross et al. (1982)	100	(N = 30)
Lietaer and Neirinck (1987)	78	(N = 41)
Llewelyn (1988)	76	(N = 40)
Brunning (1992)	94	(N = 176)

[1] The exact number is not completely clear from the text.

Table 2.2 *Client satisfaction rates from other forms of help*

Study	Client expressed satisfaction rate %	Sample size	Profession
Sainsbury (1975)	93.0	(N = 27 – families)	Social work
Sainsbury et al. (1982)	40.0	(N = 74 – families)	Social work
Lishman (1978)	50.0	(N = 12)	Social work
Maluccio (1979)	72.0	(N = 25)	Social work
Merrington and Corden (1981)	87.50	(N = 8)	Family therapy
Hunt (1985)	49.0	(N = 51)	Marital therapy
Canter (1989)	72.0	(N = 56)	Mental health centre

Table 2.3 *Client satisfaction rate (non-statistical)*

Study	Client expressed satisfaction rate	Sample size	Profession
Ryan and Gizynski (1971)	'Majority of treatments were to some degree successful'	(N = 14)	Behaviour therapy
Brannen and Collard (1982)	'Approximately half'	(N = 48)	Marital therapy
Oldfield (1983)	'More than half . . . in the pilot study'	(N = 13)	Counselling
Howe (1989)	Predominantly negative	(N = 32)	Family therapy

intense dissatisfaction with a family therapy service provided by a social work team.

Care must be taken in interpreting statistical indications of satisfaction or helpfulness, as responses may be distorted by a range of influences.

These can include contextual biases toward positive evaluations (especially when the practitioner is also the evaluator); inhibition in the communication of critical feelings; lack of response categories to reflect ambivalence; and short follow-up time scales. Also it is possible for clients to consider that a service is good – even though they feel that they have not benefited personally (Canter 1989; Sainsbury 1987; Shaw 1984). Consequently, client satisfaction rates do not necessarily accord with measures of outcome. However, notwithstanding these cautions, this research is revealing in respect of which particular aspects of therapy clients find to be helpful and unhelpful.

Helpful and unhelpful factors in the psychotherapeutic process

Overviews of process research (Elliot and James 1989; Hill 1989; Howe 1993; McLeod 1990) suggest that helpful and unhelpful factors in therapy fall into three main categories:

- those that are to do with the characteristics of clients;
- those that relate to characteristics and behaviours of therapists;
- those that appertain to the therapeutic relationship.

There is much discussion as to which of these categories contains the 'real' active ingredients of therapy, and which are 'placebos' or simply irrelevant. Sides have been taken and corners argued with surprising conviction and commitment. This hints at the significance of this question to ideological rivalries between various theories, schools and vested interests in therapy.

A 'meta' perspective is taken by researchers such as Hill (1989) and Rennie and Toukmanian (1992) and commentators such as Clarkson (1993, 1995) who argue for an holistic understanding of the interplay of diverse influences in recognition of the postmodern acceptance that there is no single truth. This is a reminder of the unlikelihood of simple answers to complex problems arising in this field. Within the three broad headings outlined (between which there is some conceptual overlap), key findings from this research will now be presented.

Client characteristics

Characteristics of clients affect the process of psychotherapy in several ways. Unlike the traditional notion in positivist experimental research, in psychotherapy a client is not a passive 'dependent variable'. Clients do not respond in predicable and consistent ways to therapeutic influences. These influences are mediated by the meanings which clients construct for their experience of them and the choices they make in response to them. Clients therefore play an active part in their interpretations of, and reactions to, the influences to which they are subject. Idiosyncratic meanings and choices stem from the interaction of: personal biographies, cognitive structures, affective states, social contexts and future expectations.

There are also wide variations in the personal resources which clients bring to therapy (Highlen and Hill 1984; Hill 1989). These include:

- types of problems;
- levels of distress;
- ability and willingness to self-explore;
- verbal skills;
- ability to form a relationship;
- psychological mindedness;
- degrees of motivation for change;
- ability to tolerate frustration;
- coping skills;
- expectations regarding outcome.

Truax and Carkhuff (1967) noted that clients who experienced high levels of 'inner' disturbance, but low levels of behavioural disturbance, were most likely to be successfully helped. Rennie (1992) described the significance of clients' *agency* or *reflexivity* as being a necessary part of a successful therapy process. Certain client characteristics appear to make therapy a more stimulating, enjoyable and rewarding experience for therapists. This plays a part in provoking increased levels of interest and responsiveness by therapists. For example, clients experienced as likeable attract more warmth from therapists (Truax and Carkhuff 1967). Schofield (1964) remarked upon the particularly positive responses offered to 'YAVIS' – clients who are young, attractive, verbal, intelligent and successful.

In contrast, a range of negative or deficit client factors which reduce the likelihood of therapy being effective have also been noted. In some studies clients described the hindering influence of their own characteristics and behaviour in therapy (Elliot and James 1989; Highlen and Hill 1984; Lietaer 1992; Lietaer and Neirinck 1987; Rennie 1992). These include: resistance, antagonism, lack of cooperation, passivity, flirtatiousness, competitiveness and mistrust. A 'clash of perspectives' can also arise when clients and therapists do not establish a shared framework for exploring and understanding human problems and their solutions (Brannen and Collard 1982; Howe 1989; Hunt 1985; Lishman 1978; Mayer and Timms 1970; Merrington and Corden 1981; Sainsbury 1975). Such clashes stem from: different beliefs regarding the cause of problems; differences in culture, social class, gender, ethnic origin; and the degree to which the therapist has ever experienced problems similar to those of the client. For example, one commonly reported clash is between working-class men (who tend to expect advice from therapy), and therapists who expect clients to generate their own insights (Brannen and Collard 1982; Oldfield 1983).

Characteristics of therapists

Beutler et al. (1994) reviewed the extensive research on therapist variables and identified three key findings:

1   Positive outcome for clients is consistently more closely associated with personal characteristics of therapists than with therapeutic orientation or techniques.
2   Some therapists, regardless of therapeutic approach, consistently produce more positive results than others.
3   Some therapists, regardless of orientation, consistently produce negative effects.

The weighting is in favour of therapists' attributes (rather than their theoretical orientations and techniques) as being the major effective therapeutic ingredient. However, it is difficult to identify what these specific attributes are, because of problems involved in isolating the effect of single factors within a complex multidimensional process. This links with an important question, which has important implications for training: 'Are effective therapists born or made?' If, for example, the ability to communicate accurate empathy is a skill, then presumably it can be taught, practised and developed. But if it is a characteristic, can it be acquired (Truax and Carkhuff 1967)?

While clients and therapists have clear opinions regarding helpful and unhelpful therapist factors, it is interesting that these perceptions can be somewhat discrepant (Caskey et al. 1984; Fuller and Hill 1985; Hill 1989; Lietaer 1992). Characteristics of therapists perceived as being helpful by clients include:

• personal warmth and likeability;
• having a non-judgemental attitude;
• being empathic, accepting, objective, patient and understanding;
• demonstrating a genuine interest in the client.

While therapists acknowledge these factors, they tend to emphasize the significance of their techniques, skills, the provision of insight, confrontation and their facilitation of clients' expression of emotions (Parloff et al. 1978). Therapist factors which are mentioned by clients as being unhelpful to therapeutic progress were noted by Howe (1993) to include:

• misperception and misdirection;
• too much or too little confrontation;
• not enough time and not enough support;
• lack of feedback;

- too deep or absent interpretation;
- misunderstanding or clash of perspective about the goals and methods of therapy;
- absence of advice giving.

Findings from research into therapists' characteristics such as ethnic origin, gender and age are equivocal (Hill 1989). It is not clear in what circumstances such factors have helpful or unhelpful effects.

The therapeutic relationship

The relative impact of the relationship versus techniques has been a central debate in psychotherapy research. The question is whether clients' experience of the relationship itself is a therapeutic factor, or whether this is simply a neutral conduit through which the therapeutic-ally active techniques are applied. The complex interplay between effects of therapeutic relationships and techniques is stressed by Hill:

> Conceptually, problems still remain in teasing out the interaction between the relationship and techniques. Some would assert that it is the relationship itself that causes the change and that the techniques are used only to give the therapist something to do. Others would claim that it is the technical factors alone that lead to change. (Hill 1989: 20)

The nature and significance of the therapeutic relationship is a focus of continued debate (Hill 1989; Dryden and Feltham 1992; Rennie and Toukmanian 1992). However, a number of commentators (for example, Howe 1993; Gelso and Carter 1985; Sexton and Whiston 1994) believe that research taken as a whole has resolved the issue in favour of the relationship rather than techniques as being the most important component of effective therapy.

Accounts from clients highlight the significance of the relationship (for example, Allen 1990; Cross et al. 1982; Dinnage 1988; Elliot and James 1989; Feifel and Eells 1963; France 1988; Grierson 1990; Hill 1989; Lietaer 1992; Oldfield 1983; Ryan and Gizynski 1971). A synthesis of clients' perspectives emphasizes the importance in therapy of having someone to talk to, being understood, and finding meaning for experiences (Howe 1993). For this to occur and to be helpful requires the development of a relationship which includes a degree of trust, confidence and con-fidentiality, as well as a therapist who is able to listen, clarify and provide support.

Conceptual difficulties and disagreements remain as to what a 'thera-peutic relationship' actually is (Gelso and Carter 1985). In this context Clarkson (1993, 1995) has developed a very useful integrative model of five types of therapeutic relating which are potentially available in response to assessment of specific client need:

- the working alliance;
- the transferential/countertransferential relationship;
- the reparative/developmentally needed relationship;
- the person-to-person relationship;
- the transpersonal relationship.

Clarkson's model has considerable clinical relevance and the potential to be a very useful assessment template for more efficacious and consistent matching of client need and therapist response. Mismatches of client need and therapist response will be very apparent in clients' accounts of therapy reported in later chapters of this book.

A number of therapists from Freud onwards have described difficulties experienced in therapeutic relationships (Dryden 1985, 1992; Hobson 1985; Lomas 1994; Mair 1989; Yalom 1989). Much of this material is anecdotal, but nevertheless does draw attention to issues considered to be relevant by practitioners. From a research perspective, Lietaer and Neirinck (1987) found that their sample of person-centred therapists identified their failure to respond empathically to clients as being the most common source of difficulty. Orlinsky and Howard (1977) and Elliot and James (1989) noted therapists' difficulties in maintaining an appropriate balance with clients between domination and passivity.

Dryden (1985) described a range of dilemmas which therapists experience involving: compromises, boundaries, allegiances, roles, responsibility and impasses. Davis et al. (1987) similarly reported on dilemmas in: responsibility, competence, fear of doing damage, technical uncertainty, lack of rapport, intrusion of therapists' personal issues, feeling threatened, stuck and thwarted by clients. Garrett and Davis (1994) and Russell (1993) reported specific concerns about therapists' sexual involvement with clients. Also, and of particular interest to the focus of this book, Frenken and van Stolk (1990) described the significant anxieties and difficulties experienced by therapists in relating to clients with histories of incest.

So far in this chapter I have described some key findings in general psychotherapy research. While this material can be a challenge to assimilate, it does seem important that therapists are aware that there is an impressive research background specifically focused on what works – and what does not work – in therapy. Many training courses pay little attention to this literature, yet it is a feature of a responsible professional that practice is grounded in research as well as theoretical knowledge.

It came as a great surprise to me when I began the study upon which this book is based to discover (in contrast to the voluminous practice and self-help literature) how little research had actually been undertaken on therapeutic approaches with adults who were abused as children. In the second section of this chapter, we will consider key points arising from the published studies in this area.

Research studies: abuse-related therapy

The literature search for this book located eight published studies on individual therapy with adults abused as children (Armsworth 1989, 1990; de Young 1981; Feinauer 1989; Fortgang 1992; Frenken and Van Stolk 1990; Jehu 1988; Josephson and Fong-Beyette 1987). A further four studies focused on group therapy, or combinations of group therapy with individual therapy (Alexander 1991; Becker et al. 1984; Bonney et al. 1986; and Haller and Alter-Reid 1986).

These studies are very varied in their purposes and methodology, which restricts the basis for comparisons and generalizable conclusions. Those of most relevance explored clients' and therapists' perceptions of the process and outcome of individual therapy in relation to the consequences of child abuse. I will discuss these studies later in this section. However, for an overview, the key studies involved are as follows.

Jehu (1988) comprised an 'in-house' evaluation of a predominantly cognitive–behavioural treatment programme at the University of Manitoba, Canada. Data regarding the effect of the programme on forty-one women who were sexually abused as children were gathered by means of questionnaires and other measures.

Armsworth (1989, 1990) explored the experiences of help sought by American female incest survivors to determine what aspects were considered to be helpful, harmful or exploitative. Thirty female respondents completed a nineteen-page questionnaire and six of these were interviewed about their sexual involvement with therapists.

Feinauer (1989) interviewed fifty-seven American adult women who had been abused as children. The interviews explored their perceptions of therapy and factors relating to successful adjustment post-childhood abuse without the need for therapy.

Frenken and Van Stolk (1990), in a study undertaken in the Netherlands, used structured interviews to investigate the social and psychological assistance given to fifty incest victims. They also elicited the views of 130 randomly selected professionals about therapy with this client group.

Fortgang (1992) explored the views of eight psychoanalytically orientated clinicians about their work with one case each of father–daughter incest. These American therapists were recruited by recommendation from 'respected analytic clinicians' and comprised five clinical social workers, two clinical psychologists and one psychiatrist. Views regarding differences in the treatment process with incest victims in comparison to other categories of clients were elicited. Seven out of eight of the respondents felt that they worked in different ways with incest

Table 2.4   *Client views re rate of helpfulness or satisfaction*

	Jehu (1988)	
Sample size	*Client evaluation*	*Percentage*
(N = 41)	'Therapy helped deal more effectively with problems':	
	'a great deal'	84
	'somewhat'	13
	'not really'	0
	'made things worse'	3
	'Extent of satisfaction with service received':	
	'very'	71
	'mostly'	26
	'indifferent/mildly satisfied'	0
	'quite dissatisfied'	3

Armsworth (1989)

Sample size
(N = 30, including contact with total of 113 different professionals)[1]

Rating scale used re helpfulness of therapy:
(5 = 'very helpful'; 3 = 'helpful'; 1 = 'not much help'; 0 = 'did more harm than good')

Mean rating of helpfulness	3.02 (*SD*, 1.93)
Mean rating of helpfulness (female professionals)	3.93 (*SD*, 1.47)
Mean rating of helpfulness (male professionals)	1.98 (*SD*, 1.91)
Clients reporting 'some form of victimization or exploitation by helping professionals'	46%

Feinauer (1989)

Sample size	*Client evaluation*	*Percentage*
(N = 36)	Rated therapy as 'very helpful'	28
	Rated therapy as 'quite helpful'	37
	Rated therapy as 'somewhat helpful'	16

Frenken and Van Stolk (1990)

Sample size		*Client evaluation*	*Percentage*
(a)	(N = 50)	'probable satisfactory therapeutic contact'	50+
		'felt let down by professionals consulted'	58
		abuse or attempted abuse by therapist	10
(b)	(N = 134 – total number of professional contacts)[2]		
		'very satisfied/satisfied'	40
		'partly dissatisfied/dissatisfied/very dissatisfied'	60

Contacts with different professional groups – proportion of these experienced in negative way:

Psychiatrists	54
GPs	52
Social workers	50
Psychotherapists	35
Women's self-help groups	25

[1] The use of the term 'professional' in this study involves a wide range of activities, training and credentialing.
[2] Many of the fifty respondents had had contact with several professionals.

victims and that differences centred around paying greater attention to the establishment of the working alliance.

Findings: outcome

These studies (excluding Fortgang 1992) presented data for perceived degree of helpfulness, satisfaction (or both), as shown in Table 2.4. While the figures are not directly comparable (because of different data elicitation techniques and evaluation criteria) they are illustrative of clients' views.

These figures show a mixed picture ranging from overwhelming satisfaction with the structured therapeutic programme evaluated by Jehu (1988) to the 'dismaying' finding of Armsworth (1989) that 46% of her sample had been 'victimized or exploited' in some way in their contacts with professionals. However, because of the methodological variations and discrepancies in training and experience of the therapists and professionals, caution is needed in drawing conclusions from these findings. Key issues stemming from these studies will now be discussed in more detail.

The key studies: discussion

Jehu (1988)

This represents the most systematic study of outcome of therapy focused specifically on the consequences of childhood sexual abuse. Fifty-one female clients who had received weekly cognitive-behavioural therapy in a specialist sexual abuse treatment programme in Manitoba, Canada, were assessed during treatment and on follow-up by means of a range of measures including interviews. The treatment programme involved a mixture of individual and group therapy as well as an educative input about sexual abuse.

Findings are presented statistically from the various instruments utilized, including outcome data relating to distorted beliefs, mood disturbances, self-esteem and overall client satisfaction with the programme. Significant and sustained changes were reported in respect of distorted beliefs and mood disturbances and to a slightly lesser extent with self-esteem. Overall satisfaction with the programme was high: of the forty-one women who completed the client satisfaction questionnaire (ten had terminated treatment prematurely) 88% rated the quality of service received as 'excellent', and 86% considered that they had been helped to deal with their problems more effectively.

The components of the programme rated as helpful by the clients were:

(a) the provision of information about sexual abuse,
(b) the acquisition of skills to deal with the problem – 'becoming one's own therapist',
(c) the alleviation of self-blame for the abuse, low self-esteem, and feelings of difference from others,
(d) the clarification of perceptions and feelings towards the family of origin and the offender,
(e) the participation of the partner in therapy and improvement in the marital relationship,
(f) meeting other previously sexually abused women in the assertiveness group,
(g) the relationship with the therapist. (Jehu 1988: 299)

Despite the impressive outcome figures there are certain limitations of this study which must be taken into account. The participants were carefully selected to exclude males, non-heterosexuals, and clients experiencing some form of crisis. These exclusions are puzzling. The absence of clients in crisis, in particular, can be expected to weight the sample in favour of motivated and receptive individuals who are more able to be consistently responsive to short-term focused treatment approaches (and the repeated evaluations contained in the research design) which is typical of the cognitive-behavioural model.

A question can be raised about the impact of the weekly evaluation procedures themselves, as it is difficult to separate out the relative impact of the therapy from the measurement procedures. Also, with 'in-house' evaluations of treatment programmes there is a need for some caution about a potential 'wanting to please' factor being present in clients' positive responses.

Armsworth (1989, 1990)

Armsworth explored the self-reports of thirty female incest survivors regarding the professional help they had received. Respondents were solicited from private therapy practitioners, a women's agency, and community groups in an urban area of mid-West USA. A nineteen-page questionnaire covered twelve preselected categories of professionals/groups frequently sought for help according to a four-point rating scale: 'very helpful'; 'helpful'; 'not much help'; 'did more harm than good'. In addition, open-ended questions specifically invited responses regarding clients' experiences of sexual involvement with professionals. From this data Armsworth's analysis of helpful factors included:

(1) the client was believed; (2) the professional was supportive and under-standing; he or she conveyed concern, care, empathy, or compassion for the client; (3) the client was not blamed for the victimization; (4) the professional was not shocked or disgusted with the incest disclosure; (5) the client did not feel alone or odd; (6) the professional helped get the incest stopped. (Armsworth 1989: 554)

In addition to eight reports of sexual intimacy or harassment, other unhelpful factors reported were:

> (1) the professional did not believe the client; the client was told she fantasized the events; (2) the disclosed incest was ignored or dismissed by the professional as not important or not damaging (since no intercourse had occurred); (3) overprescription of drugs; (4) the client was blamed for incest or was told she must have enjoyed it since she stayed; (5) the professional was shocked or disgusted from disclosure of incest experiences. (Armsworth 1989: 554)

Between them, the thirty respondents had had contacts with 113 professionals, ranging from one to nine, the mode being four. Male professionals were seen for more sessions but were rated lower in terms of helpfulness than female professionals. Eighteen of the 113 professional contacts were rated as 'more harm than good', and sixteen of these were with males. Six of the sixteen were so rated because of sexual involvement with the professional. In all, seven of the respondents reported a total of eight sexual involvements, six of which were rated as 'more harm than good'. The other two were rated 'helpful' and 'not much help'.

Armsworth went on to state that overall 'a total of 46 per cent of the sample . . . experienced some form of victimization or exploitation by helping professionals' (1989: 554). This figure requires some examination. If it is correct, it would indeed be 'dismaying' as Armsworth states. However, the figure is arrived at by widening the category of 'some form of victimization or exploitation' to include: 'clients . . . not believed, reports ignored, victim blamed' (p. 554). The number of respondents who interpreted any experience of this nature with their professional helpers is then added to the eight reports of sexual involvement to produce a sum total of 46% of the sample reporting some form of 'victimization or exploitation'.

The adoption of such a broad definition of 'victimization and exploitation' – within which almost any form of subjective experience of dissatisfaction may be included – is problematic and confusing. It is not apparent on what basis experiences such as 'reports (of incest) ignored' can be construed as either 'victimization' or 'exploitation'. No qualitative data from respondents is presented to support such interpretations. The impression is left that, as a specific focus of the study was to explore abuse and exploitation in therapy, an inappropriately loose definition was used of 'victimization' and 'exploitation' creating the 'dismaying' – but inflated – 46% figure.

If the sexual involvement figures are considered separately (as a commonly accepted indicator of abuse and exploitation in therapy), six clients reported incidents of sexual involvement with seven professionals, out of a total professional group of 113. This produces a very different figure for 'victimization and exploitation' of 6%, which is much more in line with other studies (Russell 1993).

Feinauer (1989)

Feinauer explored the therapeutic choices (including the choice not to receive therapy) and experiences of therapy of women who had been sexually abused as children. Fifty-seven respondents completed questionnaires and various instruments relating to their abuse, current adjustment and feelings about therapy they had received. The sample was recruited following a newspaper interview with the author in Utah, USA, which invited participants in the study. Interviews took place with a subgroup of twenty-five people. Both the questionnaire group and the interview group were comprised of those who had received some form of therapy as well as those who had not.

For those who received therapy, 28% rated this as 'very helpful' and 36% as 'quite helpful'. Feinauer merged these two categories to conclude that two-thirds rated therapy as being helpful. If the 'somewhat helpful' category (17%) is added, the helpfulness proportion reaches 81%. Findings also indicated that length of time in therapy and type of therapy had no significant relationship to perception of adjustment post therapy. No information is presented on the types of therapies experienced, apart from the reference to contrasts between 'marital, family, and/or individual therapy' (Feinauer 1989: 329). This precludes a consideration of factors such as training, experience and orientation of practitioners. Also, it is clear that respondents who received therapy did so on a relatively brief basis: nearly two-thirds of the sample received twenty sessions or less. This may reflect, as Feinauer acknowledges, that the sampling procedure is likely to have excluded more seriously damaged or disturbed people.

It is interesting that 36% of respondents felt that they had adjusted successfully to their abuse experiences without any therapy. The existence of support networks and a confiding relationship distinguished the adjusted non-therapy group from those who sought therapy. These are important findings regarding the circumstances in which a publicly very silent group of adults who were abused as children 'successfully adjust' without the need for therapy (see also Sanford 1991).

Frenken and Van Stolk (1990)

This is the only published study which has compared clients' experiences and perceptions of therapy in relation to childhood abuse with those of professionals. The client sample was comprised of fifty incest victims (forty-nine female) who were recruited via articles in two Dutch national newspapers. The group of professionals was a stratified random sample of 130 who had contact with incest victims, including: 'social workers, clinical psychologists, psychiatrists, pediatricians, child protection agents, general practitioners, and volunteer counselors of womens' self-help groups' (p. 254). It is not clear which, and how many (if any), of the professionals were practising recognized counselling and psychotherapy. None of the professions listed can be assumed to do so, although the authors subsume these other activities within the category of 'psychotherapy'.

Similar to the Armsworth (1989) sample, client respondents reported a pattern of multiple professional contacts averaging 3.5 each, with a range from one to nine. On this basis clients' experiences in searching for appropriate help were characterized as a 'long march through the consultation rooms' (p. 253). In the course of these multiple therapeutic encounters, just over half of the group were judged eventually to have 'found a lasting and probably satisfactory therapeutic contact' (p. 259). However, twenty-nine (58%) 'felt let down by professionals consulted'; and five (10%) spontaneously reported during the interviews that they had experienced actual or attempted sexual contact by a professional. The most frequently mentioned forms of dissatisfaction involved the failure of the professionals to elicit the history of incest or to keep it as a focus of discussion; or that such accounts were disbelieved or belittled.

An important finding from the interviews with the professionals was the extent to which they recognized the shortcomings in their therapeutic knowledge (75%), and skills (67%) in working with adult survivors of incest. Some degree of emotional strain in relation to such work was reported by 85% of professionals. Four main areas of difficulty were identified:

- embarrassment and disgust;
- powerlessness;
- identification with the victim;
- anger with the perpetrator.

Strikingly, 40% of the professionals felt that it was very difficult to maintain a relationship of trust with a former incest victim (Frenken and Van Stolk 1990: 258). This research is particularly valuable in highlighting the feelings of dissatisfaction that clients experience from their contacts with professionals, as well as the feelings of inadequacy reported by practitioners in relation to this work. The distinctions drawn by clients about the relative helpfulness of interventions from different professional groups is worthy of further consideration. In particular, psychiatrists, general medical practitioners and social workers might wish to consider why over half of a sample of adults who were abused as children felt that contact with these professionals was a negative experience.

In this chapter, we have considered the small number of studies of therapy with adults abused as children, in the context of general psychotherapy research. A significant gap exists between the volume of clinical material and research which explores and evaluates processes and outcomes of therapy with this client group. In the next chapter I will describe the methodology used in my research to explore clients' and therapists' experiences and perceptions of therapy.

Note

1 Lishman (1978); Maluccio (1979); Sainsbury (1975) – all social work. Brannen and Collard (1982); Hunt (1985); Timms and Blampied (1985) – all marital therapy. Howe (1989); Merrington and Corden (1981) – both family therapy.

PART TWO

EXPERIENCES OF THERAPY

3

Methodology

In this chapter I will describe the methodology used in research which is presented throughout the rest of this book. This involved fifty-three in-depth interviews with three categories of participants:

- clients who had received therapy relating to the consequences of child abuse;
- therapists who provide such therapy;
- therapists who were themselves abused as children.

Methodological issues are discussed under five headings: research philosophy and design; the sample; interviewing; data analysis; and validation strategies.

Research philosophy and design

This study is based on qualitative methodology utilizing phenomenological and person-centred principles. The phenomenological base stems from emphasis on, and respect for, each individual's unique experiencing and ways of attributing meaning. The person-centred aspect reflects the way-of-being as researcher in accordance with principles central to this philosophy of psychotherapy (Mearns and McLeod 1984). This approach involves the importation of attributes of respect, equality, ability to listen, empathy, acceptance and congruence into the research context. These principles are also central to the philosophy of phenomenology (Hammersley and Atkinson 1983; Spinelli 1989), and are particularly valuable in the research context because they promote rapport and trust between researcher and participants.

As has been described, the philosophical basis for the interviews was to follow a phenomenological and person-centred approach. As with person-centred therapy, this involves utilizing attributes of genuineness, respect, positive regard and congruence. Care is taken to ensure that the relationship is non-exploitative, sensitive to issues of difference and similarity such as age, gender, ethnic origin, culture, class, sexual orientation, and that the participant is fully informed and prepared for an exploratory conversation on agreed topics.

Interviewees and researchers encounter each other as real people with a range of similarities and differences which are not denied or concealed. Assumptions are not made regarding any form of prior understanding or 'conscious partiality' with an interviewee on the basis of some shared characteristic of whatever nature, for example, being a victim of abuse, being a therapist, or gender (Finch 1984; Oakley 1981). Instead, rapport, affinity and collaboration in the research relationship are seen as being earned via the unique dynamics of each actual interpersonal encounter. The challenge is to create a climate which facilitates the interviewee moving from a position of apprehension to one of full participation (Spradley 1989).

The researcher is openly receptive to whatever material is generated, including looking for 'hidden' material via techniques of probing, clarification and enquiring about exceptions to reported experiences (Hunt 1989; McCracken 1988; Spradley 1989). Being alert to opportunities for pursuing subtle or overt incongruities can be very effective in unstructured research interviews. This facilitates exploration and the provision of rich descriptions of phenomena especially with regard to areas which are traditionally private or sensitive (Lee 1993; Spradley 1989). Thus, according to McCracken (1988) the primary function of qualitative research is to gain understanding of the ways in which respondents understand their experiences rather than to measure the representativeness of such experiences:

> The purpose of the qualitative interview is not to discover how many, and what kinds of, people share a certain characteristic. It is to gain access to the cultural categories and assumptions according to which one culture construes the world. How many and what kinds of people hold these categories and assumptions is not, in fact, the compelling issue. It is the categories and assumptions, not those who hold them, that matter. In other words, qualitative research does not survey the terrain, it mines it. (McCracken 1988: 17)

Exploring opposites, exceptions, contradictions, ambiguities and ambivalence provides access to thoughts and feelings beneath the interviewee's surface level awareness and can promote new levels of insight for participants – an effect also noted by Laslett and Rapoport (1975). While such experiences are a by-product of the research interview, positive effects for participants from the experience are to be welcomed.

Being an experienced therapist with person-centred attributes is helpful in applying these principles to the research interview (Mearns and McLeod 1984; Rennie 1994b; Stiles 1993). Yet there is also an obligation to be alert to potential difficulties which may arise for 'therapists-turned-researchers' (Hunt 1985; McCracken 1988). One particularly important question must be considered: the extent to which the researcher's prior theoretical knowledge and clinical experience is advantageous (through sensitivity to the significance of key themes); or whether this knowledge can act as a blinker whereby what is expected becomes more likely to be elicited and interpreted in accordance with the therapist-researcher's existing world-view.

This dilemma about researchers' prior knowledge of the field has been discussed extensively within qualitative research theory (McCracken 1988; Schein 1987). The original view of Glaser and Strauss (1967) was that it was preferable for researchers to have little knowledge of the subject they were studying (to the extent of not reviewing the literature beforehand) to enable phenomena to be analysed almost on a tabula rasa basis, unencumbered by prior knowledge, influences or expectations. However, both the desirability and the possibility of such an approach have been questioned by later writers (Bulmer 1979; Layder 1982; Strauss and Corbin 1990). McCracken (1988), for example, noted the impossibility of being free from cultural influences and assumptions and stressed the advantages for researchers who have extensive knowledge and experience of the phenomena they are studying. This is also the view adopted by heuristic (Moustakas 1990) and clinical perspectives (Hunt 1989; Oldfield 1983; Schein 1987).

Recognizing these advantages highlights the responsibility of researchers to acknowledge and 'bracket off' the potential impact of such influences upon their interviewing and data collection processes; while utilizing prior theoretical knowledge in the analysis of the data. In many qualitative studies – including this one – data are both presented and interpreted (Howe 1989; Patton 1990). Researchers cannot avoid being the instrument via which observations are made (and not made). In the course of observational activity, a whole range of conscious and unconscious processes affect the ways in which data are pursued, perceived and interpreted (Hunt 1989). I would suggest that therapists-as-researchers, given their training and experience in observing and understanding processes at both a conscious and unconscious level, and self-reflecting on countertransference and other personal experiences, are in a good position to guard against potential biases in their interpretation of data.

The analysis presented is derived from the interaction between myself as a unique individual with each unique respondent, and also from the respondents as a whole as a unique group. My analysis is not the only possible way of making sense out of a mass of very varied data which inevitably contained many contradictions and ambiguities. Nor are the sections I have chosen to present in this book necessarily the same as would have been selected by others with a similar interest in the field. Other researchers interacting with these individuals would undoubtedly have generated their own distinct combinations of data, analysis and selectiveness.

One measure for myself of the significance of bracketing off and utilization of a pluralistic theoretical perspective on data analysis is the extent to which issues that emerged from my analysis of the research interviews surprised me, and changed my views about good therapy practice. This happened to a substantial degree. I now have major criticisms about a short book on counselling adults abused as children (Dale 1993) which I wrote before embarking on the research interviews for this study. For example, I made a number of suggestions about therapeutic approaches (such as facilitating regression and ways of working with abuse memories) which I no longer endorse.

The sample

My initial intention was to recruit a total interview sample of thirty participants, half of whom would be adults who were abused as children who had completed some form of therapy which had focused on their abuse; matched by therapists who work with this client group. I hoped for an equal balance between males and females and that all forms of childhood abuse (not just sexual) would be included.

A 'self-defined' phenomenological approach to definition of abuse was utilized. Respondents did not have to meet any criteria other than construing their childhood experiences to have been abusive in some way, and to have sought therapy in respect of this in adult life. This information was recorded in a questionnaire completed prior to each interview. Due to the impossibility of verifying their abuse and therapy experiences, and the ethical inappropriateness of questioning this in the particular context, such accounts are accepted on face value. The self-defined categories of abuse recorded by participants are shown in Table 4.2 in Chapter 4.

I did not intend that any of the participants should 'match' as actual therapist and client pairs. While such a study would be interesting (and there are examples in general psychotherapy research), I did not feel it would be appropriate for three main reasons. First, the renowned problem of access to participants in studies of sensitive subjects would make the recruitment of such pairs extremely difficult. Second, it might produce a self-selected bias in the direction of mutually appreciative therapists and clients. Third, such studies tend to focus on evaluation rather than experiences of therapy.

Researchers in the field of sensitive topics (areas which are traditionally private, secret or controversial) have described the difficulties in gaining access to appropriate respondents (Lee 1993; Renzetti and Lee 1993). In sensitive research areas, statistically representative samples of relevant populations are not feasible for a number of practical and ethical reasons. In psychotherapy research (much of which can be considered as being sensitive) there have been three main ways of gaining access to respondents:

1   Practitioners undertaking research may request the participation of their own clients or clients of colleagues (for example, Brunning 1992; Fitts 1985; Oldfield 1983).
2   Relevant agencies may give permission for their clients to be informed of the research with an opportunity to participate (for example, Brannen and Collard 1982; Hunt 1985).
3   Clients may be invited to respond by notices or articles in the media requesting volunteers (for example, Alexander et al. 1991; Feinauer 1989; Frenken and Van Stolk 1990).

In this study I considered all three of these possibilities and on reflection opted for the use of the media to gain access to clients and a mixture of approaches to therapists. Use of the media has become common in research in sensitive areas, particularly relating to childhood abuse. However, it is important to take into account the reasons why people respond to media notices – not so much as to how they might be unrepresentative of the population as a whole (truly representative samples are an impossibility in certain areas of sensitive research) – but in what ways volunteering reflects specific experiences.

It has been suggested that self-selected participants may be 'elite' members of their group with tendencies toward high levels of education, articulation and well-developed opinions (Lee 1993; Sandelowski 1986). At the end of each interview I took the opportunity to ask participants why they had volunteered to take part. There were two main answers:

● to give something back in gratitude for therapeutic help which had been of great benefit;
● wanting to warn the therapeutic community and potential clients about the damaging impact of bad practice.

Some people also remarked on additional reasons such as using the interview to evaluate how much progress they had made; and to experiment with talking about difficult issues (including talking in depth with a man).

Sources of respondents

In total, sixty-one responses were received from media notices which resulted in thirty-eight of the total number of fifty-three interviews being generated in this way. The client sample was varied in terms of age, geographical location, social and ethnic background, types and extent of abuse, as well as types and episodes of therapy. However, certain perspectives were not well represented: particularly male clients and those who had had positive experiences of 'survivor/recovery' models of therapy. The majority of interviews took place in London, the south coast, West, East and North West England. Twenty-three media respondents were not interviewed, the main reason being that their intention was to contribute in writing.

I anticipated that media notices would generate responses from clients, but that further thought would need to be given to attracting therapist volunteers. Therapists were recruited in three main ways: First, because of my practitioner activities, I was aware of a number of therapists who had substantial experience of working with adults who were abused as children. I approached six of these therapists and five agreed to be involved in the project. Three of them I knew personally and they served as pilot interviewees.

Second, contacts made at the First Standing Conference on Sexual Abuse of Men, held in London in September 1992, resulted in four interviewees (one therapist and three therapists who were themselves abused as children). Third, a notice relating to the research was distributed to therapists attending a variety of training courses relating to therapy with adults abused as children between September 1992 and January 1993. This resulted in a further six interviewees (three therapists who were themselves abused as children, two clients and one therapist).

One unexpected feature of the overall sample was the proportion of therapists who were abused as children. The interview task with this group (seventeen people) was particularly challenging as I was keen to get access to the varied aspects of their experience:

- as clients receiving therapy;
- making the transition to becoming therapists and motives for this;
- experiences as therapists working with people who have been abused;
- perspectives on the possible opportunities and pitfalls of therapists with a history of abuse working with abused people.

Setting up the interviews

Respondents were re-contacted during the period March to August 1993 by telephone. Following this, a letter was sent confirming the appointment and enclosing copies of the interview consent form and questionnaire, with an invitation to contact named university or NSPCC staff to check my bona fides. To my knowledge, no one took up the option of making such checks and it may be that the degree of rapport that was built up with respondents via letters and at least two, sometimes more, telephone conversations, as well as my associations with the university and the NSPCC as reputable organizations, provided sufficient sense of security.

During telephone conversations the respondents were also asked to consider whether or not they would prefer the interviews to be in their homes. This was felt to be an important potential safeguard for predominantly female interviewees. With a couple of exceptions, most indicated that they would prefer the interviews to take place in their own homes.

Setting up for the interview followed a casual routine: initial conversation about my journey and my enquiries about the participant's level of anxiety and whether they had ever done anything like this before. As I unpacked and set up the equipment, participants were invited to ask any questions regarding the research or my reasons for undertaking it. Many were interested in my professional and personal reasons for this particular area of enquiry. When asked, I gave brief information from both perspectives. The issue of researcher self-disclosure in qualitative interviewing is a controversial one with strong arguments in favour (Everhart 1977; Lather 1986; Oakley 1981) and reservations (Campbell 1988; Hammersley 1992). This mirrors similar debates in psychotherapy about therapists' self-disclosures to clients (Stricker and Fisher 1990).

My impression is that the nature of my responses was used by a number of interviewees as a means of 'sussing out' whether I was trustworthy or not. I was also amused that several people used their observations of my reactions to their pets (and, possibly even more importantly, the reactions of their pets to me) in a similar way.

During this preliminary conversation I went through a check list before the interview formally commenced. This is the final stage of clarifying the 'research bargain' with participants (Hammersley and Atkinson 1983). This involved:

- Receiving the completed questionnaire and interview consent forms.
- A reminder of the areas that the interview would focus on (and not focus on, that is, details of the abuse).
- A reminder about confidentiality.
- A comment that they did not have to talk about anything they did not want to, and that they could take a break or stop at any time.
- Sound check: this is vital.[1] Recording was done via a modest desktop taperecorder and two tie-clip microphones with long leads. All interviewees except one had agreed to be recorded.
- Establishing the pseudonym to be used for the transcripts.

Psychotherapy researchers working from a qualitative orientation have tended to use either semi-structured or unstructured formats for interviews. I began with the intention of using a semi-structured interview schedule which had been drawn up to reflect areas of theoretical interest generated by the literature search and my clinical experience.

Two pilot interviews using the schedule took place in February 1993. In the pilot interviews I was aware that my attention had focused too much on the schedule rather than the respondent's experiences, which felt inhibiting. From the experience of these interviews I felt that the schedule was liable to over-restrict data to predetermined spheres. Also, the pilot interviews demonstrated that the time limit of two hours for each interview was insufficient to cover all the material in the schedule in satisfying detail, which might result in superficial exploration of some areas. Consequently, the interview schedule was abandoned and I proceeded on an unstructured basis with the following fifty-one interviews.

The advantages of an unstructured format are that a far greater proportion of data is generated from the particular interest and unique experience of each respondent (Patton 1990). This approach also fits with research undertaken from a person-centred philosophical perspective. Participants feel a personal involvement in the creative aspect of each interview in collaboration with the researcher, as opposed to being someone who is being 'done to' according to criteria which they had no part in devising. The significance of this should not be underestimated with people who have histories of being abused, exploited, manipulated and neglected. A limitation of the unstructured format is that it reduces the possibility of obtaining statistical information about the prevalence of certain experiences – 'counting of instances' – as not all interviews cover every relevant issue.

Interviews began with a 'grand tour' question (Spradley 1989) along the lines of:

- *For clients and therapists abused as children*: 'Perhaps you could turn your mind back to the time when you became aware that you were experiencing problems connected with the abuse and felt that you might need some help – what sort of problems were you experiencing and where did you look for help?'
- *For therapists*: 'Do you think that in your experience there is anything significantly different in working with someone who was abused as a child compared with clients who have a general range of problems?'

From this introduction, participants were encouraged to describe their experiences in narrative style. My main interventions were to encourage, clarify, probe, explore exceptions, contradictions, ambivalence and ambiguity. Also, as more interviews were undertaken, I raised theoretically interesting experiences and views of previous interviewees and aspects of the developing preliminary analysis – inviting comments with regard to them.

In the initial discussions by phone and letter with participants I made clear that the interviews would be time limited to a maximum of two hours. I felt this was important for several reasons. Participants would know in advance exactly when I would arrive and when I would leave. This enabled them to prepare for the conversation with maximum information and control. It was apparent that several had planned contact with a friend to coincide with the arranged ending time. My impression was that the attention given to planning and structure of the interviews (including the explicit agreement that the interviews would not focus on the details of abuse) gave confidence to participants. This was particularly significant for those who had experienced unsatisfactory therapeutic relationships, or who felt uneasy with men.

Another reason for a predetermined time limit is that it is impossible to predict in advance how participants will react to the interview situation. Previous researchers on emotionally sensitive topics have noted a range of responses in interviews including catharsis and making complaints about services they have (or have not) received (Brannen 1988; Brannen and Collard 1982). In this study my intention was to interview clients who had completed therapy relating to their abuse. While from this it could be hypothesized that current distress and therapeutic needs would not be predominant, this could not be predicted with confidence. A clear time boundary provides a parameter for pacing interviews so that I could monitor and respond to any emotional distress, ensuring that the interviewee was 'grounded' by the end of the interview. The inclusion at the end of the interview of a question exploring reasons for volunteering was also helpful in this regard. It helped some people to refocus from painful past experiences (including damaging therapy) back into a present orientation; and from feelings of vulnerability into recognition of achievement.

I had considered the possibility that some participants might be so emotionally vulnerable at the time of the interview that it would not be proper to leave without offering some follow-up support. Issues in relation to 'leaving' research interviews, and researchers' responsibilities to participants, have been discussed in the literature (Brannen 1988; Renzetti and Lee 1993; Shaffir and Stebbins 1991). Arrangements were made with the NSPCC Child Protection Helpline (a free 24-hour telephone counselling service) that telephone support would be available to any person post interview if this were required. With all interviewees, either through spontaneous discussion or via probing, I gained some idea of their existing support systems. Mostly these involved a supportive partner, a network of friends, ongoing therapy, or some combination. Although a small number appeared to have very little personal support, on no occasion was I left with a feeling that it was necessary to offer the support of the NSPCC helpline.

There are also practical reasons for working within a specified time frame which serve the well-being of the researcher. The emotional impact on researchers of their research in sensitive areas is rarely reported or discussed, although Hooper (1992) and Hunt (1989) are exceptions to this. Such interviews require intense concentration on several levels simultaneously:

- The development and maintenance of rapport with the interviewee.
- Understanding the content of what is being said (and what is not being said).
- Reflecting simultaneously on the significance of the content vis-à-vis the developing analysis.
- Considering interviewing technique options: for example, which of several interesting lines to follow, whether to probe a particular issue in depth or cover several issues less thoroughly.
- Paying attention to noting and exploring unusual case examples.
- Monitoring the participant's emotional experience and well-being and regulating the emotional intensity via direction of the interview accordingly.
- Being alert to the psychodynamics of the interview situation (including countertransference reactions), and ways in which these may potentially contribute usefully or not (for example, re self-disclosure).
- Keeping an eye on the passage of time.
- Worrying whether or not the microphone batteries are going flat – it is a fundamental law of qualitative research that this will happen.

Human attention span is limited and the intensity of concentration required to become immersed within participants' worlds cannot be sustained indefinitely. This is particularly so when a researcher or therapist is attending to sensitive and emotionally intense material in conversations with vulnerable people. This is one reason why most therapists contain therapy sessions to one hour – or indeed, the psychoanalytic measure of fifty minutes. In preparing for a schedule of more than fifty interviews over a period of eight months I felt that two hours was the maximum length of time that a sufficiently intense level of concentration could be reliably maintained.

All of the interviews formally ended within the two hours, all lasting for the full length of time (apart from two therapist interviews which had been agreed to last one and a half hours). With most interviewees the final question tended to be around why they had volunteered to do the interview and what the experience had been like. This focus had initially emerged spontaneously at the end of some early interviews and in response I began to keep a separate file in relation to this for analysis.

At the end of interviews (following a suggestion made in one of the pilots) all client participants were left a simple form with the request that if they had any afterthoughts which they were willing to write down and send to me, these would be appreciated. I also sent each person a card thanking them for their participation. Eight written responses were received following interviews. Pleasingly, views expressed at the end of interviews were of the nature that the interviews had been a positive –

and often self-illuminating – experience. Follow-up written material received was also illustrative of this:

> Many thanks for our conversation last week. I hope it provided you with some useful material. I certainly found it helpful in terms of reviewing my therapy and seeing how far I've come. (Beth – 16)

Data analysis

The point has often been made that interpretation of data is as much an artistic and creative process as it is a scientific activity (Denzin and Lincoln 1994; Eisner 1981; Hill 1982; Mostyn 1985). Concepts and categorizations emerge, as patterns, regularities and exceptions in the data are noted. Hunches and hypotheses develop, decay and evolve through the interplay of the researcher's methodical observation and interrogation of data, theoretical sampling, creativity and intuition. This is the core of the process of analytic induction – an iterative process of constant cycling between interpretation and observation (Stiles 1993) – culminating in the interpretations made by each researcher. A range of methods is outlined in the research literature against which to assess the validity of such interpretations and these are discussed later in this chapter.

The method used for the analysis of data was developed according to these principles, which are outlined in key texts on qualitative research (for example, Denzin and Lincoln 1994; Miles and Huberman 1984; Patton 1990; Rennie 1992; Strauss and Corbin 1990; Tesch 1990). These approaches have developed from a long tradition of qualitative enquiry stemming from the seminal influence of Glaser and Strauss (1967). According to Bogdan and Taylor (1975) the task of analysis of qualitative data involves:

> A process which entails an effort to formally identify themes and to construct hypotheses (ideas) as they are suggested by data and an attempt to demonstrate support for those themes and hypotheses. By hypotheses, we mean nothing more than propositional statements. (Bogdan and Taylor 1975: 79)

Many writers in the field have noted that there can be no pre-set exact formula for the analysis of data in qualitative studies – rather researchers must develop a method appropriate to each particular project (McCracken 1988; Miles and Huberman 1984; Neimeyer and Resnikoff 1982; Rennie et al. 1988; Rennie 1994b; Tesch 1990). Methods involve inductive analysis (concurrent with data collection) which systematically reduces the mass of detail in the data as a whole by a process of constant comparison of similarities and differences, the identification of themes and patterns; through to the emergence or construction of concepts or categories which contain the distilled essence of the data. In Bulmer's (1979) terms, the goal is to maintain 'faithfulness' to the data while abstracting and generalizing.

The initial stage in the analysis of qualitative data is to move a step beyond the raw data into a more abstract view of regularly occurring themes and patterns. At this initial stage categories are tentative and by no means mutually exclusive. Summaries of units of meaning which did not logically fit into any of the initial categories were kept separately and allowed to accumulate until the same process of comparison and contrasting enabled new categories to be developed which included the previously unclassified material.

Each interview was transcribed verbatim by a secretary specially recruited for this purpose. The pseudonym chosen by each interviewee was used on the transcript which was also allocated a code number, which I had sole access to and which was kept separately. Each transcribed interview ran to between 20–35 pages.[2] All the interviews bar one took place between February and November 1993,[3] and transcriptions became available from April onwards.

While continuing the interview itinerary (usually between two and four interviews per week) I coded on average five transcripts per month. This enabled a preliminary analysis of categories to be developed, which could be explored and tested with subsequent interviewees, and in this way constantly refined. As Janesick (1994) notes, this practice of theoretical sampling is at the heart of the grounded theory method, facilitating constant comparisons in the collection and analysis of data.

Being faced with a mass of raw interview data is the point when a single-handed qualitative researcher can feel most at sea. As it quickly mounts up in transcript form the data can feel unmanageable and intimidating. I came to think of this as the 'sheepdog' phase, having a picture of myself constantly attempting to keep track of, round up and contain stray and unpredictable data. Control is gradually achieved by the development of an initial data organization system by means of preliminary categorization.

McLeod (1994) refers to this as 'phenomenological reduction' – a process of continually reviewing and interrogating the developing categories. Repeated many times, this promotes refinement towards mutual exclusivity between categories – referred to as 'saturation' of categories (Glaser and Strauss 1967). This is the point when incoming data no longer generate new theoretical material, only additional illustration for concepts already developed. The categorization matures in this way by clarification of subsections within categories; and the eventual 'collapse' of the categorization structure as major categories logically subsume minor ones.

Validation strategies

One of the characteristics of qualitative research is that the method develops as the study progresses – responsive to issues and questions presented by the emerging data. Unlike much quantitative research where design and testing criteria are specifically established before data collection commences, few, if any, qualitative research projects are exactly replicable. Consequently, for the establishment of the validity of qualitative research it is necessary to document in some detail the process of the research as it developed in response to emerging data and other events. This information constitutes the 'audit trail' (Lincoln and Guba 1985) which enables methodological decisions made during the research to be critically examined.

Validation of qualitative research is fundamentally based on the judgements about credibility of the description, analysis, and theoretical discussion (Janesick 1994). Validation strategies have been discussed extensively in the research methods literature (Altheide and Johnson 1994; Bogdan and Taylor 1975; Heppner et al. 1992; Kirk and Miller 1986; Lincoln and Guba 1985; McLeod 1994; Miles and Huberman 1984; Patton 1990; Stiles 1993; Strauss and Corbin 1990). These sources outline a range of established validation strategies which, when used systematically, provide criteria for establishing the 'trustworthiness' (Lincoln and Guba 1985) of non-numerical or 'human science' research (Rennie 1994b).

In this study, in addition to utilization of theoretical sampling and analytic induction procedures already outlined, validation strategies of triangulation and respondent validation give credence to the interpretations drawn from the data.

Triangulation

Triangulation involves obtaining a number of varied perspectives in relation to similar phenomena (Neimeyer and Resnikoff 1982). Assortment of perspectives can be accomplished by variety within samples, variety within methodology and variety within theoretical consideration of the data. In this study, forms of triangulation stemmed from the sample and consideration of the data from varied theoretical perspectives. The sample was relatively large for a single-handed qualitative study. It included three main subgroups:

1 Psychotherapy clients (who reported histories of child abuse).
2 Psychotherapists with experience of working with the consequences of abuse.
3 Psychotherapists who themselves reported histories of child abuse.

The overall sample of fifty-three interviews can be collapsed to reflect two contrasting perspectives:

- There were forty-seven participants with being-a-client experiences.
- There were twenty-three participants with being-a-therapist experiences.

In addition to the varied perspectives of the interview participants, further triangulation of method and data was provided by written material received from twenty interviewees; and from twelve respondents who were not interviewed – a total of thirty-two items. The perspectives within the written material were twenty-eight client, three therapist-abused-as-a-child, and one other.[4]

Data were also obtained from questionnaires which were completed prior to the interviews. In addition to biographical and personal information, questionnaires produced quantifiable data in relation to:

- experiences of abuse (for example, types, age when started and duration);
- relationship to abusers;
- experiences of therapy (for example, how many therapists seen, for how long);
- evaluations of therapy episodes;
- extent of remaining problems in life associated with childhood abuse.

Findings from the questionnaire data are presented and discussed in Chapter 4. Triangulation is also effected by considering qualitative data from different theoretical stances. As a practising therapist for more than twenty years my theoretical orientation has evolved into an integrative one, which reflects a history of theoretical influences including (in no particular order): psychiatry (my original professional training was as a psychiatric social worker); humanistic psychology; existential psychotherapy; family systems theories; cognitive-behavioural approaches and trace elements of psychodynamic theories. The developing analysis was viewed from these theoretical perspectives, as well as from standpoints with which I am familiar (but that are not central to my therapeutic orientation) such as 'survivor', feminist and trauma theories.

Respondent validation

Respondent validation strategies involve obtaining feedback from participants in relation to the developing or completed analysis. Stiles (1993) refers to this process as 'testimonial validation'. As I have already described, using non-structured interviews was one way in which respondents were able to comment on facets of the developing analysis.

Respondent validation often involves asking for feedback at a later stage from interviewees on transcripts of interviews or summaries of these (for example, Darlington 1993; Hooper 1992; Westcott 1993); or second interviews with participants at a later stage (for example, Humphreys 1990). I gave thought to the possibility of sending transcripts of interviews to participants for comment, and decided against this for two main reasons – one practical and one ethical. Practically, the transcribing of long interviews is a major task. At the beginning of the research I was uncertain how soon after interviews transcripts would be available. Also, while the transcripts were comprehensible to me, considerable further editing would have been necessary to remove transcribing errors prior to distribution for comment.

More important, however, were reservations from an ethical perspective. I was concerned about how much it was fair to ask of respondents. Undoubtedly, many would have been willing to have been further involved in this way. Others, however, clearly appreciated the one-off nature of the contact. I came to share the view expressed by Brannen and Collard (1982) that respondents' ability and willingness to be so candid were influenced by the fact that this was a single contact with a stranger who would not be seen or contacted again. In this context, it is interesting that Hooper (1992) – who did distribute transcripts for comment – noted that some of her respondents reacted negatively, considering this to be an extra chore.

I also felt reservations about the possible negative emotional impact on some respondents of receiving the transcripts. While I was with interviewees I felt confident about monitoring their well-being. However, I still have reservations about how a number of people might have been affected by possession of transcripts of interviews in which many had expressed thoughts which had surprised them. With one respondent I was left with a concern that she might have used the interview as a way of telling her story to the world before eventually committing suicide. It is impossible to predict what the impact would be on suicidal propensity of continual rumination on a transcript describing a desperate life and hopeless future.[5]

I was also concerned about the security and confidentiality of the transcripts and consequences which could follow if, in whatever circumstances, they came into the hands of significant others. Who might inadvertently come across the transcripts? Who might see transcripts after the respondent's death and what might be the family repercussions of this? It is possible that this was an over-cautious stance on my part, although it fits with expressed concerns regarding the responsibilities of researchers to establish ethical research bargains and to protect vulnerable participants from themselves and significant others (Brannen 1988; Hammersley and Atkinson 1983; Lee 1993; McCracken 1988).

On balance, in similar circumstances, I would ask each respondent whether they wished to receive a copy of the transcript. Three people did receive copies[6] and two of these specifically remarked upon the helpful effect of being able to re-read the interview.

Plausibility of the analysis

Ultimately, the validity of qualitative research rests on transparent method and the plausibility of the analysis. The focus and goals of qualitative research vary from the level of detailed description of a phenomenon to abstract levels of theory generation. Within this range, Knafl and Howard (1984) noted a level of 'sensitization' which involves reporting the results of a descriptive study with the intention of sensitizing the reader to the views and perspectives of a particular group, especially when this viewpoint has previously been under-reported or not accurately represented.

This notion of sensitization is most relevant to my purpose in this study. The emphasis is on alerting psychotherapy practitioners (as well as clients and potential clients) to key themes and issues which emerged as being particularly relevant to this sample of participants. The aim is not to generate new substantive theory about such experiencing, although I include observations on the degree to which the analysis fits with existing theories in relation to psychotherapy and child abuse. My aim is that the descriptions are convincing, the interpretations plausible and, most of all, that the account will be relevant to consumers and practitioners of psychotherapy.

Notes

1 Unfortunately, notwithstanding this, a significant amount of recorded sound was not transcribable for three interviews. Despite sound checks, microphone batteries can go flat suddenly during interviews. This happened in one interview. Fortunately it was my microphone that failed, and the transcript contains the participant's clear lengthy answers to non-recorded questions. The recording of the interview with another participant suffered from unexplained severe sound interference making it almost completely untranscribable.

2 The 20-page transcript was short because of a power cut. One interview was not transcribed because the respondent did not give permission for tape-recording.

3 For practical reasons, one took place in April 1995.

4 This was a detailed account from a male arguing that sexual contact with children is justifiable in certain circumstances.

5 This person was seeing a therapist at the time of the interview. The therapist was aware of the suicidal thoughts.

6 Two because they asked, and one to consider giving permission for the entire transcript to be included as an Appendix in the thesis. Permission was granted but the transcript was omitted for space reasons.

4

Outcomes and Benefits of Therapy

I always felt that I was like a sort of Martian – I wasn't from this planet. I was never meant for this earth. And I was waiting to die, basically, just waiting for the day. I wouldn't do it myself, I couldn't, I wouldn't because of my religion and because I haven't got the bottle. But I was just waiting to die. And I couldn't relate to anybody. I felt so inferior and all the negative things, you know, so unworthy. And nobody would want to know me anyway and things like this. But now I know that I'm alright. (Veronica – 23)

Outcomes of therapy

Overall, the research upon which this book is based generated a vast amount of data from a large sample (for qualitative research) of well-informed and highly articulate participants. In this chapter, we will consider quantitative and qualitative data in relation to the outcomes and benefits of therapy.[1]

As outlined in the last chapter, fifty-three interviewees combined to provide forty-seven perspectives on being-a-client experiences (thirty clients plus seventeen therapists-abused-as-children) and twenty-three perspectives on being-a-therapist (six therapists plus seventeen therapists-abused-as-children). A procedural error meant that seven therapists who were abused as children received the therapist version of the questionnaire (which omitted the questions about therapy received) instead of the therapist-abused-as-a-child version. Consequently, the fuller questionnaire (recording biographical information, abuse details and perceptions of therapy outcome) was completed by forty respondents who had self-perceived abuse histories. This subsample provides the basis for the statistical data and analysis in this chapter. Age and gender characteristics of the sample are illustrated in Table 4.1.

The types of abuse recorded by participants are shown in Table 4.2.

Perceptions of efficacy of therapy

Data are available for forty participants with client experiences (twenty-eight clients and twelve therapists abused as children) covering a total of

Table 4.1 *Gender and age of interview participants*

Participants	Female	Male	Total	Age range
Clients	29	1	30	25–55
Therapists abused as children	11	6	17	30–61
Other therapists	3	3	6	36–49
Total	43	10	53	

Table 4.2 *Types of abuse experiences of interview respondents and relationship to abusers*

Sexual abuse	N = 36
Fathers	15
Other family males	14
Mothers	9
Others (non-family males)	8
Other family females	2
Stepfather	1
Stepmother	1
Emotional abuse	N = 35
Mothers	26
Fathers	19
Other family males	7
Other family females	3
Stepfather	2
Stepmother	1
Physical abuse	N = 23
Mothers	15
Fathers	11
Other family males	7
Other family females	2
Neglect	N = 15
Mother	11
Father	6
Stepfather	2
Stepmother	1
Other family males	1
Other family females	1
Other	N = 3
'Financial' (mother and father)	1
'Enema' (father)	1
'Verbal' (mother)	1

130 therapy episodes.[2] As illustrated in Table 4.3, 90% of clients had had more than one episode of therapy, with a range of between 1–10 episodes (mean = 3.25).

Table 4.4 illustrates clients' ratings of the outcome of their therapy episodes from questionnaire responses.

Table 4.3 *Number of therapy episodes*

Client perspectives from questionnaires	N = 40
Total number of therapy episodes	N = 130

Ranking of number of therapy episodes:

2 episodes:	14 clients
3 episodes:	8 clients
4 episodes:	6 clients
5 episodes:	4 clients
1 episode:	4 clients
6 episodes:	2 clients
8 episodes:	1 client
10 episodes:	1 client

Table 4.4 *Clients' overall rating of counselling episodes (N = 130)*

Has the counselling/therapy you have received helped you to deal more effectively with the problems that led you to seek counselling/therapy?

Yes – a great deal	N = 48	(37%)
Yes – to some extent	N = 42	(32%)
Uncertain	N = 10	(8%)
No – did not really help	N = 17	(13%)
No – seemed to make things worse/was harmful	N = 13	(10%)
Total	130	(100%)

From these figures it can be seen that clients had very varied and mixed experiences of their different therapy episodes. There were essentially three types of overall experience:

- *Type 1*: those where all episodes were helpful to some degree (exclusively helpful).
- *Type 2*: those where all episodes were unhelpful to some degree (exclusively unhelpful).
- *Type 3*: those which involved combinations of helpful and unhelpful episodes (mixed).

Type 1 experiences: exclusively helpful

On the positive side, 40% (16/40) of clients had overall experiences of therapy which was exclusively helpful. These involved combinations of maximum and moderate helpfulness with no 'uncertain' or 'unhelpful' episodes. Exclusively helpful experiences accounted for 31.5% (41/130) of the whole sample of therapy episodes. Furthermore, of this group, just under one-quarter of all clients (9/40) had experiences (21/130 – 16%) which were ranked exclusively as being of maximum helpfulness.

Type 2 experiences: exclusively unhelpful

Exclusively unhelpful experiences were reported by only one respondent who had had three episodes of therapy, all of which were rated as 'No – did not really help' (3/130 episodes – 2.3%).

Type 3 experiences: mixed helpful and unhelpful

The mixed picture is represented by 40% (16/40) of clients who had combinations of helpful, uncertain and unhelpful experiences (67/130 episodes – 51.5%).

The positive element is reflected by thirty-nine out of the forty clients (97.5%) reporting at least some helpful effect from their total counselling episodes; and that 69% of all therapy episodes were rated as helpful to some degree.

The negative side of this mixed picture is represented by ten clients who had thirteen episodes of counselling which they felt made things worse or were perceived as harmful. This amounts to 10% of the entire therapy episodes. Fortunately, however, all but one of these clients had had other episodes of therapy which were helpful to some degree.

In this context of very mixed perceptions of the efficacy of therapy, Table 4.5 outlines participants' ratings of the degree of problems remaining in their lives post therapy.

From these data it can be seen that a very high proportion of participants continued to experience problems in their lives which they felt stemmed from abuse. None felt that their problems had been completely resolved. However, this somewhat stark finding should not eclipse the views expressed that therapy, for many, had helped to overcome substantial problems and ameliorate the impact of remaining problems.

Turning from the quantitative data to the analysis of qualitative data, examination of the life stories of participants elicited in the interviews indicates that many were very satisfied to have progressed from the 'major problems' to the 'some problems' category. Many were also confident of making further progress in that direction. The importance of

Table 4.5 *Participants' rating of residual problems (N = 40, 28 clients and 12 therapists-abused-as-children)*

*To what extent do you feel that you still have problems in your life that are connected with having been abused?**

Major problems:	7	(17%)
Some problems:	30	(75%)
Hardly any problems:	1.5*	(4%)
Uncertain:	1.5*	(4%)
No problems:	0	(0%)
Total	40	(100%)

* One participant gave two answers: 'hardly any' and 'uncertain'.

this transition should not be underestimated, even though difficulties remain.

Benefits of therapy

> Actually, this is the thing with therapy that I've found – it was like a light being switched on and a fog lifting. You know – you block off your emotions and your feelings and all the rest of it, and then, with therapy it lifted. It was like a fog, you know, it just lifted and it was like a light – there was light coming in. (Veronica – 23)

Many people described a quality of life prior to receiving therapy in which everyday experiences continually reinforced low self-esteem and chronic lack of self-worth. Some had been fixed on self-destructive pathways which included combinations of great loneliness; chronic suicidal preoccupations and attempts; repeated self-harming; a range of addictions; repetitive destructive relationships; as well as aggression and abuse of others, including their own children. Sometimes people feel that they somehow carry abusing environments around with them so that wherever they go they continue to be treated with a lack of care and consideration, or are exploited and re-victimized.

Comments about benefits derived from therapy ranged from general remarks such as literally being life-saving to details of very specific outcomes such as reduction in panic attacks, being able to control emotions, not being depressed, increased self-esteem and learning how to communicate in a clear way:

> Just being in a family like that was just absolute hell . . . it was a complete terrible childhood – and adulthood as well until probably the last couple of years. And I just learned so much from counselling – it has really done me so much good . . . It's made such an incredible difference to myself that I feel that everybody should have it. (Mary Nicholas – 55)

Positive change involves enhancement of self-image, and improvements in self-perceptions from 'bad-unworthy' (deserving all I get) into 'good-deserving' ones:

> I used to go around with my face hidden under this huge fringe of hair . . . But more and more I felt very positive and much more attractive . . . She was making me realize that I was a worthwhile person. She was helping to get rid of all the guilt I had about myself and to put it in its rightful place. To dispel all these beliefs that I had built up over, like, ten years of believing that I was just, well, like some sort of Lolita. And just to make me realize that I actually now had power over what was happening. (Emily – 15)

These changes reflect revisions of limited views of personal potential and the development of a future orientation, ambitions and creativity.

Expectations of self, others and life in general become raised, alongside an increased sense of confidence and ability to achieve desired ends. In this context, life becomes more controllable, predictable, more exciting and enjoyable and, importantly, also more ordinary:

> A lot of my life now is not concerned with having been abused – which is something that I couldn't have imagined really a couple of years ago, you know, I was, kind of, immersed in it then . . . I go for days without thinking about it – I feel freer, stronger, older, younger. (Sophia – 64)

Specific issues in abuse-related therapy

One of the questions underpinning this research was whether there is anything uniquely different in counselling and psychotherapy with adults who were abused as children, compared with clients who have problems stemming from a range of other unhappy events and losses. One conclusion is that differences may be less marked than has been claimed in much of the abuse therapy literature. As was noted in the last chapter, it is clear from general psychotherapy and counselling research that it is the provision of a safe context, as well as an understanding and accepting relationship in which clients feel able to talk honestly, feel understood, and create meaning for their experiences, which are the most helpful ingredients of effective therapy (Howe 1993). There is no obvious reason why this robust finding should be significantly different for people whose experiences include childhood abuse, in addition to what other circumstances life has held in store for them.[4]

This does not, however, detract from another conclusion, which is that there are often specific issues relating to the impact of abuse which have to be recognized and responded to appropriately, if therapy is to be experienced as being helpful – and to avoid harm. From the very varied experiences of the participants in this study, these include:

- Difficulties and challenges involved in becoming 'ready' for therapy alongside associated 'deterrents to help-seeking'.
- Challenges in establishing an effective therapeutic relationship (working alliance) with clients who may have particular tendencies towards lack of trust or over-trusting tendencies.
- Clients' inclinations toward inhibition of communication – especially regarding feelings of dissatisfaction with counselling and shameful inner experiencing.
- Dilemmas as to if, when and in what ways abuse experiences need to be discussed in detail.
- A search for understanding why the abuse occurred and dilemmas about responsibility.
- Existential questions regarding the impact of abuse on the client's sense of identity.

- Questions as to what can feasibly constitute 'resolution' of the effects of abuse.
- Questions regarding current and future relationships with abusers and other family members.
- Fears that the abuse will adversely affect clients' abilities to parent their own children successfully.
- Interpreting the nature of different types of memory of abuse – including 'recovered' memories.

In the remaining chapters in Part Two, we will consider these issues in some detail. Chapter 5 explores experiences at the very early stages of seeking help. Chapter 6 discusses what happens when things go wrong in therapy. Chapter 7 focuses on the specific therapeutic challenges involved in talking about abuse and dealing with feelings. Chapter 8 considers clients' dilemmas in reviewing relationships with significant others – especially with abusers, other family members and with their own children.

Notes

1 Material in this chapter is amended from Dale et al. (1998).

2 A therapy 'episode' consists of the total number of sessions with a therapist. Therefore a therapy episode could be between one session or several hundred sessions.

3 This amounts to more than 100% as one respondent gave two answers: 'hardly any' and 'uncertain'.

4 Particularly as significant proportions of the samples of clients involved in several decades of research are likely to have had histories of child abuse – although the researchers may not have known this.

5

Becoming a Client

I still don't think it's the therapists' fault. I think it's whether you're ready or not. You see if you've been abused by your mother, it's buried so deep that it's not going to come out until you're in your 40s. So a therapist can go on and on at you in your 20s and they're not going to get anywhere. So it's not really their fault. So how can anybody help you until you're ready? (Carol – 17)

They are often not ready to do the work anyway. They are still hooked totally into the self-destruct mode. If you try and push them, if you start by trying to tell them – it's grim. You immediately become the parent. You immediately become one of 'them' – these official carers – becoming that so-called non-abusing parent, but who actually is very abusive. (Catherine – 34)

Seeking therapeutic help can be a complex and emotionally charged experience. People are concerned about the impact of their problems, yet are also anxious about what help and receiving help will involve. Given that the consequences of childhood abuse in adult life often include low self-esteem, chronic shame and inability to trust, for some abused people the hill to be climbed between recognition of problems and being able to ask for help is particularly steep.

Processes involved in becoming ready for therapy have been discussed by a small number of psychotherapy researchers (Brannen and Collard 1982; Fitts 1985; Howe 1989; Hunt 1985; Strupp et al. 1969). Tensions involved in this process have been conceptualized dynamically as the 'push' of levels of discomfort and the 'pull' of degrees of hope (Hunt 1985); or the oppositional forces of 'problem anxiety' and 'service anxiety' (Howe 1989). Seeking therapy involves a combination of factors:

- recognizing the existence and significance of a personal problem;
- awareness of therapy as being potentially beneficial;
- motivation to invest (emotionally, time and often money) in a process of change seeking;
- some form of crisis or other precipitating event.

For the participants in this study, precipitating events usually involved combinations of significant mental health problems, difficulties in adult relationships and concerns about parenting of their own children. As the following examples illustrate, seeking help stems from a significant crisis, a cumulative build up of pressures, or a combination of both.

Veronica endured many years of depression following an extensive history of multiple abuse by her mother and two half siblings. She eventually sought help when she realized that her own violence, which was interspersed with depression, was having harmful effects on her children:

> I've always been very unhappy. I've never known why. When I look back now, it was like I'm standing on the outside looking at myself. I only recognize now this last year that I've been suffering from depression all my life. But I was terrified of anybody finding out and thinking I was a miserable sod. I used to sort of hide it and not let anybody know. I was desperate, I was really, really, really desperate. (Veronica – 23)

Some people were propelled into seeking help by intense psychological and emotional crises commonly referred to as 'nervous breakdowns'. These could be dramatic and severely incapacitating:

> The period around the breakdown, I only have sort of flashes of memory. For a year, I think, I was really out of it. I think my mother practically had to feed me and everything. She wouldn't let me go into an institution or anything. She kept me at home. Of course, now, I think maybe she had her own reasons for doing that. (Ragbag – 39)

> It felt as though you'd got bands outside your brain, you needed a hole in the top of your brain for the pressure to come out. The pressure went down your spine, through your limbs. I just had this terrible problem and it was like – it was like the right and left side of my brain were honestly being pulled in two. And somebody was actually on the outside here dragging it apart. And I was trying to keep it together. I was getting very, very close to the edge of sanity. I was ready to kind of blast out of existence. You can feel yourself getting very close to a point where there's no recovery, and I knew inside that I was getting very, very close to that point. (Sue – 54)

Experience of such 'breakdowns' was sometimes the precursor for subsequent realizations about the significance of childhood abuse:

> I actually spent many years with a lot of mental health problems that I never linked with the abuse and nor did the professionals I saw, link it with the abuse. It was all focused on the problem I had at the time and so for those years I just felt that it was me that was sick and it was my problem, until: I had a major breakdown and then the abuse came out and – well I didn't have any choice. (Zoe – 11)

> I just knew I had a big problem and then I had a nervous breakdown and went into (name deleted) Hospital here. And then I came out. And it was eighteen months after that, that I just sat in the kitchen one day and it suddenly came to the fore of my consciousness that my mother had sexually abused me. And

until that moment I had not the slightest idea that this had happened at all. (Carol – 17)

I was losing a lot of weight and became very anorexic and I eventually had what is termed a complete nervous breakdown. I sought help, basically for what I considered was the breakdown, rather than the abuse which didn't, in fact, come out until eighteen months later. (Sue – 54)

For 'Ragbag' (a self-chosen pseudonym), it was the impact of being rejected in an adult relationship which finally provoked her to seek help:

My boyfriend, we had been together for ten years – I mean, he left me about the same time. So, everything kind of caved in around me and I went because I was desperate. I think, otherwise, I wouldn't have gone. I'd have gone on skating along . . . it was a crisis. (Ragbag – 39)

An escalating crisis within her relationship also prompted Eleanor to seek help. She had a mounting concern about her increasing violence toward her partner:

I started to build this wall up because, I suppose, I didn't want him that close. I was pushing him away. And in the end I think, really, I became the abuser. I was the one lashing out and becoming violent and I didn't understand why I was doing it or where those feelings were coming from or anything. I just knew I didn't like myself and couldn't understand what had happened. I thought it was him I didn't like, and I just wanted him away. (Eleanor – 45)

Subsequent realization that part of her relationship problems involved 'taking it out on someone else' was also illustrated by Carol, who believed that her history of childhood abuse was contaminating her marital relationship:

This goes on and on and on, it doesn't matter what he does. I don't feel I'm getting affection. It doesn't matter – he can't do it for me – 'cos until I've got it all out of me towards my mother he's going to get it all. And I think he finds that quite hard. But he's learnt because I used to build up these big arguments, rages and he thought it was about us – and then he'd realise. (Carol – 17)

Having a child was an important factor in realizing the significance of childhood abuse and recognizing that problems in relationships with children could have particularly powerful impact:

That was a sort of mega crisis really, you know, there was no way of not knowing that wasn't a problem. And I could see there was something wrong with my relationship right from the start practically. I mean it was a difficult birth which I suppose didn't help but I knew I wasn't feeling the right things about him. Then when I got him home I still felt everything was wrong, you know I just didn't love him. And I just felt terrible and everything – it was really very dangerous. I really felt very violent towards my son because violence had been done to me and a lot of terrible things had happened when I was a child. Largely done by my mother who was extremely vicious and brutal and unable to love me – and this is what had to be faced. (Mary – 31)

While violent impulses towards children were mostly contained, there were perpetual fears of causing emotional harm from inappropriate parenting behaviour. This is illustrated by Eleanor who was overcome with a realization of the impact of her own abuse, after having long denied this, by her new experiences as a mother:

I never realized I'd been abused. I suppose it just never connected. I never saw myself as an abused person. I suppose because I just shut off from it. I went through a stage where nothing seemed to bother me at all – I think I had been so hurt I was just totally numb. But I never became aware that I'd been abused or how much it had hurt me until I had my first child. That's when it hit me what had happened.

I can remember one day – she was very tiny – I was changing her at the time – and I just sat and cried. And I think that was when it hit me – I just thought like, 'How could anyone hurt?' – like, 'what had I done to deserve?' Because I just kept looking at her and thinking, 'She's so tiny. She can't do anything to hurt me.' And I kept thinking, 'Well, what have I done?' The abuse, really, the sort of violent abuse started when I was two. And cruelty as well. So, I think I never realized until then that it wasn't my fault. (Eleanor – 45)

Helpful effects of therapy on clients' relationships with their own children will be discussed in more detail in Chapter 8.

Becoming aware of the significance of problems, and the availability of help only leads to therapy being sought when the person or a third party 'makes the move' to request help. Crises involving sudden deterioration in the ability to function in personal, social and professional roles often provoke urgent help-seeking:

I don't think I even thought of professional help. In fact, I know I didn't, until the crisis arose in my marriage. And that was interestingly, because I couldn't function. And that was something that I'd never encountered. Because one thing I can do is function in a practical day-to-day manner. I just went to pieces and I couldn't do anything. And that was something that was for me, new – and something I couldn't handle. I couldn't handle not managing. The reaction was, 'We've got to get some help, so that this doesn't fall apart'. (Georgia – 51)

Making the move to seek help is commonly characterized by a very ambivalent process of approach and avoidance involving high levels of anxiety and uncertainty:

It took me ages to pluck up courage to do it . . . I've never jumped out of an aeroplane with a parachute strapped to my back, but I can imagine the feeling is much the same – 'it's now or never!'. (Beth – 16)

These moments often follow long periods of denying the need for help, of being unable to ask for help when the need is recognized and uncertainty about the nature of help. Important factors deter people from seeking help which need to be overcome.

Deterrents to help-seeking

Inhibitions in seeking help involve the interplay of ignorance, anxiety, denial, belief systems, practicalities and previous negative experiences. A number of examples follow to illustrate these processes. One scenario involves a belief that the problem predominantly lies elsewhere:

> My then boyfriend had been saying to me for a long time: 'I really think you should go.' And my attitude was: 'I don't need it. There's nothing wrong with me!' I think probably people don't go until the situation gets desperate. (Ragbag – 39)

> At that point in time I still didn't recognize, really, that there was anything wrong. You know, the fact that I couldn't relate to people and that I was very critical and various other things, was just the way I was, other people were always wrong and it was always their problem, it was never mine. That kind of attitude pervaded at that point in time. (Georgia – 51)

There may be an increasingly painful awareness of the significance of problems but little conception that any sources of help exist which could be of benefit or accessible. The experience of intensifying personal problems without knowledge that these are amenable to help and change is a very isolated and desolate position, but thankfully one which media attention to child abuse over the past twenty years has done a great deal to ameliorate. Sometimes people are aware of their problems and of potential help, but feel restrained by beliefs that help should not be sought or is not deserved. Examples of these beliefs include: one has no rights to any help; one should be 'self-sufficient' and conceal vulnerability; be able to resolve one's own problems, or cope with them alone:

> I was utterly convinced that I hadn't got any entitlement to any help anyway, that I shouldn't need it, and if I did need it there was something wrong with me. (Sue – 54)

This reflects the low self-esteem, pessimism regarding potential for change and fear of stigmatization which is characteristic of the thinking at their lowest moments of many adults who were abused as children. Pressure at the time of the abuse 'not to tell' can also linger, reinforcing silence and deterring help-seeking:

> I'd always thought, 'Well, there must be something dreadful about me and I must keep my mouth closed about it as I've been told to'. (Anna – 19)

Others feel ashamed about their need for help and are afraid of being labelled by involvement with helping agencies:

> Having to admit that I have got a mental problem – it's something which you don't admit to, really, because there is a stigma attached to it. (Veronica – 23)

Fear of stigma was poignantly evident for abused adults who worked or who had worked in the helping professions and who found themselves desperately needing help. Myrtle felt great discomfort in the role transition involved in becoming a patient in the psychiatric unit where she had worked:

> I really, really went to pieces, and I didn't know where to go for help. Because having worked in the Mental Health field, I know just how bad it can be – you know, I really do – how abusive it can be. Their attitude is 'blame the victim', it's really punitive. The attitude of people being to blame for having problems is so pervasive. I went to (psychiatric clinic- name deleted) and it was really funny going there, because some of the people I'd treated were still there – they thought I was going as a member of staff. I was slightly embarrassed – I didn't want to meet any of the staff. Because I'd never asked for help in my life for anything – it felt like a real confession of weakness. (Myrtle – 22)

We will return to Myrtle's subsequent experiences of therapy in this and the next chapter.

People can be keen to obtain help, but feel thwarted by practicalities which stem from the problem itself, or other factors such as lack of local services, absence of suitable childcare facilities or inability to travel. Carol, for example, who lived in an isolated community, described the effects of panic attacks and flashbacks which significantly impaired her normal ability to drive safely:

> I can't drive – you can't possibly drive, it's dangerous. You might be going through a time of anger – that's OK, you can drive. But supposing it changes to terror – how are you going to carry on if you're in a state of extreme terror? (Carol – 17)

A particularly notable deterrent to seeking therapeutic help stemmed from previous negative experiences of contact with professionals, especially psychiatrists and social workers. The style and authority of these professionals regarding admission to psychiatric hospitals, having children taken into care and repercussions on employment had major impact, especially when this involved insensitive, dismissive, critical and punitive responses. Psychiatric interventions had left particularly bitter residues:

> I was horrified that I was classed as a mental patient. I was put into a locked ward because of the suicide indications. That will stay with me for ever and ever – to be in a locked ward with people who behaved strangely. I was

depressed and suppressed, very unhappy, very frightened to be faced with this. (Rose – 20)

I've had a lot of psychiatric treatment and I didn't get anywhere with any of them so I don't really trust them. When you get into the hospital there isn't anybody to talk to – they don't want to hear you – and I think some of the nurses were sadistic, they really were. They were really cruel to the patients actually, a lot of the patients talked about this. That hospital: worse experience than the abuse, it really was. It was terrible, you know, people were taking overdoses and everything, but there wasn't any sitting down and talking to people at all. I really think that it was a very dangerous place to be in. (Carol – 17)

They didn't talk about it in there. All I could do was cry, all I wanted to do was cry. And the Charge Nurse said: 'You can't stay there and cry all day, that's not what you're here for.' It was more or less: 'Pull yourself together.' So, I was just, like, forced. I'd go for meals I didn't want, go into rooms I didn't want, but nobody sat down and talked or said: 'Why are you depressed?' Why couldn't they just talk to you like a normal person, instead of doing all these stupid things like they do in hospital? I mean, you think you're mad any-way being sent in there, and then the things they do! Just confirms it really. (Mary – 53)

Since I was abused by a male school-teacher, I have had no therapy at all, except drug therapy. At 23 years of age I was diagnosed as having schizo-phrenia. I asked a doctor whether I could have psychotherapy. I was told 'For psychotherapy you need insight – and schizophrenics don't have insight.' When I asked what insight was, I was told, 'Look it up in the Library.' I did look it up in the Library. And discovered that I do have insight – into the years before my breakdown. (Written contribution, male)

Dismissive responses provoke frustration and anger for people when their experiences of abuse are not believed, or are not taken seriously:

I had this Freudian psychotherapy for two years and it was totally useless. She kept saying: 'These ideas towards your parents are fantasies, sexual fantasies.' So that was a dead loss you know. (Carol – 17)

Sometimes the things that the doctor said, I was shocked by. I don't know now whether it was because they were trying to make me angry or what. The doctor said: 'Well, your father slept with you – so what?' – like it was nothing. And I didn't know whether it was right or wrong, or whether I was right or wrong. And now, I find, when people say: 'Well, it's not your fault' – I don't know. (Mary – 53)

Critical and punitive responses left people feeling hurt and angry many years later:

I was approximately 16, still very desperately unhappy at home – and over-dosed at that time, and was taken into hospital. And a Policeman was the first person I saw, and he said 'If you do this again, we can arrest you'. So I didn't approach anybody for help – I didn't seek therapy. (Rose – 20)

This level of insensitivity and lack of human concern is striking, and typical of many people's experiences. The impact of previous professional interventions where these involved combinations of dismissal, criticism, insensitivity and punitiveness was enormous. They reinforced existing feelings of anxiety and suspicion about 'help'. They deterred many for periods of time from seeking further help (a few for good) and exacerbated the challenge for subsequent therapists in establishing trusting relationships.

Initial sessions

> I wanted all my mind unjumbling and all my thoughts unscrambling and straightening out. I had my handbag with me, and my handbag was like a complete – all sorts of stuff crammed into it. And I said to her, 'See that bag – that's what my head's like.' (Veronica – 23)

Having overcome anxieties and deterrents to help seeking, potential clients face the challenge of how to find a suitable therapist. For many this is a much more complex and difficult task than they imagined, particularly for those who have no previous experience of contact with helping professionals. One client summed up this predicament as 'avoiding the minefield'. The transition into the role of client for the first time may also involve bewilderment about the 'rules of the game' of therapy and what is expected of participants in the process. At this point clients may be in high states of confusion or even despair. Some prepare themselves for the worst:

> I didn't have any expectations because I'd never done it before, but I imagined it would be fairly unpleasant. (Jamie – 12)

Given such trepidation, the sort of experiences people have at this point are crucial as to whether the initial rapport necessary for the development of a positive therapeutic relationship can be established – or whether the client will flee, dismissing any prospect of therapy being helpful. Clients with no previous experience of therapy (naive clients) can feel very confused, particularly during the initial stages. They often do not know what to expect from the therapist, or what the therapist expects from them. It appears that some therapists do not appreciate this and relate to new clients assuming a shared understanding which does not recognize the effects of the client's naivety.

What sort of responses do clients meet in their initial contacts with therapists? How do they interpret such responses? Above all, what effect do they have on perceptions as to whether therapy is likely to be helpful? Clients describe strong initial reactions to the personal characteristics of therapists and the contexts within which they work. These often suggest meanings which powerfully influence their initial sense of ease or discomfort. In addition to actual characteristics, there is potential symbolic significance in almost every aspect of a therapist's characteristics or context. Such characteristics can be reminiscent of other significant people and circumstances – influences on perceptions and interpretations which are often construed theoretically as transference. Clients have a great deal to say about how these characteristics can unexpectedly have positive and negative effects on engagement and the subsequent process of therapy. A number of examples follow to illustrate this.

For Mary, confidence in her new therapist was raised by an incidental observation:

> It sounds daft, but when she was talking, there was a wasp trying to get out the window. And she said, 'Hang on, this is going to distract us.' So she just got up, got this tissue, got hold of the wasp and just threw it out of the window. I thought, 'Well, she's not scared of wasps' – I was really impressed. (Mary – 53)

Positive feelings and expectations also stem from contextual features which the client shares, admires or aspires to:

> A lovely house – it was the sort of house that I could quite happily live in. And it was the kind of room that I could quite happily have, and the sort of furniture and schemes that I could happily be with. And therefore I felt very comfortable. But you don't get that from an office. (Georgia – 51)

> She lives in a lovely old stone farmhouse – the kind of house where I'd like to live. Before I even saw her she was going to be my type of person. (Myrtle – 22)

Negative reactions are equally commonplace. Clients can feel inhibited, distracted and discouraged by specific contextual features which have personal significance for them:

> Taste in their surroundings is indicative of how much people are aware of themselves. I'm here to be helped: if you give me a bright green wall, bright yellow wall, bright pink wall and a bright purple wall – are you trying to send me round the bend? If I walked into a room like that now, knowing what I do, I'd say, 'Piss off, Mush, I'm off! – I don't trust you at all – not with this lot. What are you trying to do?' (Sue – 54)

> She was just very 'right-on' – she might have been gay, I'm not sure. But very – one of the 'Sisters' you know. And I was a businesswoman. I was going to see her in my business clothes, with my briefcase, and I sort of wondered what she thought about that, and that became inhibiting. I wondered if she thought, 'She's not very right on.' I wondered whether I was being treated differently because of the way I looked, or my life style. She lived in a council flat, I thought, Oh, is she sort of thinking, 'Well really, this isn't the thing to do – for one to be so material.' (Ellen – 13)

Most private practice therapists in the UK work in their own homes using either their own living space or a room separately set aside for seeing clients. In addition to the stimuli this provides for clients to react to and interpret, it is interesting that being seen by others in such environments could either raise significant anxiety or be reassuring. Mary, for example, appreciated the steps that were taken to prevent her being observed:

> And when she sees you out she says, 'Oh, I'll just make sure there's no-one around.' Because when you come out from talking about something like that, you don't want to have to walk past people and, like, put on your 'normal' act. You just want to get out and go. (Mary – 53)

However, for Esme, such behaviour had completely different meaning and effect:

> I don't know why it is, but if therapists work in their home and they have family around it's almost like the family aren't allowed to see you. I felt very like, 'Well, what's wrong with me that I can't even be seen by other people in this environment – am I that, sort of, horrendous? – I'm not contagious!' – I felt really weird. (Esme – 42)

At a stage when she was extremely naive about therapy, Esme remembered sessions with a therapist where she was not sure whether or not the presence of a third party was standard practice:

> I can't remember saying very much at all. She had a baby daughter who was a very sweet little thing, but she used to run around in the sessions. She was under two, so, you know – this was her mother sitting here! And I did feel that I was actually in the way. (Esme – 42)

The confusing and distracting presence of the therapist's daughter (despite the fact that she was paying for the therapist's time) reinforced Esme's existential theme of not belonging and her longstanding feelings of being unimportant and unworthy.

For people receiving therapy in agency contexts, the experience begins with contact with reception arrangements. Clients are highly sensitized to the friendly or unfriendly impact of their initial welcome. Unwelcoming responses easily reinforce feelings of non-deservingness and poor self-esteem. Eva remembered not knowing what to do and feeling invisible when she arrived at a clinic for her initial session:

> I remember going there and it didn't seem clear to me whether I was meant to go and present myself at the office or go and wait in the waiting room. So anyway, I put my head round the office door, and people ignored me, it seemed for ages and ages. Nobody looked up or anything. So, I didn't like that very much. (Eva – 57)

In agency settings there were particularly strong senses of stigma at being visible to other staff and other patients:

> I didn't want people to know that I was actually getting help for anything – being thought of as being in need of psychiatric help – that was all very strange. I often remember thinking, coming out from time to time, that I would look like one of the counsellors as opposed to one of the patients. I didn't want to look like one of the patients. I used to carry a bag with me, or something like that, so I could look like a counsellor. (Sally – 65)

Experience of initial sessions is of great significance for clients, and strong impressions about helpful and unhelpful potential are formed at this stage. Almost all forms of therapy acknowledge the importance of the relationship formed between therapist and client, either as being a central component of change in its own right, or as providing the vehicle for the effective utilization of therapeutic techniques. Many therapists seem to pay insufficient attention to the impact of their behaviour, and the therapeutic environment, on clients who at this stage are particularly emotionally sensitive and vulnerable. The initial establishment of rapport in the very early moments of contact is fundamental to the development of a positive therapeutic relationship. There is widespread acceptance of the underlying importance of the Rogerian 'core conditions' in creating an effective therapeutic relationship: careful listening; communicated understanding and empathy; a respectful, congruent and non-judgemental attitude. The extent to which clients in this study did not experience this approach is a surprise and a matter of concern.

This is particularly important as, by definition, adults who were abused as children invariably have histories of lack of appropriate care. When seeking help their perceptions of the potential for genuine care are very significant. Of all the many accounts given by clients relating to negative experiences with therapists, time and time again the key theme involved a lack of 'humanness' on the part of the therapist:

> I couldn't trust the second one, you see, she was too cold, she was too detached somehow. It was like she didn't really want to know. It was that sort of attitude, 'I'm here, but I'm not really here'. She just hadn't got the human touch. (Alice – 04)

Ellen – a very naive client at this stage – had travelled for a couple of hours across London early one morning for her first session with a psychoanalytically orientated therapist:

> I felt uncomfortable in the room with her. It was like a feeling of not being accepted, you know. Because if I had been accepted she would have been nicer to me, and smiled, and said: 'How are you?' and 'Do you want a cup of tea?' And I didn't understand the game. I didn't understand the rules. And I just felt, 'You don't like me, you don't want me here, I'm not accepted.' (Ellen – 13)

Myrtle, as already mentioned, found herself seeking help from the hospital psychiatric psychotherapy unit where she had recently worked as a professional. Many years later she remained distressed and angry about the way her two initial interviews had been conducted:

> So I went to see her and she just didn't like me, and I didn't like her from the minute I went in. I was very paranoid and very disturbed, but I'm a therapist and part of my mind always keeps working and I know what a good therapist is. And, she kept looking at her watch while I was talking, and she answered the phone while I was talking. She never offered me a cup of tea. And she sat behind her desk, you know, and however paranoid I am, I know that that's not what you do with somebody who is deeply distressed and distraught – it was so cold.
>
> And I can't remember things she said, but it didn't feel sympathetic or understanding, so I didn't want to talk about my Dad with her. I didn't trust her. I didn't like her, and this was the first session. Anyway, I went back a second time – I wasn't happy about going back – (but) I was desperate. Even through my terrible distress, I knew this woman was crass. I knew that she was useless. There was that bit of my brain that was a therapist saying, 'This woman is the pits – you'll get damaged if you continue seeing her.'
>
> And I just wanted to die. And she said, 'Well, I think I can offer you six more sessions.' And I said, 'Thank you very much!', and left. Oh, and the other thing she said, in the session, was, 'I can see you find this boring.' This is the woman who'd been looking at her watch and answering her phone! Well, I didn't find it boring – distressing and whatever else – I didn't find it boring. She was saying she found *me* boring. I thought, 'Lady, can't you even see when you're projecting.' She was unbelievable. (Myrtle – 22)

These sorts of responses by therapists are not only hurtful, disrespectful and potentially damaging in their own right, but they can be poignantly reminiscent of early experiences with caretakers:

> As an abused child, all affection is very conditional. It's very conditional – very much on your toes to know how to behave so as not to incur their wrath, you know. So I was always frozen by people who were cold towards me. (Ellen – 13)

The extent to which some practitioners can be seemingly oblivious to their anti-therapeutic characteristics and the negative impact of these on their clients is surprising. However, as will be further illustrated in the next chapter, part of the complexity of this dynamic is that clients have strong tendencies to conceal their negative reactions and this deprives therapists of feedback about the unhelpful effects of their practice. These experiences reinforce negative self-images of being to blame and a sense of hopelessness from being unhelpable. In turn this serves as an additional deterrent to further help-seeking:

> It just makes you feel more hopeless than ever, you know. You sort of think, 'Am I so, kind of, mad or ill?' I had no idea on a scale of how disturbed,

distressed – I had no kind of diagnosis. And I didn't know why I couldn't do this therapy thing. So that was upsetting, made me feel quite hopeless and, also, it felt like it was a shut door. I thought: 'Well, I can never try that again, I'll never do that again.' (Ellen – 13)

In comparison, positive experiences of initial sessions involve the establishment of rapport, through being listened to attentively, with warmth and gestures of caring. Idiosyncratic, but clearly genuine, aspects of the 'human touch' were crucial for many:

Always the same routine. She would always offer me a drink of tea, and because I had herbal tea, she always gave me a little glass that I could put the bag in. I quite liked that. It was kind of nice, I liked it – she didn't have to give me a cup of tea. It communicated that I was kind of a person, if you like, rather than just a client, I suppose. (Eva – 57)

You know when rapport is there, don't you. It's in eye contact, or things people say, or it's in body language – things you can't really define. (Mary – 53)

I'm much kinder since I had this experience of therapy myself. I think I always was a kind therapist, but I've been a lot kinder, and a lot more gentle. Do you know, I say to my students: 'the distillation of 25 years of experience – the most important thing is to be kind'. (Myrtle – 22)

For Bea, the human touch was literally so. This was facilitated by her therapist's willingness to offer physical contact and comfort at the very beginning of what became a long-term relationship which she felt had had a profound positive benefit for her:

She just asked me if it was tears or if it was sweat running down my cheeks. I can't remember my answer, but I really liked that. In a way she said, 'It means something to me if you are crying right now.' That was, in a way, what she was saying, and that touched me deeply. I remember at that time I was so desperate, so my arms reached out for her. And there must have been a bit of conversation in between, but then she said, 'Come over – if it means so much to you, then come over.' And then she just took me as a child, and just held me tight – and I was sold, immediately. (Bea – 18)

Establishment of rapport is also affected by the context and dynamics of control and authority. Given that the experience of being abused as a child invariably involves exploitation of adult authority, it is not surprising that the power dynamics of relationships, and relationships with authority in general, are frequently issues which are problematic. It is likely that therapists of both genders are not fully aware of the degree to which they are perceived by clients as being powerful and controlling figures; and the intensity of clients' experiences and reactions to this, particularly at the initial stages.

Clients often experience a dilemma about power: a therapist is needed who is powerful enough to help, yet encountering someone with power raises anxieties about control and harm. This can be an extremely vulnerable position. As will be seen in the next chapter, damage stemming from domineering therapists can be great. Yet some therapists seem oblivious to this.

Myrtle expanded on her two initial sessions on the psychiatric psychotherapy unit:

> She wanted me to be weak and dependent, I think. But I'm not. Basically, she was 'blame the victim'. She embodied what I find distasteful about people who want power over other people. This woman saw me as somebody who should be a patient, but who was coming in trying to be a professional. I've seen it happen with other people who are professionals. I think she saw me as being in competition in some way. She lacked goodwill. She was punitive. I actually think its something about psychotherapy reinforces that, you know – Freudian psychotherapy, analytical psychotherapy. It's very anti-women, and it's very, well, it's very much about power. (Myrtle – 22)

Myrtle's reaction to the second initial session, described earlier, provides an illustration of a fortunate process of flight transforming into fight:

> I walked out of (NHS Psychotherapy Clinic, name deleted), and I walked down (name deleted) Road to the railway station, and I was really, really low. And I stood on the station, I was shaking all over. I was going to jump under a train, but of course, I couldn't because of my daughter. And then I just flipped – like I always did with my mother. She became my mother, somebody to kick against. I thought, 'I'm not going to let that bloody woman ruin my life – like I've always thought with my mother. There's no way that I'm going to become what she wanted me to become. I'm going to get better, and that's it.'
>
> I was just filled with rage. I just flipped into anger, out of depression into anger. It was a turning point. It gave me the energy. I wrote a very polite letter saying that I'd decided I didn't need the therapy but thank you very much anyway. I made a positive decision that I wasn't going to let that woman stop the therapeutic process for me. (Myrtle – 22)

It is not known whether Myrtle's therapist considered this to be a successful brief 'cure'. Fortunately, Myrtle was not deterred for ever from seeking other help. She later experienced a very different therapist:

> She brought her empathy and experience. First of all the position she took in relation to me, which is sitting near me and not with a desk in between. Giving me a cup of tea, making sure I was supplied with tissues. You know, the head nods, the body language, the eye contact, the concerned expression, all that stuff. It's body language mostly. (Myrtle – 22)

There is little discussion in the therapeutic literature about inappropriate power and control dynamics between female therapists and female clients. In the study as a whole the extent to which problems and dissatisfaction arose in female–female therapeutic relationships was striking. Statistically this would be expected as in the UK the majority of therapists and clients are female. In much therapeutic literature the merits of female therapists working with abused female (and male) clients is often stressed and recommended on the basis of avoiding further potential abuse of male power. However, experiences reported in this study suggests that such a single factor gender analysis in relation to male power is limited and simplistic. This view underplays the clinical reality of mother–daughter conflict, neglects the role of mothers as active or passive abusers and adopts an idealistically generalized benign view of female therapists.

Participants in this study reported preferences for therapists of both genders and often no preference. The reasons given for gender preferences indicate that two main motivations influence this choice: a desire to avoid a specific gender; and a desire to encounter and explore contact with a person of a specific gender. Avoidance can be fearful, angry or aversive and is sometimes based on a recognition of intense representational influences. Sue, for example, had been abandoned by her father at an early age and described being sexually abused by her mother and grandmother throughout her childhood:

> The only criterion that I'd asked for with my doctor was that it was a bloke. I didn't want a female therapist – I don't want to be near women. (Sue – 54)

The desire to encounter and explore stemmed from awareness that difficulties in relation to a significant person could be generalized to all people of that person's gender. This can be a very limiting position in relating to the world as a whole. Consequently, from this perspective, therapy is seen as an opportunity, albeit a challenging one, to experiment with making a satisfactory relationship with a person of the sensitive gender. This could involve searching for restitutive relationships or positive role models:

> I'd not had real help from my father ever. I really felt that Dad had let me down on a lot of scores, and what I was trying to do I was trying to build up at least some kind of trust relationship with a man, even if it was only verbal. (Sue – 54)

> I had been very concerned that he was a man. I'd always regarded my father as a bright star in an otherwise sort of murky skyline . . . he was the saviour and my mother was the demon. I actually said to him at the time – and I think it is probably right – that it could be useful for me that he was a man, because it's something I have to deal with. (Georgia – 51)

> So it came to me thinking, 'Well, it would be useful for me to work with a man.' Because I wanted to be able to relate and feel comfortable with men. And so I did. That's how it came about really, and it was very useful indeed. Very helpful. (Mary – 43)

> I think I would definitely look for a woman. Although, in fact with seeing a man, I think that would give me a very clear indication about how I actually

felt now about the abuse. Although going to see a woman would obviously be easier – its not so much that I would feel unsafe, although that is still around. And so that is what I would want to explore. And whether I had another part of me that felt safe enough to let that happen. In a way, I kind of think for me at some point – that is necessary to do. (Eva – 57)

Like Eva, some clients who feel aversive to a particular gender at the initial stages of their therapy come to recognize the need in later stages to work with a therapist of the abuser's gender. As has been illustrated, this is not specific to female clients avoiding male therapists. Furthermore, for many who experienced abuse by both men and women the 'avoid therapists of the same gender as the abuser' arguments are irrelevant.

Checking out therapists

Clients' perceptions of therapists and their contexts are affected from the earliest moments of contact by reactions to a wide range of character-istics and behaviour. This is a confusing time for clients who may have high levels of anxiety and uninformed fantasies and fears as to what therapists are like and what therapy involves. Anxiety, fantasies and transference responses all combine to affect perceptions during initial meetings. It is interesting to explore what people remember about such moments, and how they try to judge whether or not a particular therapist is likely to be of help to them.

The transition from therapeutic naivety to becoming more discerning about therapy involves development of an ability and willingness to question the therapeutic process. Sophisticated clients have learned ways, often through prior negative experiences, of 'checking out' poten-tial therapists in initial meetings and throughout the early stages of therapy. Checking out takes place at both direct and indirect levels. Direct checking out requires a degree of confidence and assertive-ness and includes asking questions regarding therapists' qualifications, theoretical orientation, levels of experience, attitudes towards abuse and about the structure and boundaries of the proposed therapeutic work.

At another level, there is simultaneous indirect checking out which relies heavily on intuition and the generation of negative or positive feeling states, which is much less perceptible to therapists:

I always suss people out within about fifteen seconds. It must be more to do with smell than it's got to do with looks. It's literally smell and eye contact – and the way they respond. It's the body, the way that the body moves and whether that feels honest or whether their voice feels as though they are resolved. There's a lot in people's voices that gives them away orally – some people sound very false. (Sue – 54)

I did trust (therapist: name deleted) a lot. Quite how I arrived at that I don't know. It was entirely gut. She was very patient with me, which was very important as far as I was concerned. She didn't chivvy me, or hassle me, or demand to know what had gone on. So I set the pace, which was important. And neither at any time did it feel like she was being voyeuristic, and if I'd had any sense of that, I'd have been out of the door. (Beth – 16)

The antennae are out and I'm looking for any hint of rejection, or that it's false, or that there's some hidden agenda, or that I'm going to get manipulated. (Zoe – 11)

Bea remembered her intense need for emotional attachment to a therapist, and her way of checking this out intuitively:

I can see what I have in me – if I can recognize that in the other person's eye then I think I might get emotionally attached. It's a deep trust. If they can see my little girl who once suffered a hell of a lot. I don't know how to do it, but normally when I have asked for help I will know immediately, or within a few minutes, if that person can see a hurt spot in here – or if they can't. (Bea – 18)

The role of intuition or 'gut feelings' is particularly complicated for naive clients who have had little or no previous experience of therapy. For many people who were abused as children, one consequence is a diminished capacity and confidence to trust their own perceptions. There may be a habitual tendency toward mistrust (or generalized over-trusting); an over-valuing of and deference to the opinions and perceptions of others, especially when those others have authority status. Self-image can be so poor that people feel they should accept and be grateful for whatever is offered. For some clients, the notion of questioning whether or not the potential therapist was suitable had simply not occurred to them.

An interesting way of 'checking out' occurs through clients being 'difficult' or 'different' in initial sessions and observing responses to this:

I think it's almost an unconscious thing. I mean I was watching and noticing his every move, his every expression. Every little detail I would watch. It was, sort of – terribly, very, very, very, acutely observing how he reacted to what I said . . . and gradually testing. And I remember testing him out by being quite rude to him sometimes . . . I'd get a bit stroppy . . . just refuse to say anything, answering back – just all the things I was never allowed to do as a child – just to test him out. (Mary – 43)

Clients may or may not recognize that their testing out or awkward behaviour sometimes represents desperate attempts to deny their pain and needs; attacking to remain in control; needing to be noticed; or creating conflicts to provoke rejection or retaliation which would confirm that they were unhelpable:

I think I was very antagonistic, hostile, or whatever the word is. And I got the impression that she didn't really like me very much. I think she felt a bit threatened by me. I hated everything and I hated everybody, quite frankly. (Veronica – 23)

I always dressed in a kind of self-covering way – just not to draw attention to myself. On this particular occasion I wore a bright orange skirt that was slit – it actually had buttons – but I had it undone, practically to the top. And it had a very bold black pattern round the bottom of it. And I wore purple. Why did I do that? – I just felt that I ought to look weird. And also – I was trying to express some kind of sexuality. Because I had learnt that sex was a way of getting noticed and attention. (Ragbag – 39)

These forms of behaviour transmit covert messages to therapists about clients' problems. When a therapist is able to decode the behaviour and reach through to the underlying meanings and feelings this can be the starting point for the formation of a very beneficial therapeutic relationship.

At the first session, I've learned since, that I actually terrified the living daylights out of her. Because I'd turned up in my business suit and did my power act – made her feel utterly useless and inadequate. What I was doing was very much hiding my vulnerabilities and being very in control.

I turned up in the BMW with the filofax tucked under my arm, and the business suit on, and talked in a very highly intelligent and cognitive way with her. And, she said I made her feel very inadequate and scruffy and useless. But also she could see that somewhere there was a little hurting kid in me. And this front I put on as being very tough and very successful – I didn't know that it was intimidating, and I didn't know that I was doing it to protect myself. I wasn't aware at that point that I had this really false sense of self, and false persona that I hid behind. (Zoe – 11)

Following initial sessions, clients make decisions about whether or not to continue. Most people who felt that a degree of rapport had been established in the initial session did return for ongoing therapeutic work. Non-returners opt out because rapport is not established, because of feelings that the initial experience has been negative or harmful and because of the absence of a sense of hope. However, some clients who experienced the initial session as being negative also returned. Many regret this subsequently, wishing they had trusted their instincts to keep away. Others, however, were pleased that they had persevered against initial feelings of uncertainty, as gradually overcoming them had resulted in the development of therapeutic work which had become beneficial.

Seeking therapeutic help when one has no knowledge as to what the process involves can be a bewildering experience. Many clients feel that their therapists are not sufficiently aware that they do not understand the culture, context and processes of therapy and that this ignorance can have negative impact which clients often conceal. As will be seen in the next chapter, the culmination of this complex help-seeking process (the client asking for help) does not always result in a service that is actually helpful. Many are then deterred from seeking further help. Others have a number of mixed positive and negative experiences before giving up or eventually finding the help that is right for them.

6

When Things Go Wrong

'Excuse me – You're meant to be focusing on me.' (Emily – 15)

I had terrible trouble getting away from them – especially the paid ones. The National Health ones couldn't wait to get rid of you because they've got so many to see. (Ellen – 13)

In this chapter we will consider clients' experiences of dissatisfaction in therapy, including surprising difficulties which were experienced in attempting to end unhelpful therapeutic relationships. Overall, there has been relatively little discussion in the literature regarding clients' feelings of dissatisfaction with professional help. Exceptions to this have been provided by Mayer and Timms (1970) and Howe (1989) in relation to social work/family therapy services. Armsworth (1989, 1990); Frenken and van Stolk (1990) and Walker (1992) have illustrated abuse survivors' negative experiences of a range of helping professionals. Rennie (1992) and Thompson and Hill (1991) noted the reluctance of psychotherapy clients to express dissatisfaction to their therapists. Pope and Bouhoutsos (1986) and Russell (1993) reported on the phenomenon of sexual intimacy between therapists and clients. France (1988) provided a compelling account of the difficulties which arose with her three psychotherapists.

In focusing on clients' experiences of dissatisfaction in this chapter, it is not my intention to eclipse the important benefits which many people report from helpful therapy. The book as a whole will illustrate that adults who were abused as children can experience great gains from effective therapy. However, in view of the extent, variety, unusual nature and detrimental effects of negative therapy experiences reported by participants in this study, this merits detailed consideration. This is particularly so as it involves phenomena which clients believe therapists are often unaware of.

The term 'dissatisfaction' is chosen, following Mayer and Timms (1970), to represent a general category of negative or unhelpful experiences, including the episode of therapy as a whole. It is important to recognize that dissatisfaction is a broad, fluid and complex concept which subsumes many types of feelings about therapy experiences, including ambivalence, ambiguity and contradictions. However, just as clients' satisfaction evaluations do not necessarily mean that the therapy was efficacious, feelings of dissatisfaction do not necessarily imply that there has been no benefit. This highlights a consistent underlying theme that experiencing in therapy is multidimensional and is resistant to reliable evaluation by use of single process or outcome measures.

Except when led directly by the concepts and words of participants, I have resisted using language in this description and analysis which necessarily construes therapist behaviour leading to client dissatisfaction as 'abusive'. The reason for this is a desire to remain true to the phenomenological subtlety of participants' experiencing and their ways of understanding, without superimposing a constricting 'abuse lens' on any event which at some point felt uncomfortable, inappropriate or harmful. Routinely to label inexperienced, ineffective, clumsy, questionable or dubious aspects of therapists' behaviour as 'abuse' without first understanding the meaning of the behaviour both for the therapist and the client, risks introducing a false, but fashionable oversimplicity which distracts from an understanding of the complexity of the phenomena.

However, this is not to ignore the prevalence or the research into abuse within therapy (Garrett and Davis 1994; Jehu 1994; Pope and Bouhoutsos 1986; Russell 1993). The existing literature on abuse and exploitation in therapy focuses predominantly on scenarios involving male therapists and female clients. In contrast, as mentioned in the last chapter, one surprising feature of this study is the extent to which female clients felt significant dissatisfaction with female therapists, some construing this as having involved abusive dynamics of control, power, exploitation and domination. This phenomenon is largely unreported in the clinical or research literature and will be a significant focus of this chapter.

Experiences of dissatisfaction

Clients do not expect that therapy will be a pain free, pleasant or magical cure. Rather they tend to anticipate that helpful therapy involves challenge, frustration and set backs, as well as progress. Effective therapy, therefore, invariably includes elements of frustration and disappointment. As a consequence, some degree of intrinsic dissatisfaction is to be expected even within therapies which are ultimately considered to have been successful. However, in contrast to inherent dissatisfaction, some clients have negative experiences which cannot be attributed to an intrinsic inevitable process. Instead, these are often related to the impact of therapists' characteristics, contexts, attitudes and behaviour which range across a continuum from the extremely subtle to the blatantly overt.

In the last chapter, the significance of therapist factors were noted in relation to their impact during the initial stages of therapy. In this chapter it will be seen how therapists' characteristics can have a serious detrimental effect throughout a therapeutic relationship. In such situations, all manner of distortions can develop in the relationship between client and therapist. Clients who have no previous experience of therapy (naive clients) face major problems in interpreting the appropriateness of therapists' behaviour. They also tend to construe uncomfortable feelings as being a part of their problem. It is also apparent from participants' accounts that significant levels of dissatisfaction with therapy can be experienced without clients being able to communicate this. In such scenarios, clients feel completely stuck and at a loss as how to extricate themselves.

'Weirdo shrinks'

Uncertainty about interpreting the difference between common, unusual, questionable, inappropriate, bizarre and abusive therapeutic practice was graphically illustrated in the following excerpts from the interview transcript of Sally's account of her contacts with a therapist to whom she referred as the 'weirdo shrink':

> *Sally*: I went to my doctor and he decided to send me to a psychoanalyst[1] I think it was called, at the hospital. And this guy, I thought, was supposed to be giving me will power, and the will power was – he used methods of electric shock – using an electrode on your hand. And then it got that I would have to sit in his office with a paper bag over my head – a big envelope it was – over my head – and this was to give me will power! And then it got to the stage after several weeks of going to him and doing various things – leaving me in the office with this bag over my head – of him suggesting that he came round to my house one evening. Remember, I lived on my own at the time. He came round to my house, put me into a swimsuit, put me in the bath, tied me up, put a bag over my head, gagged me, and left me there for a few hours – which was slightly bizarre, I thought at the time. My friends – also at home during that time had to tie me to the bed and leave me. And my friends also had to tie me up on a chair and put me in a cupboard – these were all methods of giving me will power!
>
> *PD*: On his recommendation, his instructions?
>
> *Sally*: On his instructions, yes. They were all sort of methods of giving me will power and strength to cope with my eating! I used to go to a group session of weighing in and when we had to weigh in – and this wasn't just me, this was other women – if you didn't lose weight he used to make them wear either bunny rabbit ears or a swimsuit with bunny rabbit tail and bunny rabbit ears. And we had to parade like that in this group and it was quite bizarre.
>
> *PD*: I'm supposed to take a neutral stance here, but I have to say that sounds pretty odd and pretty bizarre to me.

Sally: I went through a long time of this, and I didn't know. In the end when he started suggesting he come round to my house, I stopped going. I didn't report him to the doctor, I didn't report him to anyone. Because I thought it was me, as I've done all of my life.

PD: How long did that go on for?

Sally: Probably getting on for a year, or a good length of time. And it was towards the end of that time when he suggested he should come over to my house. But it was very odd. He actually had photographs in his office of women who he had done that to – he actually showed me the photographs. Polaroids – so when you see that you think: 'Oh, well, this is quite normal, this is obviously what other people have done.' But in my heart of hearts I knew that I was going because I had been abused. And it was ringing bells again and I realized that things weren't quite right. So, I didn't report him back to the doctor or anything. Needless to say I didn't lose weight either! (Sally – 65)

Sally only gradually came to recognize how bizarre and inappropriate this behaviour was. Her toleration of it, despite her growing unease, stemmed from a combination of deference to the authority status of the therapist and lack of confidence in her own perceptions and judgments:

I remember thinking: 'No, I can't have this man coming round to my house, I can't have this happening.' And I was in fear for quite some time afterwards because he lived so close to me. And I remember thinking at the time 'Well, I should say something to the doctor – No, no, no, no – that's just my imagination. All these other women accept it – it must be just me – forget it! Just ignore it – I haven't got a problem really.' (Sally – 65)

Reflecting on this experience in the research interview, Sally stressed the connection between childhood abuse and subsequent difficulties in interpreting therapeutic contexts which inhibits self-protective responses and increases susceptibility to re-victimization. She continued to ponder on having remained in this relationship while increasingly feeling that it was not right:

I think it's because you're afraid to report things. Like, as a child you were afraid to report things because people won't believe you. I was abused – I was sexually abused at work once and this guy came into my office and started to fondle me. And I just froze. And I thought: 'Oh, my God.' And eventually I had enough gumption to say: 'If you don't go, I'll scream' – and I was absolutely shaking. Then a friend came up to me and said: 'You've got to report it' and so I did. And I was told: 'Oh, no – not (name deleted) – he wouldn't do that sort of thing'. And the blame was put onto me. And I never forget these experiences. I've gone through quite a number in my life and that just sums up how I feel and what people would say. (Sally – 65)

Expectations of trustworthiness in a person in authority and deferent responses are key factors in the toleration of the uncomfortable behaviour:

> *Sally*: He was a man of responsibility, he was, in effect, to me a doctor. And like, you trust your doctor. You thought they were doing what they were trained to do. My friends who were supposed to give me the treatment at home also thought it was very odd. In fact they thought it was quite amusing – it was quite funny really. At the end I just felt he was weird – just a weird guy.
>
> *PD*: Do you see it now as an abusive experience?
>
> *Sally*: Yes. I consider that he abused his position with me. Because I stopped it, it didn't go any further but I think effectively it would have become sexual abuse. But I consider it an abuse to my being, to myself, my self-esteem too. Because one of the things of the abuse in my life is that my self-esteem has been hit. And that didn't help – that guy was just so weird, was so odd.
>
> *PD*: Was there anything within it that did actually help you?
>
> *Sally*: I don't think it did in the end. It was actually an horrendous experience really – with someone you trust! But then again, always the abuse is from someone you supposedly trust. (Sally – 65)

Without having access to the therapist concerned it is impossible to be clear what lay behind the behaviour described. It is known, however, that therapists do continue in practice while experiencing all sorts of major emotional and psychological impairments (Guy 1987).

Out of their depth

The stories of Rose, Grace and Beth illustrate situations where clients feel they had been led into areas which were beyond the competence of their therapist to handle. For Rose, the scenario involved a therapist using techniques to induce her into a regressive experience which resulted in both therapist and client panicking when he was unable to manage what followed. The therapist then neatly disowned responsibility, blaming her instead:

> All hell let loose – and he said: 'I don't understand what's happening.' And I suppose subconsciously I thought: 'Christ!' – and panicked: 'If you don't understand, well, what do I do now?' And then, he said: 'If you don't behave you have to leave this therapy.' And he reported to my doctor that he wasn't happy with what was going on within my life. And he didn't tell me he was going to do that and he hadn't told me he'd done it. It was when I went to the doctor, the doctor told me. (Rose – 20)

Despite this incident, Rose continued with subsequent sessions because of her lingering hopes that benefit might still be forthcoming:

His approach was sort of 'palsy, walsy' – crawling on the floor and saying: 'Oh, you've got that cushion in front of you because you are putting up barriers against me.' And I did want to put up barriers against the man because he was so gushing. And one day he said to me: 'I love you.' There was something about him that made me uneasy. (Rose – 20)

Naive clients have a tendency to presume that their adverse reactions are part of their problem. Rose was sufficiently inexperienced at this stage not to have the confidence to trust her gut feelings of discomfort. Often, it is only from hard lessons learned that progress is made towards therapeutic sophistication, whereby clients become more discerning as to whether the basis of unease lies within themselves or with the therapist.

This was not the end of Rose's story. Things became even more disturbing when the therapist began imposing interpretations regarding her problems and behaviour – supposedly from a transactional analysis perspective:

Rose: It was done graphically – the Adult, the Parent and the Child. Instead of all overlapping nicely, going from one into the other – mine were all merged into one you see. He suggested to me that it was probably psychotic behaviour – because of these circles, or something, merging.

PD: Was that a helpful concept to you?

Rose: No! I rushed to the library and I'm looking up 'psychotic'. And I thought: 'Dear God, perhaps I am psychotic.' And then I got to the realms of psychotic people. So I shut the book up, heart thumping and worried about it and determined if I were, I'd hide it. And I went to the doctor and got some tranquillisers. (Rose – 20)

During the research interview, several years after these experiences, Rose remained disconcerted about the notion of psychosis:

Damaging?!! it damaged me, and even now I still wonder, I just wonder, maybe there's a tinge there. And then I try and comfort myself by saying: 'Perhaps everybody has a little bit of psychosis.' (Rose – 20)

The impact of the therapist's incongruous behaviour, compounded by the suggestion of psychosis, was frightening and profoundly unhelpful for Rose. Having eventually managed to extricate herself, she gave up for ever on the prospect that any therapy could help. Like a number of other dissatisfied clients in the study, she turned to other sources for healing – in her case a Buddhist spiritual path which had profound positive impact on her life.

Beth also encountered a therapist whom she felt got severely out of her depth. The therapist worked in a religious order and cheerfully and openly acknowledged that she 'broke all the rules'. Despite Beth's knowledge from a previous positive therapy that her new therapist's behaviour was very inappropriate, and notwithstanding her feelings of mounting dissatisfaction and anger, she felt powerless for a long time to influence or end the relationship:

> This is when I learned that you can be in a very powerless position as a client and she was really abusing that power. I couldn't win in this relationship. I absolutely could not win. On the one hand this Nun was telling me off for not following the rules, and yet on the other hand she was the one that was breaking them. Although I knew I shouldn't be socializing with this woman – she was specifically seeking me out to invite me to do things, to take part in things. It's just a nightmare – you are aware that the power relationship is wrong again. You know that things are wrong but you don't have it either within yourself or within the circumstances to do anything about it.
>
> I remember one session we actually talked about this. She said: 'You do realize that I'm not treating you in the way that a therapist would normally treat a client – well this is because I've decided that I realize what you need isn't to talk about this (the abuse) – I think this is all something that happened a long time ago and you've already dealt with it anyway. You are just lonely – and you wanted somebody who would just take time and spend time with you on a one to one.'
>
> And, I mean, I just sat and listened to this and thought: 'She really believes this!' And the response in me was to think: 'Is she right? Is this all I'm doing? Do I have a crush on this woman? Is it just an ego trip for me?' And I really thought that it was! She really had me like a puppet on a string, bouncing everywhere. (Beth – 16)

Eventually, Beth realized that she had to extricate herself:

> It wasn't a particularly easy decision to make because I wasn't sure whether I was acting out what she said I was acting out – whether it was just that I needed this kind of special relationship. So I wasn't sure about it. But once I'd made the decision: 'I don't have to carry on seeing this woman' – once I'd made that decision it was incredibly liberating. And I went to see her. And I got this very offhand reaction: 'Why are you here today?' And I said: 'Well hang on a minute, haven't we got something rather unresolved here? Aren't you supposed to be acting as my counsellor?' And she said: 'Well I think I've made it quite clear to you that you don't need counselling.' And I said: 'Well, as it happens, I've come here today to tell you that I'm not going to come again, that I don't think that this is being very helpful.' (Beth –16)

Beth reflected on the significance of this experience:

> *Beth*: I needed to have it clearly defined for me that this relationship had ended. But she, I think, was just hoping it would just fizzle out and go away. I think she got herself into something which was much more than she could deal with. And having got herself in so deep and made such a bloody mess of it, she didn't know what on earth to do. And she was just hoping that I would quietly go away.
>
> *PD*: That's quite a story isn't it?
>
> *Beth*: Yes, it's a real horror story. And again, if that had been my first experience of counselling I really do not know where I would be today. (Beth – 16)

Although it did not prevent her from getting ensnared for quite some time, Beth's previous experiences of positive therapy gave her some baseline against which to measure the unpredictable behaviour of her second therapist. At the time of the research interview she was seeing a third therapist and deriving great benefit from this. She is one of several clients in the study who pursued further therapy largely to ameliorate the effects of previous damaging therapy.

Grace (who had experienced five unsatisfactory and ineffective therapies before turning her back on therapy for good) remembered an encounter with her last therapist – a hypnotherapist. She illustrated a common misconception about the ability of hypnosis to ascertain the truth about childhood memories:

> I was so fed up with the dreams that I decided I would have some hypnotherapy and be properly regressed and see if we could just absolutely one way or the other decide whether I had been abused or whether it was all in my imagination.
>
> She put me very deeply under and took me back to the age of about four or five and established that, yes, I certainly did have grounds for believing that my father had sexually abused me. But her method of dealing with that was to put me under and reprogramme me. She created this tape which went along the lines of: 'This is how I've been in the past' – and gave some of my negative ways of being and my fears – and then it went onto something like: 'And I look around me and I see other people who are successful at this and successful at that, and that's how I want to be – and so that's how I'm going to be from now on.'
>
> And I said: 'No – that's not how it is – that's your stuff, that's not mine. I've never said to you that I envy anybody else or that I see other people being in ways that I want to be and can't.' I said: 'All the time I am looking for ways of changing my way of being where I see that it doesn't serve me. But that must come from me. I can't lay here and let you pump this into me.'
>
> What she said to me in defence of her methods was: 'Well, I'm not used to dealing with people like you. I am used to dealing with people who want to give up smoking or lose weight – and this is the method I use.' (Grace – 63)

Clients' concerns about therapists' vulnerabilities

A number of clients felt adversely affected by the psychological and emotional states of their therapists. It seems quite common for clients to sense and respond adaptively to perceptions of vulnerability in their therapists:

> *Mary*: I went to the first one, and it was this young woman, and as I was talking I could see her eyes were filling up, and I just thought 'No'! So I stopped and thought: 'I can't see her.'
> *PD*: What went on inside at that moment when you were talking and her eyes filled up?

Mary: I felt awful. I couldn't really do anything to help her except stop talking. And just say 'Oh, it's OK – I'll give you a ring in a week's time.' And I didn't phone her back. And I thought: 'Well, if she can't take what I'm saying now . . .' And I felt I shouldn't have said anything. (Mary – 53)

Georgia had felt for some time that her therapy was not progressing beyond the sorts of conversations she could have free of charge with her friends. However, she had been anxious about raising this with her therapist through fear of upsetting her:

I find it very difficult to actually state my needs. And this was – not only was I sort of stating a need, I was actually, maybe, threatening somebody's self-esteem. And actually I was potentially saying: 'You're no good at your job.' And I didn't want to do any of that. I did spend time being distracted within sessions with these sorts of things going round in my mind. And I remember coming to think: 'Right, this is what I'm going to say' – planning it out in my head and then getting to a session and not saying it. And coming away again still not having said it. (Georgia – 51)

Emily was aware that her therapist was feeling pressured by other responsibilities and felt frustrated by not being given regular appointments. She was silently irritated that she was preoccupied with other matters and did not remember her issues from previous sessions. She too was unable to express her dissatisfaction and found herself resentfully being concerned about her therapist:

The first few times I think I did walk away thinking 'Am I at the right place?' But, I don't know, I guess I didn't have the guts to sort of say like: 'I'm not coming again' or whatever. Because I didn't know where the next therapist might be. In some ways maybe I excused it because I knew that she had a lot of work on – fund raising and things. At the same time you are meant to be the focus. It's sort of like, 'Well yes, that's all very well, but you know – excuse me – huh – you're meant to be focusing on me for the next hour.' (Emily – 15)

Emily also felt that her difficulty in expressing her annoyance stemmed from her childhood experiences:

It's tied up with the problem. In that the fact of being abused made me very secretive – not secretive in a wicked kind of way – but secretive of my own feelings. (Emily – 15)

Other important concerns about the vulnerability of therapists included situations when they knew, or suspected, that they were still struggling to deal with the consequences of their own abuse:

I said to my husband: 'You know, she's an unhealed one – she's one that's working at it before she's healed herself.' That was what I felt. I can remember going home and saying: 'I think (name deleted) is trying to dump a lot on me – she's trying to get me to do the work for her.' (Alice – 04)

Therapists with their own 'unresolved' abuse issues were perceived as exhibiting combinations of the following features: being emotionally fragile; over-confident; somewhat zealous; seeing abuse as the explanation for every problem; using clients to satisfy their own needs and dominating clients with stereotypical 'recovery' programmes:

> I felt she wanted to control me – that was it. She wanted to be able to set a plan for me with what I should be doing with her and where she wanted me to go. It felt as though she was using me as a guinea pig . Oh, I carried on, yes. I was back in the victim role. (Alice – 04)

While these are important observations about the negative impact on clients of therapists' vulnerabilities, the conclusion should not be drawn that therapists who were themselves abused as children are at an inherent disadvantage. This is clearly not the case and accounts of very positive outcomes pay tribute to the special skills and sensitivity of many such therapists. Further discussion regarding factors which influence whether a therapist's own history of abuse impacts in an helpful or unhelpful way on clients is presented in Chapter 7.

Many clients who were abused as children have histories of behaving in adaptive or caretaking ways with abusers and other family members. Retrospectively, they often note the irony of this dynamic becoming replicated in their relationships with therapists – sometimes while they are paying for the privilege. A good deal of clients' attention may become devoted to behaving adaptively in ways which respond to the perceived needs of their therapists. In attending to their therapists' vulnerabilities, clients inhibit recognition and expression of their own needs and do not communicate disappointment, frustration and dissatisfaction, so as not to upset the therapist.

Another notable area in which clients feel dissatisfied is when the therapeutic relationship begins to mirror and replay the dynamics of other problematic relations, without the therapist appearing to recognize or respond to this. Therapeutic relationships, like other intimate relationships, often involve the generation of close bonds and significant emotional investment by both parties. This can be a powerful mix with the potential to be of great benefit, yet also to go seriously wrong.

One of Grace's several unhelpful therapies had begun in an unusual way when she was approached at a meeting by a therapist who suggested that Grace should become her client. She had initially been flattered by this expression of interest, but came to experience familiar disappointment:

> Somebody else said to me, you know, this is something you need to talk to her about. But again it was like I *should* go back when the feeling was that I really didn't want to go back. It's something to do with my way of being in that if you don't give me what I want, I'll look for it somewhere else – I won't try and get it – 'It's too hard to try and get it from you.' And that's the link with my

mother. There were other areas where I felt she wasn't going where I wanted to go, and so I kind of allowed all that to accumulate. And I really recognize this now because she's not the only person that it happened with. Obviously it happens in my relationships – I let things accumulate and then I can use them as a reason for moving on. So I mean, I can't say that the fault was hers. (Grace – 63)

By this stage in her client 'career' Grace was therapeutically sophisticated and quickly became suspicious about her therapist's personal motives. She was also assertive enough to be able to extricate herself, despite considerable emotional pressure:

And it all came to a head one day when I was late. And I said to her: 'Look, I'm not even sure I want to come any more.' And she said to me: 'If you don't come, I'll have this empty space in the middle of my day.' So I said: 'Well, sorry, but I think that's your problem and not mine.' (Grace – 63)

Grace's description highlights her awareness of her tendency to re-enact with therapists the dynamics of earlier and concurrent significant relationships. She believed that none of her several therapists had been aware that she was repeating significant patterns of behaviour with them and that this had been the key issue which she needed to address. Many theoretical perspectives on psychotherapy expect repetitive, transferential processes to occur in some form in the therapeutic relationship. Therapists' lack of understanding and response to this significantly impairs the effectiveness of therapy.

Dependence in therapy

Experiences of emotional intensity, attachment and dependency on therapists are described by clients in many different ways. For some this is very helpful, indeed essential, for effective therapy, while for others it reflects an unexpected and disturbing phenomenon. Emotional dependency (with positive or negative impact) may develop in response to therapeutic styles which are either distant, withholding and abstinent, or those which convey warmth, personal involvement and physical nurturing. Dependence on a controlling or emotionally abstinent therapist can be excruciating in its own right, and even more so if this replicates childhood experiences with emotionally cold and unpredictably punitive parents:

I was in Jungian analysis – a very good Jungian analyst. But the process of analysis seemed so cold in retrospect. That's a very lonely way to experience recovery, really, to be separated from the therapist by the transference. (Abida – 09)

Emotional dependence on a nurturing therapist can be a mixed blessing, combining a tantalizing taste of what it must feel like to be unconditionally loved which may, however, trigger painful, sometimes unbearable, feelings of yearning and frustration. The need for dependence and nurturing in a therapeutic relationship (an experience which can be profoundly beneficial) may however become dangerously distorted. Fears of abandonment or smothering may emerge, as may compelling fantasies and preoccupations that the therapist is willing to evolve into the role of parent or partner. The dangers of this are most acute when the therapist fails to keep this aspect of therapy as a focus for regular discussion and review.

These sorts of experiences may be particularly intense for some adults who were abused as children, especially those who have histories of significant emotional deprivation and who did not experience secure attachments with consistent nurturing figures during critical stages of childhood. Anxious attachment patterns of abused children can be replicated as a dynamic in therapy, contributing towards clients remaining in relationships with therapists against their instincts and better judgement.

Dependency in therapy is not always uni-directional. Relationships do develop in which therapists become very attached to and sometimes highly emotionally committed to their clients. This can result in therapists becoming emotionally dependent on their clients. While this is not necessarily harmful (so long as the focus is consistently held on the needs of the client rather than the therapist), such high levels of emotional involvement produce significant risks. The therapist's conscious or unconscious needs may begin to predominate, manifested in a range of ways including domineering and prescriptive attitudes which were characteristic of many of the negative experiences of clients in this study.

Like many other powerful factors in psychotherapy (such as touch and therapist self-disclosure), high levels of commitment and involvement have the potential to be either enormously helpful or ultimately very damaging. Esme felt that a significant part of the many problems which arose in one of her therapies stemmed from the intense interplay between her own needs for – (and fears of) dependence – and her therapist's dependence on her for professional status:

> *Esme*: I was frightened because she was quite punitive. She'd say things like: 'If you do that again – like if you hurt yourself – you're out of here.' It used to scare me because there is a sort of dependency on these people. When you're in that, you don't think: 'Well, this is it – I've got nowhere else to go.' But what you don't realize is that there is somewhere to go. She was more dependent on me in a sense. I didn't really ever feel that close to her. The other clients used to say that I was the 'star client' – because, I don't know – whether my history was more interesting, or whatever. But they were all quite envious of how that therapist saw me.

PD: So, you were getting some messages that you were special to her?

Esme: Yes, but the trouble is that that message to me was not a good one to have – because I didn't respect her skills. So I just felt that being special to her was for her gain, not mine.

PD: What was she getting out of it? What was she getting out of being dependent on you? What was in it for her?

Esme: I think she got, like – she was after fame and fortune really. Not that I'm famous or anything – but she worked in a therapeutic organization and she was one of the therapists who specialized in working with survivors of child abuse. And I think in the organization she would say things like: 'Oh, gosh. She's a really difficult client, but I'm getting there.' And they used to really admire her and think she deals with some hard people. What they didn't realize was that she didn't really. (Esme – 42)

Esme's ultimate dramatic escape from this therapy will be described later in this chapter.

The combination of dependence and intense emotional experiencing in therapy can generate a sense of disorientation for clients. An example was provided by Carol who illustrated how this can be the precursor to a transgression of ethical boundaries in therapy, given a therapist with sufficient predisposition.

At the time my relationship with him was extremely powerful – the only person I lived for was him. If he clicked his fingers, I would jump. I was also very sexually attracted to him, there was no doubt about that. So I invited the re-abuse, and there's no doubt about that either. (Carol – 14)

The combination of her need for attachment and dependency, the intensity of her erotic feelings and her susceptibility to the therapist's seductiveness eventually led to sex during a session:

We got into a deep compilation about my sexual habits. He asked me direct questions. He had his hands here and he started to slide down the chair as though he was completely mesmerized by me. And I was mesmerized by him. (Carol – 14)

At the time Carol experienced this as an inevitable and welcome aspect of their contact. Only several years later, in the context of subsequent therapy, did she begin to construe the therapist's behaviour as improper and abusive. This situation mirrors that of a small proportion of adults abused as children who experience some pleasure from erotic responses and physical contact with their abusers, only to realize in adulthood the inappropriateness of this.

It is interesting, notwithstanding the research and clinical opinion in relation to the harm which is usually caused by client–therapist sexual relations, that Carol and another participant who described a similar event were both left with mixed feelings about these experiences and the therapists concerned. They considered that they had had a part to play in what happened and that their role should not be completely ignored. Just as many adults who were abused as children experience ambivalent feelings towards their abusers, clients do not always have straightforwardly negative feelings about abusing or exploiting therapists, particularly when at the time the relationship had been experienced as important and rewarding. To assume that they will do so, or should do so, can misjudge an important aspect of their experience and render it even more incommunicable. On this basis it is important to recognize that there is a difference between disapproving of an activity in principle, while respecting each individual's unique experience and interpretation of that activity.

This is a significant point for therapists to bear in mind when working with clients who were abused as children. It can be counterproductive to oversimplify notions of responsibility and blame. As will be discussed in Chapter 8, repetition of the mantra 'It wasn't your fault' can completely miss the point for some clients who do need to explore and understand the ways in which they perceive that they contributed to the abusive relationship. In these circumstances, 'It wasn't your fault' can be experienced as naive and patronizing and can reinforce beliefs of clients that they should conceal their 'dirty secrets' – even from their therapist.

Hoping that benefit will emerge

The lingering hope that some benefit may eventually accrue is a key factor that keeps many people in therapy which they feel is going nowhere. This is illustrated by the experiences of Alice and Anna.

Alice continued seeing her second therapist for two years despite feeling dominated and never trusting her:

> I thought: 'This is the only person I've got to turn to, so this will work eventually'. She had got me and I hadn't the strength to say: 'No, I'm not having any more of this.' I kept hoping for the miracle, I suppose, that we would get somewhere. We didn't. (Alice – 04)

Throughout these two years, Alice was never able to get to the point where she could assert herself effectively enough to terminate the therapy. The relationship only ended when the therapist changed jobs:

> *PD*: Was there anything within that two years that was helpful?
> *Alice*: Her leaving, I think. That sounds awful, but really – I think that was one of the best sessions I had with her when she was telling me that she was going in a month's time. It was a strange thing because I'd been without periods for six months and like a fortnight after she'd told me she was going, my periods came back! So I don't know whether that was relevant or not – but it was like this relief – this huge relief. (Alice – 04)

Anna was seeing a Jungian psychoanalyst and had many reservations as to whether this orientation was too 'esoteric' for her. She had read a great deal about therapeutic theory and suspected that a feminist or gestalt approach would suit her better. However, she felt inhibited in pursuing this because she did not have confidence in the discretion of therapists of such orientations to guarantee the degree of confidentiality she required. She knew therapists in her social circle and felt they had a tendency to talk too freely about their clients. Feeling aggrieved by the occasions when her psychoanalyst's attention did not appear to be fully present, Anna did eventually manage to communicate, albeit in writing, her feelings about his lethargic behaviour:

> I saw him for six weeks and then I had one session where he sat and yawned all the way through it. And I wrote and told him that I wasn't going anymore. I wrote him quite a long letter and said: 'You sat and yawned all the time – I felt this was really bad.' Anyway, I went back and said to him: 'I can't go and see another therapist until I've sorted this out.' So I started seeing him again. He did apologize and said he was sorry and that he gets very tired.
>
> And so, I've just been seeing him ever since. I mean, most of the time when I've seen him, I just come out thinking: 'This is hopeless, it's absolutely bloody useless.' But I don't know what to do about it. On the other hand, I know when I don't see him I really miss seeing him. He tells me I have a great resistance to therapy which I'm quite prepared to believe. There must be a limit, really, to how much therapy one can have. And if it's not productive, then maybe I should stop. But then I feel if I do stop, I'm just taking a great big leap into nowhere. (Anna – 19)

In this case the therapist was able to acknowledge, by means of honest and helpful self-disclosure, that the reasons for his behaviour were located within himself and were not a reaction to Anna being tiresome. This is important, as many clients are inclined privately to perceive and construe such behaviour as being a reaction to their own negative characteristics. Having the courage to raise her dissatisfaction and to receive the subsequent explanation and apology, was sufficient for Anna to remain in the relationship, which she was still in three years on, at the time of the research interview. Notwithstanding her thoughts that she was an 'unhelpable client', Anna continued for a combination of reasons: her liking for her therapist; feeling that she would miss the sessions; feeling deterred from undergoing a search for an alternative suitable therapist; and out of a hope that some benefit would emerge.

'Getting out' of unsatisfactory therapy

It is of great concern that many clients in this study had similar experiences of being 'stuck' in therapy which they had come to recognize was unhelpful, but were at a loss to know how to 'get out'. A number of examples of this phenomenon follow. Ellen's difficulties in 'getting out' of unsatisfactory therapy were evocative of processes in other intimate relationships:

I sort of think it's like trying to get out of relationships with lovers, you know, not that I've done it that many times. But, I think 'I want to get out of it but what can I say? What can I say? They haven't picked up the hint.' And sort of trying to steel yourself – to build yourself up to start to say. And it's really difficult. (Ellen – 13)

One participant remained puzzled about why she had continued for six dissatisfied months with a therapist who ultimately made a sexual proposition to her. Desperate hope that benefit might somehow occur had also been an important factor:

I know it was a fair length of time and it baffles me when I think about it because I know that I never had any real respect for him. He was the last in a line of people and I was just desperate. And, you know, you really want help and you think: 'Maybe if I stick with this'. And of course, he must have put it across that he was doing me good. (Ragbag – 39)

The sexual approach was the critical incident which led her to leave:

I mean, nobody ever listens to you, especially if you're a girl. And so I said to him: 'I'm not coming back, I just can't see the point.' And he said to me: 'You'll come back.' And I said: 'Why?' And he said: 'You're in love with me. And, in fact, you want to have sex with me, and I think we should do it now.'

And my mother, who took me – I was living with her all this time – she remembers that I went in there in my usual state – sort of, kind of really low, not speaking. And I came storming out with red face and bright eyes and got in the car and said: '*That's* the last time I go.' I mean – I was *furious*. At least he made me angry, I suppose, for the first time – I got angry and I got out. (Ragbag – 39)

This illustrates that some clients retrospectively construe key negative incidents as paradoxically having been helpful in promoting change via an energetic (usually angry) reaction against the therapist. In the study as a whole, there were several instances of incidents experienced as being negative at the time, subsequently being viewed as major positive turning points. I gained no impression that this reflected therapeutic behaviour which was carefully considered to promote such a reaction in the clients' ultimate interests – as would be a conceivable (if dubious) theoretical rationale in forms of paradoxical or provocative therapy. Rather, the positive effects seem to stem from the inherent capacity of some clients to create positive value and meaning from negative situations.

Difficulties in 'getting out' were not restricted to naive clients. Ellen had considerable experience of therapy and still struggled to be allowed to leave:

Ellen: I was verbally more skilled – I knew the language, I had more self-awareness. But it was still tough. It was still tough. And I knew that it would be tough but I just kept supporting myself saying, 'Come on, you've got to do it – you know you hate going there.' I just hated going there – I really hated it. I thought it was another hour of feeling beaten up, you know.

It was a real hassle trying to get permission to end the flaming thing. And again, I think it's about not knowing the rules. Even with the last one, ending it was really difficult. I had to be like a sort of bleeding barrister – putting my case. And it felt like it's a battle, you know, me saying: 'I can't stand it, I've had enough' – and expecting this onslaught from her.

PD: Did you get the onslaught?

Ellen: Yes, yes, yes – I got the onslaught. (Ellen – 13)

Katie's experience was similar:

I felt under pressure to talk about things that I may not have been ready to talk about at that particular time. And when I did decide to stop – she was absolutely furious and gave me a really bad time and said 'We've only just started.' I don't think a professional person would have taken that attitude or that stance. She was just very – just totally angry. I can only call it obsessional. I mean if she had her own unresolved problems and that's why she was getting angry with me – I don't know. I really couldn't care less. At the end of the day the only thing she was to me was totally unprofessional and that was enough, you know, to make me feel I'd made the right decision. (Katie – 32)

The continuing story of Esme most dramatically illustrates this difficulty. Esme's childhood had included significant emotional deprivation in addition to abuse. She had had numerous changes of caretakers and scores of professionals who had fleetingly passed through her life during a long progression through the 'care' system. As an adult she had seen five therapists. The previous extracts in this chapter and the extract which follows relate to the disastrous fourth therapy. Esme was all too aware that her inability to form relationships and her intense need for them heightened her susceptibility to dependency on her therapists. This also rendered her vulnerable to abandonment and exploitation.

With her fourth therapist she initially felt confidence in her charisma and public reputation as an expert with 'Survivors'. However, these factors fuelled the therapist's domineering power to exhort compliance with major boundary violations. Esme remained extremely angry that she had been manipulated by the tantalizing prospect of much desired maternal attention:

Esme: She's quite charismatic and she can be, sometimes, very maternal to the client and she really hooks them. And then sometimes she can be really nasty to them – really, really nasty, and terribly wounding. She knew nothing about boundaries – I never felt she understood Survivors. I knew a lot of times working with her that: 'there's something not right here'.

PD: What do you think was not right as you look back on it now? What was her business? What was her agenda?

Esme: Fame. I hate to say it, but fame and fortune, basically. She wanted to be, kind of, like a leading light in working in child abuse and so on. I just think she's very destructive. It's really sad because I know she gets some quite young clients, you know, terribly vulnerable people – and she's got a really amazing way of hooking people. (Esme – 42)

'Getting out' for Esme was a dramatic and memorable experience which took a great deal of preparation and several false starts:

> *Esme*: I was with her in all about eighteen months, but it took me six months to get out of it. It took a lot of guts actually. I tell you it was one of the hardest things I ever did. For a long time I just used to go and I used to say: 'Right, this week I'm going to say it' – and I'd rehearse it all week. And the amount of time I put into that is unbelievable! And I'd get there and I just couldn't do it. For months I did that.
>
> I knew that she was going to be angry – and I wasn't wrong. She wasn't going to like it one little bit. And what I had to do was to get into a position where I no longer cared enough about her anger, that she really couldn't touch me. So I had to really detach myself completely from her to be able to do it. And when I finally said: 'I really don't want to come any more' – she went *nuts*. She screamed and yelled and yes – she went completely nuts.
>
> *PD*: Was this damaging to you?
>
> *Esme*: It hurt me. Yes, it really hurt. I knew this was going to happen but it really hurt me. But it really just confirmed everything I'd thought of up to that time. And I was prepared to go through that, because I wanted to do it properly. I was ending this and I wanted to do it, like, properly. Because I'd had one (therapist) retire, another just up and leave, and this one – I just wanted to do this. To start doing something properly because I'd felt almost like my whole therapy with her hadn't been proper and I just needed to end it properly – do something proper in this whole relationship. (Esme – 42)

The intensity of this was reinforced by a further recollection:

> What was really bad about the actual time it happened was that I'd gone with this other person whose session was supposed to be before mine and I was prepared to sit and wait. This person wanted me to go as a bit of support for her. So I did that. But when we got there, what happened was the therapist changed us round and said: 'Oh, I'll see her first.' I said: 'But actually, her session was before mine.' But she said: 'No, no. I'll see you first.'
>
> So I had to go in there. But what was the really bad thing is that this poor woman was in the kitchen and she could hear this shouting going on and then had to go in for her session after it. I was quite concerned about that – I thought that wasn't on. Because she was scared – she was really scared. She said: 'My God, I didn't think you were going to come out of there walking!' (Esme – 42)

At the time of the research interview Esme had found a new therapist and was hopeful that this would help her to overcome many of the major problems she continued to experience as a result of her extensive childhood deprivation and abuse, as well as her damaging therapeutic experiences.

As has been emphasized in this chapter, naive clients in particular find it difficult to judge the significance of inappropriate therapeutic behaviour and sometimes assume that this must be a somewhat mysterious but relevant aspect of therapeutic practice. Being stuck in such situations stems from combinations of factors including:

- doubts about the validity of their perceptions;
- ignorance about effective and ethical therapeutic practice;
- deference to the authority of the therapist;
- inhibitions in communicating dissatisfaction;
- repeating helpless patterns of behaviour;
- hopes that benefit might yet emerge;
- emotional dependence;
- fear of the therapist.

A distinction can be drawn between: clients who leave without communicating their dissatisfaction; clients who are able to communicate dissatisfaction and work towards improving the therapeutic relationship or leaving it; and those who are unable either to communicate dissatisfaction or to leave the therapy. For the latter group, the most commonly used exit strategy for 'getting out' was to pretend to be better. Ellen and Sally remembered presenting their cases to their therapists to be given permission to leave:

> A couple of them, I think, I said everything was an awful lot better than it was. Because I thought 'I don't need this every week, everything's fine, just let me go!' (Ellen – 13)

> It was a case of: I felt we were going over and over the same ground. And I was going round in a circle and I wasn't getting out of the circle too. And I'm sure I said that to her – that I'm coping with this very well. I'm always very good at giving out impressions that everything's OK and not really sorting the problem out. (Sally – 65)

It is ironic that 'pretending to be better' gives false positive feedback to therapists, presumably reinforcing confidence in methods which are then applied to subsequent clients.

The experiences of dissatisfaction described in this chapter led some respondents to abandon hope of receiving benefit from any form of therapy. Thankfully, as was also noted by Sanford (1991), many were able to find other routes toward healing and resolution of their childhood experiences. Notably these pathways involved various forms of spiritual development and expression of creative abilities. Others were able to find subsequent appropriate therapy and to gain benefit from this.

Note

1 It became clear from the conversation that this was in fact a hospital-based clinical psychologist.

7

Talking about Abuse

One area which by definition is unique to adults abused as children involves talking about childhood abuse as part of the therapeutic process. In this chapter we will look at this from two perspectives: clients talking (or not talking) to therapists about their abuse and the impact of the converse situation which occurs when therapists who were themselves abused as children self-disclose to their clients.

Clients talking about their abuse

> I couldn't talk about it, I was mute about it really. And it was something that I hadn't talked about to a living soul. And at the time I was seeking help I just couldn't actually bring that into the conversation. I couldn't introduce it on to the agenda at all. (Jamie – 12)

The opportunity for clients to talk about experiences of abuse as part of the therapy process can be problematic for a number of reasons which we will now consider. One important factor is that the context of being abused often involves an absence of authentic communication which continues to have an effect in later life:

> The hard thing about therapy is they want you to talk. And the problem with being an abused child is that you are told not to. (Esme – 42)

Esme associated both her adult difficulties in communication in therapy and her ability to write with her muteness as an abused child:

> I had always written, and I just found it very useful – partly because for a lot of my childhood I had no speech so it was one way of getting stuff out, I suppose. (Esme – 42)

Children retreat into silence and adaptive responses through threats, fear, shame and inhibited hostility. It is important to appreciate that these communication patterns often continue in adult relationships – including relationships with therapists. Establishing a process of and language for communication may therefore become a significant focus, challenge and goal of therapy. Participants felt that many therapists were insufficiently aware of the excruciating difficulty posed by the expectation and act of talking. Not being able to talk was sometimes the major problem. Some clients had initially got round this difficulty by developing non-verbal forms of communication, including writing, painting and sculpture. For many, written and artistic creative expression was a very important and valued feature of 'resolution' of abuse and one which provided great personal satisfaction and sense of achievement.

In contrast to a total inability to talk about abuse, others were able to do this – but only in an emotionally disconnected way:

> I never have, really, talked about it in the way of reliving it and reliving the pain of it, with somebody else. I've never felt sufficiently, whatever it is – trusting or safe or accepted enough to be able to say, 'This is what happened.'; 'on this day this happened and this is how I felt.' I find it easy enough to say in a kind of intellectual way, not an emotional way. It's easy enough to say: 'Look, I was sexually abused by these people.' But to actually relive it and get in touch with the feelings is something that I try to stay away from in all the therapy I've been in. (Ellen – 13)

An important question arises as to what extent it is necessary to talk about the abuse, in what detail and with what level of feeling, for therapy to be beneficial. There is not a consensus view among clients on this matter. Some feel that a specific abuse focus is vital; others are less keen. Also, as will be seen later, some feel that active emotional expression is necessary, while others do not.

Jamie and Mary's comments are illustrative of the views of those who found a specific focus necessary and helpful:

> I've wanted to focus on it a lot – different aspects of it. And between sessions I've gone away and I've thought about it. I needed to talk, first of all, about what had happened. And I needed to talk about why it had happened and I needed to talk about why it was happening now to other people. And I needed to talk about what was going on in my family at that time which allowed it to happen. (Jamie – 12)

> It was helpful. I'm glad I did say what I said, and she didn't put any pressure on me. She just said: 'You say what you want to say about it – but I feel it would help you a lot if you could talk – even if only a little bit – about it.' And once I'd started talking a little bit about it, it just came out. But she never once said: 'What else happened?' or 'Was there anything else? Or, you know, really trying to delve. She just said: 'How do you feel about that?' She just had the right kind of approach. (Mary – 55)

In contrast Myrtle found it much more helpful for the focus to be on her present life:

That's another thing that I've liked, surprisingly enough, is that she concentrates very much on the here and now. And she told me that at the beginning. She said: 'We might consider how what happened in the past has influenced the way you are now, but it's in the past and it's what happens now that's important.' That's another difference between sort of traditional psychoanalytical therapy and this. In psychoanalytical therapy I could go on talking about what happened for ever and nothing would change necessarily. We don't really talk much about what happened at all. We talk about who I am now, and parts of me now that are still acting like that child. But we talk about it now, very little about the past – which I actually prefer. (Myrtle – 22)

Therapists noted that careful consideration of each individual client's needs and wishes was vital:

I think it varies from person to person. I was thinking about myself and my own childhood experiences and the importance of talking about the bits that I've labelled as sexual abuse. It's not *that* important to talk about the mechanics of what actually happened. (Mike – 62)

I think it's a very sensitive subject. I think, usually, a client should be encouraged to talk, in detail, about what actually happened. But not if that's to satisfy the therapist's prurient curiosity – that's no part of it. Although it's very difficult for the therapist *not* to be curious, especially if they've been abused themselves. I think if the encouragement to describe the gory details is, again, gratifying the therapist's voyeurism, it's potentially extremely destructive. But it's equally, I think, destructive for the message to go across: 'Well you don't need to tell me exactly what happened' – because that's just what the other parent usually did. It's a classic triangular arrangement. (Robert – 07)

Inhibitors in talking about abuse

Although clients realize that therapy is likely to involve talking about the abuse in some way, this is often a very difficult step to take. A number of factors inhibit their ability and willingness to talk about abuse. This involves the emotional challenge of speaking the unspeakable; facing embarrassment, guilt and nausea; as well as shameful anticipation of therapists' disgust, disbelief, rejection or excitement.

For Anna, these feelings contributed to prolonged silences in sessions and a strong sense of lack of progress in her therapy. She was frustrated that she could not overcome her aversion to talking about the abuse, and felt that things were unlikely to move on until she was able to do so:

He hasn't told me not to talk about the abuse, or that I can't talk about the abuse. But somehow I feel inhibited. I think that's my problem – talking about it. Because basically I find it so distasteful. (Anna – 19)

Inhibitions also involve challenges in finding adequate language to articulate the experience of abuse. There is sometimes a need to desensitize certain words (for example, for sexual organs or actions) to which strong aversions may have developed. This is encapsulated in a sense of muteness within which some clients are unable to mention abuse at all.

> Well, to talk about something like that when you've never – all you have is the memory – you've never talked about it at all. Well, I'd never talked about it at all. And I didn't have the words. (Mary – 53)

> In fact she never really, really ever got to know what happened. Because I still won't bring that out of myself, my subconscious or whatever. But she would often try to work her way round to talk about what actually happened and then we'd go back the other way – I'd twist it again the other way. (Sally – 65)

Having finally told her first counsellor of the abuse, Mary's immediate reaction had been to flee for three months, driven away by reactive feelings of guilt, shame and aversion. She had never been able to speak about it again:

> I just think, as soon as people know, they must be so – I don't know, disgusted. I still can't believe it now with the counsellor I see. The first time I told her I stopped the counselling for about three months. (Mary – 53)

Another internal inhibitor involves feelings of disgust and shame stemming from a degree of enjoyment of the erotic component of the abuse experience. The inhibiting effect of erotic responses is particularly powerful and is compounded as this is rarely discussed in clinical or popular literature. Clients who have such experiences can be left with feelings of being uniquely bad, responsible, complicit and very alone. This is further enhanced when they encounter therapists who expect stereotypical 'victim' reactions such as rage and disgust and who do not recognize the significance of the erotic and ambivalent feelings:

> It was the combination of having the feelings of disgust, mixed with the feelings of quite high eroticism, that had obviously given me quite a lot of conflict. Because there was disgust at me, disgust at my mother, mixed with the fact that I must have been feeling pretty erotic at the time. And instead of just giving me a cuddle and making me feel happy and close, she did something more than that. It was the real conflict between enjoyment and disgust which I was having a big problem with. It was the admission, not of the disgust, but of the enjoyment that I found very difficult to actually say. (Sue – 54)

> It raises very ambiguous sorts of feelings because part of the guilt of abuse, I've learned, stems from the fact that children can enjoy aspects of the abuse. Because they've derived enjoyment from it, they get the subsequent guilt that, 'Yes, it's partly me.' (Jamie – 12)

These experiences are highlighted here because of their poignant significance for clients so affected. There is no published research which indicates the extent of this reaction within the wider population of adults who were abused as children. When erotic responses to abuse memories are a part of the client's experiencing, this may underlie an otherwise puzzling lack of therapeutic progress or setbacks. In such circumstances, self-defeating (and sometimes self-harming) guilt feelings can be frequently (but secretly) negatively reinforced by clients' self-blaming reactions to continuing erotic responses to memories of the abuse, or to current sexual activity which evokes such memories. Given careful consideration, in the context of an established good therapeutic relationship, tentative enquiries which acknowledge that this is a recognized reaction to abuse can bring relief and understanding, and can constitute a significant step forward in the progress of therapy. Consequently, therapists should be aware of the potential for such experiencing, but should not assume that it is present. To introduce this possibility indelicately, or inappropriately, is likely to cause offence.

Similar inhibitions also occur in relation to the legacy of sexual abuse by mothers. Again, stereotypical assumptions held by some therapists that all sexual abusers are male inhibit clients revealing and discussing their sexual abuse experiences with women. This reinforces beliefs that they are uniquely tainted and incapable of being understood or helped.

Inhibitions related to therapists

> They can't win can they? – the one that was cold, I couldn't stand her. And the one who was nice to me, I couldn't actually tell her. (Ellen – 13)

Difficulties in talking about abuse also stem from the nature of the therapeutic relationship and reactions to specific characteristics of therapists. These factors affect perceptions of the potential levels of acceptance, security and safety which are felt to be necessary for this focus in therapy. Clients are sensitive to their impressions of therapists' attitudes towards abuse. These include feelings that they might not be believed, and that some therapists seem uncomfortable with abuse material:

> Well I think there's a problem with discussing abuse because, even for me now, there's always the fear that you're not going to be believed – and I think that's inhibiting. (Anna – 19)

Clients who have some doubts about the truth of their abuse memories may expect not to be believed by others:

> I certainly went through the very common phase of getting to the point and wondering whether any of it was true. And a bit of me wishing it wasn't and wondering what the hell am I doing? – I wouldn't be in so much pain struggling so much with my life if I wasn't going to therapy and unearthing all of this stuff. So that ambivalence was certainly there. And it was very important for the therapist to continually stand firm and believe and accept everything. (Zoe – 11)

Clients can detect therapists' inhibitions through their avoiding or curtailing a focus on abuse:

> This is something I've come up against – I don't know whether it's just my choice of therapist – but there always seems to be for me areas where the therapist won't go. I think it's because they have unaddressed stuff in their own backgrounds. (Grace – 63)

> My feeling is that even therapists, even experienced therapists, don't want to hear about abuse. That is my feeling – that there can be an initial discussion of it, but I just have the feeling, even now with my current therapy, that this is something, somehow, that isn't very nice and mustn't be talked about. I think there's a massive level of denial about it. (Anna – 19)

> I wanted to carry on with my childhood and she said that, 'Really, we should put the childhood behind us now and get on with the present.' And I still felt there were some problems in my childhood and I felt that she'd kind of shut me off that area. It was like a cop out. (Sarah – 30)

Sometimes, therapists respond emotionally to hearing accounts of abuse. Nobody in this study suggested that an impassive reaction in these circumstances would be appropriate. Indeed, a key feature of establishment and maintenance of rapport is a degree of real human involvement. However, a particularly unhelpful response to hearing details of abuse involved therapists expressing their own anger. In contrast to some models of therapy which suggest that therapists modelling anger may be helpful, it is apparent from experiences in this study that therapists' angry responses regarding the abuser often served to reinhibit clients talking about abuse. Sonya, for example, initially felt scared that the therapist's anger was with her for talking about such things:

> He was very angry and no way could I cope with that – to see him angry. Initially, it was, 'Is he angry with me?' He said he wasn't, that he was angry with the abuser, but I didn't like the anger. I didn't like to see him angry, I felt very responsible for it. I made a conscious decision then never to talk about it. (Sonya – 33)

This angry reaction effectively ended the therapeutic potential of the relationship. Sonya retreated back into the familiar pattern of inhibited communication, adaptation and concealed dissatisfaction:

> My hurt wasn't being acknowledged, I felt – it was only his own anger that was being acknowledged. If I started to talk about it again, would he get angry? Would he be able to listen? And then I thought: perhaps I don't need to talk about it. After that I didn't really get much help. I thought when I went back for any sessions it was seemingly to please him in some way. Very censored and very aware of what I say rather than just talking. Whatever came out – I'd rehearse it in my head first. (Sonya – 33)

Strong emotional reactions of any type could have this effect. Anna suggested what she felt was the most helpful type of response:

> No revulsion should be shown – I think that's very important, no matter what's being described. And I don't even think sympathetic comments are appropriate because I think they could be construed as patronizing. I think it should be, even though it's awful, I think it should be treated quite matter of factly – almost as if you were talking about the weather! I mean, there can be recognition of it, but I don't think expressions of horror or sympathy are appropriate at all. There should be a sense, I think, that one is believed and that, no matter what you've said, you can still actually be construed as being a human being, even though one might feel like an animal. (Anna – 19)

Therapists focusing on abuse

Clients experience a dilemma: recognizing the need to talk about the abuse and fear of adverse emotional reactions from doing so. They want therapists to 'back off' from the abuse and also, conversely, wish to be 'pushed' into this focus. This presents a complex challenge for therapists.

Emily and Veronica found it helpful to be encouraged to talk about the details of the abuse:

> She was helping to get rid of all the guilt I had about myself and to put it in its rightful place. I think by making me really look at what I was saying. By making me talk in as far as possible, as detailed as possible, about what happened to me. And to take an incident and say: 'Well, look – this happened and this happened and you had nothing to do with this and you weren't in a position to say no.' Just to kind of break it all down, and sort of start making me believe that it wasn't my fault. (Emily – 15)

> I've never spoken to anybody about it previously – I've always kept things to myself all my life. And when I spoke to the therapist about it, it was like somebody here is actually listening to me and believing what I'm saying and taking it seriously and taking me seriously and wants to help me as well. To be honest, I think I wanted to talk about it, but I think the therapist drew me on it mostly. Because I would sort of skate over things and she would sort of make me stop and – as I say, I would avert my eyes when something came into my mind. And she'd say: 'Just let's stay with that' – and then explore that more. That was the painful stuff which she managed to draw from me. (Veronica – 23)

Ellen felt her therapist pushed too much:

> I got away with that a lot, in a sense, in therapy. It wasn't until the last therapist I saw said: 'I'm going to challenge you there' – which was very threatening. She said, 'You know, you're telling me things but it's like you're telling a story.' And she said: 'Well, you need to relive the emotion in order to

sort of dispel it' – words to that effect. And I thought: 'Oh shit! Have I? – Ohh NO!' And I just felt I can't imagine doing that. I can't imagine doing that with that particular woman. (Ellen – 13)

In contrast, Eva and Mary felt frustrated that their therapists did not focus and encourage enough:

I would give a response which was usually, 'No, I don't want to talk about it now.' And my feeling is, had she had followed up with a kind of: 'Well, what is it? – what's happening in the moment when you are saying no?' – then that would have been going into something even though it wasn't actually going into what her question was about. But she didn't. She took the 'no' – which I think was a mistake. And that's why I say she was a bit cautious. Because she didn't want to push me and yet the opportunity was missed. (Eva – 57)

The first counsellor – I felt that she wasn't really drawing it out of me. I felt it was really hard work. I felt that I wanted her to help me more and she wasn't really giving me that help. I felt it was always all coming from me – but she wasn't kind of drawing out the things that needed to come out. I knew she was listening but I felt she wasn't really understanding what I was saying. She wasn't giving me much feedback. She didn't really say very much at all and I don't think that helped very much. (Mary – 55)

The challenge for therapists is to establish an optimum position of encouraging and focusing. When this balance is right, the benefits can be great:

I didn't particularly want to go through what happened between us and how it happened, but she got that out of me as well. And when I was talking about it, I was so embarrassed that I could hardly look at her. But I knew that she wasn't going to be embarrassed. I mean, at one point she just said: 'Right, we'll swap seats now – and you're the counsellor and I'm the person who is going to tell you what you want to say about what happened. What do you think I would say back to you?' And I just said: 'I've heard it all before and it doesn't embarrass me.' And there we are – I just swapped places and I just kind of reeled it all off. (Mary – 55)

She was very patient with me which was very important as far as I was concerned. She didn't chivvy me or hassle me or demand to know what had gone on. So I set the pace which was important. And neither at any time did it feel like she was being voyeuristic – and I think if I'd had any sense of that I'd have been out the door. (Beth – 16)

I think that it's like something that's buried inside you and until you dig it out and look at it, you know, put it there and look at it, it's like it's doing you harm inside. And as soon as I'd brought it out, I felt better. And because I'd got recognition from another adult that I respected that this was wrong and it shouldn't have happened and it wasn't my fault, and so on. (Jamie – 12)

It just suddenly happened one day. I said to myself: 'Right, I'm going to talk about it today.' And I did. It was very important that I talked about it – to prove that I was still alright having talked about it. I mean I knew intellectually, 'Gosh, it wasn't my fault' and I'd read enough books and I knew enough about it in *theory*. But the emotional – the inner child part of me didn't know that. So the inner child part of me had to actually be able to say that to someone and that person still to actually like me – still feel respect for me. I had a great – huge – feeling of relief. Not immediately, because I had to test his reaction. But it was a relief once I left and went home. Gradually the weight came off – you know, like a big weight. (Mary – 43)

The question arises as to how therapists should respond when they intuitively suspect a client has been abused, but the client does not raise this. There is a dilemma involved in enquiring directly about abuse:

I think you have to be careful when it comes to asking directly. I think if people are ready to talk about it, if they feel they can talk about it, then they will. It's a difficult one because if you feel that somebody has been abused and they would talk about it if you asked them, it may be that some people won't ever be able to talk about it unless they're asked – it's difficult. (Anna – 19)

Esme appreciated the caution a valued social worker had shown about this:

She said she knew for five years before I ever said anything about it. She kind of sat on the itch basically. (Esme – 42)

She felt that this stance, whatever its motivations, had been the right one:

Yes, yes, I really do. Because I did have a therapist who believed in doing that – if she thinks someone has been abused, she'd just tell them. I really don't think that's very helpful because I do think from what little bit I do know about psychology, that the mind is a pretty clever thing and it will let you know something when you are able to deal with it.
What that therapist could have done is just very gently help the person to perhaps focus on a certain area of their life, rather than just say, 'I think you've been abused.' Particularly if they're the sort of person who hasn't got memory of an incident, but only has a lot of feelings about something. I mean, I do think it can add to the fear and confusion that's around at the time. Also, it's like the therapist then is doing it for you and I don't know how helpful that is. (Esme – 42)

Others stressed the potential disadvantages of therapists using their intuitions about abuse before a client is aware of this, or shares it themselves:

I think asking someone head on: 'Were you abused as a child?' is probably going to be a hell of a shock. Because people may not realise it – it may be so buried it may never come up. (Sue – 27)

Well, it could be catastrophic. The client could cut off. I mean, the mind isn't ready until it remembers itself – it is not to be forced – it is not. It will have to be recovered layer by layer. Not to remember is a protection and I don't want anyone to break down that protection – that's a disrespect to a high degree. (Bea – 18)

Well, for instance, there's a man I am working with at the moment and I am absolutely sure that his mother sexually abused him. And, there's no way I would give him that piece of information. I feel that I might be ready for him to hear that he was sexually abused but if he's blocking, he sure needs to block. And it would be very bad practice for me to give him information that he himself wasn't psychologically ready to hear. I don't need to be the smart cookie that gives the information. (Inga – 03)

In contrast, Soraya regretted that her father had not been more alert about the abuse and its effects to which she was subjected by a babysitter as a child. Aware of the transference connection, she also felt that it would have been helpful had her therapist been more inquisitive about the background to her problems:

I think it would have been, Yes. But probably a lot of transference with my own father. I think probably I wished my father would have asked me if it had happened. Because it was a childminder who did it and he was trusted by the family. And maybe I was transferring that onto my Dad – this counsellor – and wished that somehow he should know and that he should ask me if I was alright. (Soraya – 52)

Many publications from a 'survivor' perspective have encouraged therapists to share their hunches about abuse with clients. As Soraya illustrated, some clients wish that therapists had been a little more proactive in enquiring about non-disclosed abuse histories. Tentative enquiries of this nature by therapists are unlikely to do harm, and may be the trigger which facilitates clients becoming able to talk about abuse:

There's nothing wrong in mentioning it as maybe a thought, 'Do you think you have been sexually abused or anything like that?' . . . I mean, that's just to feel whether there are any memories or not and whether the person is ready to look at whatever – that's OK. (Bea – 18)

However, a clear distinction needs to be drawn between tentative open-minded enquiries and therapists repeatedly suggesting and inculcating beliefs that abuse must underlie a client's particular constellation of problems. Great caution in this area is indicated to avoid the possibility that a suggestive single-minded therapist could inappropriately lead a client to believe that he/she was abused as a child, when in fact this was not the case. This issue will be discussed further in Part Three of this book.

Therapists underlined the importance of providing the opportunity for clients to talk about abuse, while being very careful to avoid being over-inquisitive or invasive:

I think it can vary from person to person. I believe that people do – it is a very important part of the process to disclose the intimate details of what has happened. And, as a therapist, I would endeavour to make the environment safe enough for the client to disclose at whatever level they wish to. Some clients find it easier to do this and this becomes part of the healing process. Some people find that they are unable to do so or can only do so in a very limited way. I don't take the stance that a client has to talk about every intimate detail – every intimate part of every intimate detail – unless they feel the need to do so. (Cliff – 05)

We have to be very attentive to what people can cope with at any particular time and monitor that all the time – rather than going fishing for material. My sense is that people who do that anyway are almost kind of voyeurs and just into the story or the account of how awful or how dramatic it is, without having a strong sense of what that means for the particular individual and how helpful that is for them. (Nor – 35)

To achieve an effective balance includes paying attention to safety – monitoring what each client can cope with at any given time:

It's when they are getting material which emotionally is too much for them to cope with and they go into emotional overwhelm. I have a technique which I call 'permission to suppress' – because opening the unconscious sometimes is like opening Pandora's Box. So that's one of the things I offer them – that they can actually say to themselves: 'Look, right now I'm not able to deal with this feeling or this memory.' (Sarah – 10)

Virtually all of the clinical literature on therapy with adults who were abused as children notes that a necessary part of the process includes talking about the abuse in some form or other. Therapists shared this view but, with one exception, were remarkably consistent in saying that this should be at the clients' pace, to the extent that the client wishes, and not be forced in any way.[1] While clients focused predominantly on inhibiting factors, therapists may occasionally experience some clients inappropriately talking about the details of abuse:

If somebody starts to tell me a great deal of detail in the first session, I shall close them down quite explicitly. It's quite a complex communication because it has to be phrased carefully to indicate that I am, in principle, willing to hear it – but my judgement is that it's not the right moment to do it. (Robert – 07)

An important practice principle is that work on establishing the therapeutic relationship should normally precede detailed discussion of abuse. Without the relationship being established, particularly in respect of open and clear communication, motivations behind presentation of explicit abuse details can be difficult to discern and the outcome unpredictable:

I think there are two groups. One is the kind of exhibitionist bit where the person will come along and tell you lots of very lurid stuff and there is a kind of sexual transaction going on. They are actually sexually abusing the therapist in telling them that. And it leaves the therapist feeling dirty and contaminated just like abuse does. And the other one, I think, is when somebody comes along and blurts it all out, having never told anyone before. And goes away feeling that they have completely undressed themselves – they have raped themselves. I think in both situations the therapists is well advised to contain that. (Robert – 07)

Perhaps the most important conclusion from participants' experiences in talking about abuse in therapy, is the variation in types and intensity of experiences. Talking about abuse is a delicate and sensitive part of the therapeutic process. Great positive gains were described when this was successfully achieved, although at times this could feel overwhelmingly painful. When therapists make assumptions about clients' needs in this area, dissatisfaction can arise. Clients may feel coerced into talking or frustrated that therapists are over-cautious and avoiding with the result that important opportunities to do the real work are being missed.

On this basis therapists should not make advance assumptions about what they think will be helpful. Instead, consistent efforts are indicated to explore each client's unique hopes, expectations and fears about this aspect of therapy. Discussing the pros and cons of talking about abuse before the client makes an informed choice whether or not to proceed in this direction is an important preliminary process. Failing to explore and identify each client's idiosyncratic needs in this way can lead therapists to miss the optimum mark by either being under-focused on abuse or over-intrusive.

Therapists' self-disclosures

I think if people set themselves up in a more open way it is easier to ask them questions and I think that would be helpful. Because when you are in therapy with somebody, you are revealing massive amounts about yourself. And in some sense I feel it's the least you can do to ask them to reveal something about their selves. (Anna – 19)

It's helpful that I don't know much about her. (Esme – 42)

It is a fundamental expectation in therapy that clients disclose personal information about themselves, yet the question arises as to how far this also applies to therapists. Theoretically, different stances are taken on this question. Analytic and behavioural forms of psychotherapy discourage therapist self-disclosure. In contrast, most humanistic and 'conversational' psychodynamic therapies include degrees of self-disclosure as an important part of the therapeutic relationship. Little is known overall about how clients react to receiving personal details (sometimes intimate ones) about therapists. In this section the mixed experiences of clients and the views of several therapists will be described.

Before doing so, it is relevant to note that clients are also affected in positive and negative ways by the non-self-disclosure of therapists. The most unhelpful scenario of therapist non-self-disclosure reported in this study involved relatively naive clients seeing analytically orientated therapists. These clients found the perceived absence of warmth and rapport to be particularly uncomfortable. In contrast, those who preferred therapist non-self-disclosure tended to have some knowledge of the process and culture of analytically orientated therapy. Consequently, they were more critical of therapists who self-disclose, seeing this as diminishing the potential for valuable transference experiences:

> Well I was more curious about (name deleted) because I had really fallen for her, you know, in the transference – and I wanted to know everything about her of course. But luckily she didn't go into a lot of detail – or any detail – because it would have had a stifling effect on a therapeutic relationship. (Mary – 31)

A second reason for preferring non-self-disclosing therapists stemmed from previous therapy in which this had been unhelpful. For example, after a disastrous experience with an intrusive therapist, Liz felt clear about the value of a non-self-disclosing stance:

> The sessions are about me. I've been visiting (name deleted) weekly in her own house for the past $2\frac{1}{2}$ years, but I don't know her – her likes, dislikes, her family. I find it very helpful to have such a one-sided relationship. It relieves me of any burden of worrying about my therapist. Her needs and concerns are not expressed. (Liz – 16)

For Mary, it was the exception to her therapist's general stance of not self-disclosing that was important. This, and Carol's experience, indicate the potential significance of minimal, well-timed self-disclosures:

> She very rarely spoke about herself – a couple of things she did tell me and she said, 'Keep that to yourself.' So there was an element of the fact that she was trusting me with some things as well. I felt very close to her, like she was a confidante and that I could tell her a lot of things because she trusted me with some things – I felt that I could trust her with anything. (Mary – 55)

> The Gestalt one, I sensed that he's been abused, but he never talked about it and I don't want to know. But what I did find useful was that he did say in one session, 'I know it's difficult, I've been there.' And I thought, 'He knows how I'm feeling.' And that was very, very useful. But (not) if I'd had details. (Carol – 14)

Therapists self-disclose in three main areas:

- sharing thoughts and feelings openly in sessions about a client;
- sharing aspects of their personal life and experiences;
- sharing their own experiences of childhood abuse.

When this is experienced as being helpful, the beneficial effects for clients include:

- learning from feedback about how they are perceived and the effect they have on others;
- development of rapport, trust and confidence in the therapeutic relationship;
- helps promote a sense of understanding and being understood;
- experience of role model of someone who is coping;
- aids reality testing re perceptions of others and validity of intuitions;
- experience of authentic contact with a 'real' person;
- experience of a sense of equality.

Therapists' willingness to self-disclose and give feedback about the effect a client has upon them can help clients learn how to distinguish between fantasy and reality in relationships and to develop confidence in the accuracy of their inter-personal perceptions. To come to know a therapist as a person, as well as a professional, invariably diminishes the extent and impact of transference fantasies and misperceptions. To be able to discuss these fantasies and to receive honest feedback regarding their accuracy assists clients in understanding their tendencies to mis-perceive significant others. The benefit of this is particularly important for those who had been troubled by mistrust and the intrusion of repetitive fantasies in their relationships:

> It's important for me because of this need to reality test – that's what I call it. I need to know what's my fantasy and what's real. And if she's having an off day – I need to know she's having an off day – that it's not me having paranoid fantasies. (Myrtle – 22)

A therapist's self-disclosure can influence client feelings as to whether the therapist will be able to understand:

> She said she'd had a difficult life and I'm sure she had. She understood because she'd felt it. And can you understand things if you haven't felt them? – I don't think so, I don't know. I think you can imagine, you can empathize with somebody else's pain – but whether you can actually understand? (Sarah – 30)

> As a therapist she's very open about her own – well she's a Survivor herself. And so right from the beginning I felt that, here, finally, was somebody who understood. And she also quite early on talked about me not being the only one. And hoping that one day I might be able to meet other Survivors because there's a sort of sisterhood or something like that you know. We are special, we are different. (Zoe – 11)

> Intuitively I said to him one week: 'You've suffered haven't you?' And he had. There's the difference. That's why I don't particularly recommend psychiatry –

because that's all textbook stuff. It's excellent. It's factual – but when one human being has suffered and they are helping others – that's a big difference. (Rose – 20)

Sarah found it surprising, yet hope inspiring, to learn that her counsellor had had similar experiences which she appeared to have overcome:

> *Sarah*: Toward the end of my counselling I became aware of the impact that my mother had had on my life. Whereas in my first counselling session I was saying that my mother was wonderful and I didn't want to discuss her and I didn't want to hurt her and all this. And then I became increasingly more aware of the impact that she had had on my life. And the counsellor said that she had had a very poor relationship with her mother and had always been frightened of her mother too.
>
> *PD*: What effect did that have on you – to have that sort of disclosure from the counsellor?
>
> *Sarah*: It made me feel better – yes. Because having negative feelings about my mother still, I think, made me socially unacceptable – or that's how it seems to me. I mean – it is a taboo really. (Sarah – 30)

The encouragement gained from a therapist as role model in being able to 'deal with' events was also illustrated by Georgia:

> And he shared with me the fact that he's got a very eccentric mother and now she's elderly a lot of people are putting her down as a very eccentric old lady. But to him she's always been exactly the same. And that sort of felt: 'Gosh – he can deal with that now – so it's possible to deal with that.' (Georgia – 51)

Self-disclosures can help clients to recognize that therapists are often people with vulnerabilities – who nevertheless cope well with life:

> I think I benefited from being sort of pulled up short – being made known that I had another human being in the room with me who had also suffered pain and anguish – It humanized him. It made me realise that I was dealing with a person. There can be a tendency to sort of put a halo around a counsellor's head. This tendency to forget that they are also human. (Georgia – 51)

> I get snippets about him which I found helpful. I'd know what was going on a bit in his life. He wasn't one of those remote figures who sat over there and I didn't know the first thing about them. I knew if one of his children had been ill. The equality was very important to me. Very important that he was vulnerable too – I wouldn't be able to relate to somebody who wasn't. He never went very far into what was going on in his life – obviously not. He was very professional in that way. But it was nice getting a straight answer about things. (Mary – 43)

> We're not robots are we? We've got feelings. And if the therapist has feelings that he can offer back to you, then that's OK. I did go through a phase of saying: 'Are you alright?' Because he had admitted his vulnerability. And I don't know why I became so concerned about this, but I did. But he said: 'You

can rest assured, I'm OK. While I'm here, I'm OK.' And I respected that. And it is – it's OK. (Rose – 20)

However, other people felt confused and silently irritated by receiving unwanted personal information from therapists. When therapist self-disclosure is experienced as unhelpful, the negative effects involve:

- feeling of intrusion across personal boundaries – simply not wanting to know;
- feeling inhibited, distracted, confused and angry re the unwanted information;
- inhibition of the development of transference phenomenon;
- becoming overwhelmed when vulnerable or regressed;
- creates feelings of comparison and rivalry;
- promotes role reversal: client caring for therapist;
- feeling frightened by therapists' vulnerability;
- takes attention away from client's needs;
- reinforces clients' tendencies to be compliant and adaptive;
- disturbing intuitive feelings that the therapist is not psychologically healthy;
- lack of trust in authenticity of therapist's self-disclosures – sense of manipulation.

A number of people commented on disconcerting reactions to blurring of boundaries which therapist self-disclosures can provoke:

I knew a lot about the other one – that was the trouble. I felt it wasn't real because there was no boundary there – nothing was real – it didn't help me. (Esme – 42)

I find that I like boundaries and I am not particularly happy with fuzzy boundaries. I think that perhaps the odd bit of self-disclosure like 'Gosh – I've got a cold' is OK. I think there's a tremendous *danger* in the therapist bringing too much of themselves into a session that is for the *client* not for the therapist. I do find self-disclosure intrusive. (Jean – 36)

I think it could be morally wrong – I think it is almost like incest. It could be damaging because it could stop people recalling and facing up to the hurt, deprivation and helplessness – all the things that are at the root of the problem. Because somebody is stopping you doing that – somebody is papering it over a bit. A therapist's got to show a sort of altruistic love – I think there is such a thing. I have certainly experienced it – where they do love the person they are dealing with but it's in a way that is totally detached from any expression of it. (Mary – 31)

Therapists' self-disclosures of their own abuse:

Does it hurt for them as much as it does for me? (Esme – 42)

I think it's usually people who go in for therapy because they have had some sort of problem themselves – but the nature of it should be private to them. I wouldn't want to know. (Mary – 31)

I'm quite sure I'm working through my own abuse in my work and I needn't pretend otherwise. I don't think I'm that altruistic. (Inga – 03)

One area of particular significance concerns therapists' self-disclosures of their own histories of abuse. Many clients had experienced this and strong feelings were expressed both in favour and against the practice. One view was, as with the sharing of other forms of personal information, that this could be helpful and reassuring, especially in contributing to a feeling that the relationship was with a 'real human being'. Beth, for example, found her therapist's matter-of-fact disclosure about her own abuse very helpful in developing trust and hope during a first session:

She said, 'Well, I'll say to you that I have quite a lot of experience dealing with people who have been sexually abused. At this point I will also say to you that I was also sexually abused as a child and I have been through counselling myself for it.' It was very refreshing – here was a promise of an end to all this mess. I found it helpful to know. I felt able to go back to (therapist) and ask her about it. We didn't dwell on it – it was just: 'Can you tell me the circumstances' – and she did. I mean, as much as anything else, you spend a lot of time (thinking) that you're the only one it's ever happened to, and you don't get opportunities to meet people who have shared that experience and who've worked through it. (Beth – 16)

These combinations of understanding, human contact, positive role models for having successfully 'dealt with' their own abuse and effectively managing vulnerability were especially valued. Anna and Katie acknowledged the potential helpfulness of therapist self-disclosure of abuse – so long as the therapist's own issues are resolved:

Yes, I think that would be helpful knowledge. Yes, as long as it wasn't something that was currently going on and was upsetting. If it was something that could be seen to have been worked through, I think, yes – that would be helpful. (Anna – 19)

I think the most important thing for therapists is to come to terms with their abuse. If they've been abused I think they must have come to terms with it. When you can hear somebody say how it might have had beneficial effects in some ways, then maybe they are starting to accept. But all the time they're trying to find out why did it happen I would be a bit worried about whether they were the right people. (Katie – 32)

Alice, however, remained uncertain:

I don't think they should. If you can see that they are healed and through it, maybe. It's a dodgy situation. Would I want to have the responsibility of knowing that my therapist had been abused as well? I don't know. I suppose it would depend on the therapist actually, and the relationship. It wouldn't necessarily be helpful to know it straight away. (Alice – 04)

A number of reservations about this practice were expressed including:

- boundaries becoming blurred between roles of therapist and client;
- confusion developing as to which abuse material is the client's and which the therapist's;
- 'unsorted' and 'driven' therapists seeing abuse everywhere and the explanation for every problem;
- therapists' being unable to work on issues with clients which they have been unable to resolve for themselves: over-emphasizing or avoiding issues which are personally relevant for the therapist;
- using clients to do the therapist's own work by proxy;
- therapeutic relationships becoming collusive and self-indulgent – stuck on abuse issues – not moving on to non-abuse issues, post-abuse functioning and future orientation.

A key distinction for clients is their impressions of the degree to which therapist self-disclosure about abuse stems from a 'healed' or an 'unhealed' position. Particularly disturbing experiences involved therapists telling clients of their own abuse, when this raised feelings in clients that the therapists were practising without having resolved their own problems. Clients sensed that they were being used by their therapists to help sort out their problems – and paying for the privilege:

I'm actually quite good at listening to other people's traumas, so I'd just switch into another mode at the time. Afterwards I would feel let down and – I don't think one can discount the money element in this. I feel I'm paying for a service – it's £27 per hour – it's quite a lot of money to me, I don't earn that much. I like to think that I'm getting something for it, that that person is there to listen to me for that hour. I'm not at all sure that I want to pay them to listen to their life events, really. (Anna – 19)

The third therapist would bring too much of herself into things. Now I found that intrusive and – particularly because I was paying her you know – felt like saying, 'Well, whose session is this supposed to be mate – yours or mine?' (Mary – 31)

For others, therapist self-disclosures, especially about abuse, were markedly unhelpful, leading clients to feel more inhibited in talking about their own painful material:

I was thinking, 'Give it time – over time I will be able to say it.' But I wasn't and I became more enclosed in this kind of iron room. I felt that because she'd been abused she might be judging me in some way – it was just very inhibiting. (Ellen – 13)

In these situations clients come to feel protective about the revealed vulnerabilities of their therapists and concerned not to upset or harm them. Role reversals may occur in response to hearing about therapists' personal issues – especially abuse – and clients find themselves feeling responsible for their therapist:

If you're going through some really painful stuff at that time and this therapist who's supposed to be 'supporting and taking care of' – inasmuch as they do – then it's almost like you've got a role reversal here and it feels to me like I'm to take care of them so to speak. Or, maybe I couldn't land them with too much of mine because I'd be working through theirs. (Esme – 42)

Soraya also experienced the potential inclination toward role reversal:

Soraya: I didn't really like it too much if she did talk about herself – I felt the session was just for me. I think if she said anything it would have had to be very short and quick and not dwell on it. Maybe that would have been useful – I think it might have been. But I might have felt uncomfortable, maybe. I don't know if it was because I was used to being the centre of attraction in the sessions.

PD: So, if she had shared it, she had dwelt on it – what would have gone on in your head in reaction to a therapist doing that?

Soraya: I would have wanted to protect her then – like the way my mother is, or was. I would have put myself aside, and I'd have got back into that – and I didn't want to! (Soraya – 52)

These examples highlight the susceptibility of some adults who were abused as children to be drawn into inappropriate caretaking of others, while inhibiting the expression of their own feelings and needs. For these reasons Myrtle was clear that she did not want to have any knowledge as to whether a therapist had been abused or not:

I don't want to know that. I liked (therapist) saying: 'Other people who have had this experience also feel that way' – because that made me feel normal. But I don't want to take on my therapist's problems – because therapy time is for the patient. It's like if your therapist voluntarily tells you, then it's almost as if she's asking for sympathy. It's not that I expect my therapist to be strong, you know, it's not that I expect her to be Superwoman and not have any problems. But therapy time is time to deal with my problems and she should be dealing with her problems somewhere else. I don't want her to bring her problems to my therapy session – because then I would feel I have to offer something and I don't want to. (Myrtle – 22)

Also in these scenarios some clients came to contrast their abuse experiences with those of their therapist, wondering 'whose abuse was the worse?' Esme and Ellen were both wary about the potential for rival comparisons to become part of the client–therapist dynamic:

> I think sometimes if I'd gone into the therapist and she's said to me: 'I'm a Survivor as well' – I'd have felt a little bit like: 'Mmm – am I going to be in competition here? Is everything I'm going to say – they're going to say: 'Yes, well, that happened to me.' I'd rather not know any more than my gut allows me to know. (Esme – 42)

> And she would bring it up at other times when she thought it might be helpful. But it wasn't that helpful in the long run because I thought: 'Oh, she's probably been more abused than me, so mind what you say.' (Ellen – 13)

Another surprising factor was the extent to which some clients did not trust the authenticity of their therapist's self-disclosures. This reflected an alertness to a sense of incongruity and suspicions about therapists' covert behaviour and needs:

> Although she said to me that she was a Survivor – she actually disclosed to me at some stage – but I just felt she wasn't. I didn't believe her. I felt she had told me and what she was really trying to say to me is: 'I'm one of you as well' rather than, 'I understand this'. It didn't come over as real to me. I felt really uncomfortable with that because I suddenly felt that she wanted to talk to me rather than listen to me. I didn't feel good about it at all. (Esme – 42)

> One thing that I did find disconcerting – another thing that would happen in sessions – was that she would spend quite a lot of time talking about herself and her family. Telling me how wonderful they all were. But then, at the same time, I also learned from her that there was an awful lot that wasn't right. (Beth – 16)

One consequence of such intrusions is that clients become distracted from their own needs. This results in a state of confusion, with clients privately trying to figure out 'what is going on' and adapting into passive and compliant responses. Ironically, these dynamics often mirror clients' ways of adapting in their original abusive environments, which contribute to a sense of dissatisfaction, resentment and exploitation. As was seen in Chapter 6, many had had experiences of feeling trapped, compliant, and preoccupied with trying to meet the needs of their therapists. Emily linked her own compliance in such circumstances with her family background:

> *Emily*: With my second counsellor, she told me things about her being divorced and there were a few times when I just thought: 'Why am I paying her twenty quid to sit here and listen to this?' And, in fact, rather than empathizing I just got quite fed up and thought: 'When are we going to talk about what I'm here for?'
>
> *PD*: What was going on? It sounds like it was unsatisfying for you to hear the counsellor's business in those moments. What do you make of it? What was happening?

Emily: I don't know. I think in some ways maybe it was a thing of trying to set up a more sort of normal relationship – a more friendly relationship. Rather than being sort of a counsellor and detached from you as a person. I think it was just a bit too much in that situation, because then you do start worrying about her, personally and: 'Hang on – is she alright?'

PD: How did you deal with this in the moment when you were feeling irritated?

Emily: Oh, I'd politely sit there and nod and agree, you know – the way I was brought up to. (Emily – 15)

Emily's final comment reiterates one of the strongest messages from clients in this study – the extent to which therapists can seem unaware of the amount of 'nodding and agreeing' that goes on in therapy. At best, such experiences involve frustration about paying fees to listen to therapists' problems. At worst, clients felt imposed upon and exploited in ways which phenomenologically replicated the contexts of their childhood abuse – through a sense of not being listened to or valued for themselves, with the other person's needs having to be put first.

Therapists' views about therapist self-disclosure

Overall, clients' views about the positive and negative effects of therapist self-disclosures were expressed with more feeling than the reflections by therapists on the subject. This suggests that the impact of receiving such a disclosure (whether positively or negatively experienced) is greater than that felt in providing it. The therapists with whom this issue was discussed felt that self-disclosing to clients about personal material, while potentially helpful in some respects, had to be carefully considered and balanced in view of the possibility of many pitfalls:

Sarah: I think there are enormous disadvantages. That's why I think to just share that you were a Survivor and you've been there and you know what it's like, is enough. I think if you start off-loading, that is a total No-No. Absolutely not. I mean, that's the biggest danger and I think that comes with not being conscious about yourself. And that doesn't mean to say you need to work with all the issues and have gone through it all – because this is a lifetime's work as far as I am concerned. But it's really staying conscious to yourself and if something is like bubbling – just to note it, and disidentify from it in your work.

PD: And if a therapist doesn't notice, doesn't disidentify, but carries on self-disclosing to a client – what would go wrong?

Sarah: Well, first of all role reversal could happen. Secondly, I actually think it's abuse. I think you are actually reenacting an abusive situation because you are using the client for your needs and not paying attention to theirs. It's so immoral and I get so angry. (Sarah – 10)

Therapists expressed two distinct views about self disclosure in a therapeutic relationship. As one would expect theoretically, caution about

self-disclosure was more typical of therapists influenced by psychodynamic theories than for those influenced by humanistic theories. For
the former, self-disclosure tends to be seen as either inappropriate or
ineffective:

> I don't put myself in saying: 'This is how I am' – because of my more
> analytical type training I am taught to keep myself away. And I do think it is
> ever so dangerous. Because with the transference, if you want to start sharing
> yourself – with the power and destructiveness of some of the people that we
> work with – it can be horrendous. (Catherine – 34)

> I have been through phases when I've shared and then felt: 'What's this for?'
> Or I've thought: 'Well, what's actually happened by my sharing – I don't think
> I have brought the session on at all.' I don't think clients care a toss about my
> background – I think they care about theirs. I know that Rogers says about
> sharing when appropriate – I just don't find it is appropriate because nobody
> gives a toss really. I find them here to be interested in themselves – so I don't
> bother. (Inga – 03)

The second view inclines toward some degree of self-disclosure occurring routinely with clients:

> I believe that there is a place for self-disclosure. I would disclose things about
> myself, particularly if I felt that would be helpful within the therapeutic
> environment. I think that there is a very, very fine line between self-disclosure
> and turning the table round so that your client becomes your therapist. And
> that's why you have to be aware that the disclosure takes place as *part* of the
> therapy and not as you talking about your own material. Because then it is a
> total waste of time and takes away from the important issues of the client . . .
> The closer relationship I have with my client, the more honest and open I am
> with them – the easier it is to self-disclose. I do not have to pretend to be
> anybody. I can be a real Human Being – warts and all. Self-disclosure is
> appropriate because I am a Human Being trained as a counsellor – I am not a
> counsellor who is inhuman. (Cliff – 05)

> I couldn't give you a rule about that but there's a definite time when it can
> help. I'm aware of transference and countertransference and I've worked with
> that in the past. But I tend to work more alongside people now. My whole
> thing has been to try and find ways that are more merciful to work with
> Survivors than what I experienced myself. (Abida – 09)

Therapists also recognized the potential for unresolved personal abuse
experiences to contaminate their perspectives and actions. A psychiatrist
observed:

> What I've seen emerging is a number of staff members who have come to wear
> their own abuse almost like a badge of pride: 'I've been abused and therefore
> I have a particular ability to work with abused people' – and I think there are
> dangers in that. There can be advantages too – because there is something
> about having been there which can be very important. But I've become deeply

uneasy about it because a lot of those staff members have clearly a very great level of passion for this kind of work and I don't think they have fully sorted out what they're trying to do.

There is a great deal of over-identification which I think is potentially really quite damaging because it perpetuates the sort of Victim–Rescuer thing. Only a Victim needs rescuing – an ordinary person doesn't. So I think the kind of *driven* therapist, who is still in some way working through their own abuse experience is quite a dangerous commodity. (Robert – 07)

In this emotionally complex area it is apparent that there is no simple answer as to whether a therapist should or should not at some stage, and to some degree, give a client information about their own background of abuse. Therapists' self-disclosures in general appear to have the potential to be both particularly helpful and equally unhelpful. The right balance has to be struck: too much personal information given too soon is likely to be unhelpful. The strongest message from clients overall on this point is that it is not so much whether a therapist has been abused or not that is important, but rather the degree to which an abused therapist is 'sorted' before embarking on work with other abused people.

Note

1 The exception was a psychiatrist who made extensive use of sodium amytal assisted interviews – described in Chapter 10.

8

Reviewing Relationships

Reviewing the state of current and potential relationships with significant others is invariably an important focus of therapy. One of the generally reported benefits of effective therapy is improvements in mood, self-image and self-esteem. It is common that when a client's depression lifts the world is seen as a very different place and this often has reverberations (sometimes uncomfortable) for partners and other relationships. Changes in perspectives include: reduced tendencies toward withdrawn, inconsistent, aggressive or destructive behaviour; less passivity and deference to the needs and opinions of others; increased sense of independent real self – rather than identity being defined in relation to others (for example, wife, daughter); greater ability to communicate effectively and assertively; better understanding of the perspectives of others; and being able to deal more successfully with differences, conflict and all forms of intimacy.

In this chapter we will focus on three areas where these changes affecting relationships were notable. These involve exploring emotions in therapy, relationships with children and with abusers and other members of the family of origin.

Exploring emotions

> I wouldn't have known what a feeling was if it had come up and hit me on the nose. (Zoe – 11)

> What I've been able to do there – is actually to be physical about my feelings. It's the opportunity to lose control, physically, and still come out of it alive. And, the opportunity, in my case, to kill my mother on a number of occasions and still come out of it not having harmed her. (Georgia – 51)

It is well established that histories of childhood abuse can affect the adult mood states of people, contributing in particular to depression which ranges from pervasive sadness to suicidal severity. Other effects on mood include: a general numbing of emotional responsiveness (in which feelings of pleasure become disconnected or dissociated alongside feelings of pain); general irritability; unpredictable mood swings; and outbursts of explosive anger. Some people try to avoid or block off painful feelings through substance misuse or compulsive activity. Others fear the destructive potential of their anger and need to learn how to prevent this from damaging relationships, especially with their children and families:

> I mean, I've got my mother in me – I can get really violent – and I know I can. (Sue – 54)

> It was very frightening because I thought: 'Well, if I really do give vent to these feelings, where the hell are they going to take me?' And I still feel that – I still feel if I really let these emotions take over, I'm afraid of what they will allow me to do. So, I was just afraid that I was going to run havoc with a shotgun. Not that I've ever had access to one – but the fantasies were very real. (Beth – 16)

> I found that while I was actually going through therapy I couldn't see my mother. Because after that one visit, the whole time she was chatting to me I just kept seeing her as this monster, this evil. And I hated her. I wanted to get up and punch her, and I found it was really difficult to control. I kept thinking: 'You've done this to me and I'm still suffering, like, at thirty-two years old – I'm suffering because of things you've done to me when I was two years old.' (Eleanor – 45)

> I've always been very good at being angry – my family are a very violent, angry family. She's worked a lot on empowering me, giving me the skills to handle my own feelings. She's helped me to learn how to step outside my feelings and not be overwhelmed by them. She's helped me to take control so that I'm not controlled by what happens. So that even when I'm frightened or distressed or depressed or doubting or whatever, there's always part of me that can stand outside it. (Myrtle – 22)

Progress in these areas involves:

- developing greater awareness of the complexity of feeling states and the circumstances in which they arise and change;
- better understanding of their origins, meanings and impact on others;
- increased ability to learn and to make conscious choices about ways of safely acknowledging, expressing, containing or avoiding them.

Working with anger in therapy

Beth and Zoe illustrated how therapists had helpfully enabled them to recognize and express their anger. After two unsatisfactory therapies, Beth reported great benefit from her third experience. In the context of a positive relationship she was able to respond to gentle teasing:

> I'm still not very good at expressing my anger, so I tend to become quieter and quieter the angrier I am. I don't rage and shout – it's all internalized. I

remember laughing one day with (therapist) because – we were talking about my father and how I was feeling about him. And he was being a bloody pain at the time. And I was getting quieter and quieter and in the end she said: 'Well, can you tell me how you feel?' And I just whispered: 'I feel bloody angry.'

And she just fell about laughing! She said: 'You're "bloody angry" and that's all you can say!' You know – it *was* funny – this was as much as I dared to give expression to my feelings. But she was prepared. She wasn't going to push me into ranting and raging when that wasn't something that would have been helpful to me. But equally, she was going to make sure I knew what I was feeling. (Beth – 16)

While driving herself to significant success in a demanding career, Zoe also described having spent a considerable part of her life feeling emotionally disconnected, interspersed with significant eating disorders and powerful suicidal urges:

I actually believe that I never got angry, and I never lost my temper – I didn't know I was angry. It took a lot of time for my therapist to actually facilitate anger out of me. I had it absolutely battened down, you know, because of what a lot of Survivors experience. And that is that we are *so* angry that just getting in touch with a little tiny bit of it is just going to let the whole lot out of the bag and the world's going to be devastated. (Zoe – 11)

She recalled with amusement how her therapist had carefully encouraged her to begin to recognize and express anger about her childhood:

Well, I wish I had it on video! The first thing she did was she got a bean bag out and she said to me: 'Come on Zoe, get down on the floor and beat this bean bag.' And I just sort of got down on the floor and went: 'I can't, I can't.' I was frozen, absolutely frozen. So she said: 'Watch me' and went: 'Aaaargh' on this bean bag. That was my first step toward actually expressing anger and then gradually working toward being able to be very directly and spontaneously angry now. And feeling OK about that, and it being over and done with. (Zoe – 11)

The usefulness of this was that it was a painstaking process which developed over time, more than an intense – or cathartic – explosion:

I've never had any mega-cathartic things. It's been – I liken it to peeling an onion or going on an archeological dig – going through things layer by layer as it's safe to do. So in none of my work have I been over anything just once. It's been a continual revisiting at a deeper level each time. So dealing with it bit by bit. So there's the 'tell the story with no feeling', and then beginning to get in touch with the reality of what happened, and then beginning to get in touch with the feelings that might have been around at the time and expressing some of them. (Zoe – 11)

In addition Zoe reported great benefit from creating and destroying artistic representations of the objects of her anger:

What was much more useful for me was doing big drawing work. Using sheets of lining paper on the wall and drawing my abusers. And then kneeling in front of them and being facilitated to communicate with them about what I felt about them and what I wanted to do to them. And at one point there were a couple of times where a cushion was put behind the drawing and I punched that and then, sort of, tore it in pieces and I threw them in the sea.

It puts the feelings – the anger where it belongs – and puts it out there in a way that there is a result. So even if it's using red coloured pens, at least there's something being done to that image of the person that one has. And then things like burning them – it's all going to be a bit crude, but I've actually gone through that sort of ritual at times here where I've done little figures and set fire to them. I've spat on them, and I've flushed them down the loo and I've pissed on them. (Zoe – 11)

These experiences highlight an effective combination of a measured expression of anger alongside symbolic retaliation and revenge. Other participants reported that more intense cathartic angry expression was helpful, indeed vital, for releasing pent up emotions. The following accounts of Georgia, Sue and Bea show the benefits of intense emotional expression: Georgia had worked with three therapists over three years, two of whom had proved to be beneficial:

So one thing I have gained is the ability to sit there and actually say things like that about my own mother and, initially, feel guilty about it because: One doesn't hate one's mother, does one? One loves one's mother!

So it's sort of getting things like that out of my system, without actually harming her directly and being left with something manageable. I mean in my case – I ended up strangling a pillow. And I was getting furious because I couldn't get my hands around it properly – my hands wouldn't meet. And that's an occasion when I lost all control. And I realized just how strong my feelings were and how it's no good for me holding all that inside my body. (Georgia – 51)

Sue had spent approximately three years in therapy with two male therapists. Both had been very helpful in different ways. Her second therapist was of a bioenergetics orientation:

Bioenergetics is all about touch and feeling safe, and skin-to-skin contact – which takes one hell of an amount of trust for somebody to do. And I think it took about a year to get to that. I needed somebody to be able to touch me, and me not feel frightened – to feel incredibly safe. I needed somebody to hold me without doing anything else, so that I can feel safe with another human being's contact, without it being sexual. (Sue – 54)

Sue was acutely aware of her own violent potential and found active expressive and regressive work with her second therapist to be the most effective way to discharge and defuse the intensity of her rage:

And he eventually got me back inside my Mum. The therapy with him was much more painful and I can't remember crying so much in my life than those eighteen months. And, you know, you've got to choke back the tears while you're walking through the streets, because people think you're loony, don't they? And I used to go to school some days with my eyes puffed out and I'd hardly been to sleep. I'd spent the night bawling – but I'd be getting rid of so much body tension it was absolutely untrue. I hardly cry, now. (Sue – 54)

Being struck by the intensity of such therapy, I asked her how she formed a view during these experiences as to whether they were helpful or not:

You don't. You just go with it – you can't stop. Within that hour you'd get half an hour of experience – because you've got the lead in, and then you've got to be cooled off to get yourself back out into the big, wide world – to get you home. So it has to be very, very carefully guided through. You can't be put out on the street in a state of just about ready to kill somebody! (Sue – 54)

Bea had worked with two therapists (both female) over a total period of eight years, the second of which she regarded as having been very helpful. She recalled actively beating beanbags and cushions:

The beating was just to beat. And I didn't know why I was beating, or who I was beating. And then, a bit later, she would say: 'Who are you beating?' And then maybe I would realise who I was beating. And then the next question was: 'What are you doing it for?' And then I would get a specific situation and that's when the beating gets really effective. And then, after that, I remember she asked me: 'How do you feel now?' and then, always, something positive came up.

We always got that positive feeling growing up afterwards. We talked about it. So that was a reward for the beating. It was not to kill my mother – I mean that was maybe my unconscious mind or whatever in the beginning – but after that I was beating to find my positive feeling underneath. I remember: love – and then I would paint that positive feeling. (Bea – 18)

As can be seen in these examples, for those who found catharsis helpful the impact revolved around a sense of significant release of tension; the ability finally to 'let go' in safety after many years of containment or displacement of anger into other moods, especially depression; and to experience the emergence of more rewarding feeling states.

However, there is a need for some caution about the facilitation of cathartic emotional expression in therapy. While Georgia, Sue and Bea illustrate the potential benefits, others had found their therapists' beliefs in the need for this and their attempts to provoke it very disconcerting and unhelpful. Cathartic expression of anger is not a therapeutic pathway that is helpful for all clients. While regular active expression of angry feelings can be an important factor in diminishing depression and developing assertiveness, it may also become routinized as an end in itself. Sarah commented on the potential for expression of anger to be self-reinforcing:

The anger's so healthy because it begins to empower you. Suddenly you are using this energy in which you are experiencing power. So yes, the anger. I can understand people wanting to stay there because it certainly fires you up. (Sarah – 10)

Concerns were expressed about anger being ritualized and cathartically celebrated, rather than being a stage of therapeutic development. This involves 'action hungry' therapists who see being angry in itself as the preferred way-of-being in the world for 'survivors', and consequently the desired end point of therapeutic resolution. This may be true (and appropriate) for some people who can use anger to drive towards achievements which previously they would not have dreamt of. However, this is not a universally desired outcome. Other people feel that perpetual anger can serve as a barrier to the development and expression of other aspects of their personalities and satisfying relationships.

Christopher had strong reservations from his experiences both as a client and therapist about the value of cathartic expression:

I have never beaten a cushion because, partly, it feels like doing it for the sake of the therapist. Because 'It's a gestalt session, and we believe in the beating of cushions.' I remember saying when I started therapy: 'I'm not going to beat up any cushions or talk to any cushions – bollocks – I'm not going to do it!'

I work with a lot of Survivors who are glad they don't have to. I'm very suspicious of therapists who are very much into cathartic work – action hunger – getting somebody into an excited state and then saying: 'There, there – how can I help you?' Wanting to see big changes – well it's bullshit! Shifts are minute, and long term, they're not going to come from somebody screaming for a minute – it's got to be integrated. (Christopher – 59)

This thinking was also illustrated by Abida from his personal and professional experiences:

To some extent I suppose I personally made quite a personal ritual about celebrating my anger toward these people. It had become like a way of being in the world. And so, to let go of that, is like opening up another space that needs healing. Because anger fills a lot of space. So if anger goes, much more healing has to happen. (Abida – 09)

From his perspective as a therapist he recalled his response to one patient:

I just think of them as encapsulated rage patients – who have had a lot of therapy, a lot of Fellowships – so they've acquired whole walls of therapy words – and there's no context to it. With one fellow, his whole life was therapy with no movement. He was going to his Men's group, and he was in two or three Fellowships. He goes to see a Healer. He goes to some kind of spiritual counsellor. And each place he goes he just acquires the words. And would talk endlessly, or cathart in a very stereotypical way that he'd been doing for seven years with his other therapists. Which was: sit down – start howling.

A very particular mask of anguish would come on his face and he'd spend the whole of the session doing that. And there was rage in that, but there was also: 'You're no good – you'll never be able to help me.' And with him, I confronted him every time. I'd say: 'OK, we're going to negotiate how many minutes of catharsis' – I would call him a 'Catharsis Queen' or a 'Survivor of Therapy Syndrome.'

So, after the third session, I just said: 'Look, you've done this. You've done this for seven years, and you're not going to do this here.' I could be very firm in those cases. And then the *real* rage came out – the 'f-ing' and the 'blinding' and: 'How dare you?' – and stuff. And I just stayed very, very still. At the end of it – he giggled. Because he'd found somebody he couldn't kill. (Abida – 09)

Robert also felt that getting stuck in a therapeutic culture of constant catharsis could impede progress:

One of the things that used to happen in Gestalt and those therapies a lot is that people would go round beating pillows and screaming at their parents. And that's actually, in my experience, of virtually no therapeutic consequence. It may be the first step in getting a process to unblock – if a person has never expressed their rage – yes, that's very important. But it's only a first step.

And I think that for a long time it was seen as an end in itself. And it became almost like a cameo of certain types of therapy – that people would scream things at pillows. And using that particular approach as an example, if somebody only externalizes their hostility and doesn't switch around and become the object of the hostility, in my experience, no resolution will occur. They may have got a little bit further than they had before – at least they can own and express the rage. But it's something about being able to see both good and bad in the person who abused. (Robert – 07)

These disparate views signal that there is no simple formula for the expression of feelings about childhood abuse in therapy. Some people need to do this, and find it helpful for therapists to facilitate and encourage. Others find such suggestions pressurize and the experience itself to be unhelpful or harmful. There are indications that some therapists do not recognize this and prescribe, provoke or model angry expression without prior exploration and assessment of its relevance for each individual's personality, feelings, needs and wishes. In response, some clients report 'going along' with such suggestions – 'play acting' anger to satisfy therapist's expectations and to fulfil the role of 'good client'. Alternatively, they dissociate from the emotional impact of the experience – as they may have done when being abused. This cannot be considered to be beneficial therapy. Indeed, the effects may be re-traumatizing and harmful: enhancing dissociative responses; ritualizing anger as a character trait and inhibiting other feelings (including positive memories).

Working with other feelings

Anger is by no means the only emotion central to therapy with people who have been abused. Other complex and poignant feelings arise which may require therapeutic space and attention, such as betrayal, loss and love towards abusers and significant others. Abuse is not a unitary category in which essentially similar things are done to children, are experienced in similar ways and have similar long-term effects. Rather, there are many different types of harmful actions and inactions to which children are subject and different children experience and react to these in different ways.

To illustrate this, three common scenarios can be summarized which would be classifiable by most people as constituting sexual abuse. They involve, however, very different contexts, impacts and consequences, and are likely to present different challenges in subsequent therapy. In one context that we might call tyrannical type abuse, children are simultaneously and chronically abused physically, sexually, psychologically and emotionally in every conceivable way; including consistent rejection and deprivation of affectionate attachments. In these violent and   unpredictable contexts there is no experience of abusers and other 'carers' as positive figures. Consequently, in later life, there is no loss of positive attachment to feel ambivalent about.

From this background the therapeutic challenge for clients is most likely to focus around:

- revising learned inappropriate self-concepts that they are bad (therefore deserving of abuse);
- recognizing and expressing anger and hatred;
- finding ways of protecting themselves more effectively from the continuing influence of abusing family members;
- giving up the deep sense of yearning for love from a family that is manifestly unable to provide it.

Invitations from therapists in these circumstances for clients to explore ambivalent feelings towards their abusers are likely to be either experienced as incongruous or offensive.

The second scenario involves sexual abuse of children who otherwise are generally well cared for. Typically this involves a child having 'special' status with a primary caretaker or other significant figure where there is an established affectionate and nurturing relationship. However, the relationship of genuine attachment and affection is subtly and gradually sexualized by the adult over a period of time, precipitating a premature sexualized responsiveness in the child. This form of abuse often involves fathers and daughters. One consequence of the daughters' sense of special status can be a disproportionate sense of powerfulness which contributes to dynamics of rivalry with mothers and dominance over siblings. This scenario illustrates that a state of powerlessness, as reported by Finklehor (1984), is not necessarily a factor and consequence of sexual abuse.

A third scenario of sexual abuse involves a pseudo-affectionate relationship in which the adult provides attention and affection to a child with the ultimate deliberate intention of manipulating the child into sexual activity. These children are often emotionally deprived and lonely, living in families where parents are preoccupied with other matters. They are easily identified by adults with paedophile tendencies who gain access to them in a variety of ways as extended family members, neighbours, or through forms of community, recreational, pastoral or even professional contacts. Under the guise of providing much needed attention, pseudo-affection, games and rewards, children become subtly sexualized to the point where they may subsequently seek out the adult and initiate sexual contact. This offence against childhood naivety is then ironically compounded when such abusers construe this behaviour as the child seducing them – a claim which will be used in their defence if criminal charges are brought.

The experience and effects of abuse for children between these categories is very different. For those who were sexually abused in the context of an affectionate, or pseudo-affectionate relationship, a significant focus of therapy in later life often involves recognizing and reconciling a sense of loss about what was valued in the relationship with the abuser. Loss can be excruciating in respect of a relationship which was experienced as genuinely loving. Feeling betrayed can be equally devastating when what was perceived as love and affection has to be reconstrued as manipulative pseudo-affection.

This raises key questions about resolution of abuse experiences. I have already noted that one view sees the ability to express anger (sometimes directly to abusers via confrontation) as being the optimal and ultimate therapeutic achievement. It is likely that this outcome is more congruent (but not necessarily inevitable) for those who experienced 'tyrannical type' abuse. People who were abused in the context of affection and pseudo-affection may also benefit from exploring and expressing anger in therapy about the abuse and its circumstances. However, it is more likely (but again, not inevitable) for this group that this may be a transitional position which opens a pathway to experiences beyond anger in which both the 'good' and 'bad' elements of the abuser can be recognized, understood and integrated.

Central to work beyond anger is that this focus involves clients exploring and acknowledging ambivalent feelings towards abusers and significant others, and struggling to understand the complexity of feelings towards parents and other attachment figures who were both caring and abusive. One illustration of this was provided by a therapist regarding a male client who had been abused by his father:

He just said that when his father had died, he hadn't grieved at all. He'd sort of said: 'Oh, I'm glad you've gone – it's good to see the back of you, you bastard' – you know, all the totally negative stuff. He did some really cathartic stuff like hammering a ten-inch nail into his father's grave – into the stones that are there. He painted over a portrait of his father – a portrait painted by a famous artist. And he did some really powerful stuff.

But the gift I'm talking about was that at the end of counselling he told me that in doing all this and getting all the hate and the anger out – he had allowed the love to come back in again, and could actually mourn. He could remember lovely things that he'd done with his father. He'd blocked out the good things. (Jane – 24)

This area of exploration is vital for some clients and may include the development of feelings of forgiveness and desire for family reconciliation. Progress in this direction can be impeded by therapists who do not understand or accept the nature of such ambivalence. However, it is equally important that this potential to move beyond anger is not adopted and presented by therapists as a formulaic expectation:

Well, it's nice if it happens but you can't make it a goal for everyone because for some people, as far as they seem to get for many years is that they've identified the abuse, managed to be angry and managed to confront, and that may be as far as they want to take it for many years. Indeed, for ever sometimes . . . you can't force people to go down a path they're not prepared to take. (Abida – 09)

Relationships with children

All through school and that, you're taught all the basic things, but no one teaches you how to become a parent. (Eleanor – 45)

As noted in Chapter 5, problems in relationships with children were often the trigger for seeking help. These concerns have a powerful and poignant impact:

I realized there was something wrong when I had my first child. When I did something about it and confirmed to myself there was something wrong was when I had my second child. I realized that I wasn't bringing my children up as I wanted to bring them up. The main thing was that I was physically abusing the oldest one – it became uncontrollable. In my conscious mind it was my mother and her coming through me. (Carol – 14)

I abused – because that is the word – my youngest child Not sexually – whether it means anything to qualify it, but I suppose it does to a degree. I certainly played out a lot of violence with him. But the interesting thing about that is that if that hadn't happened between he and I, I wouldn't have started looking at me. (Grace – 63)

To their great relief retrospectively, many parents had been able to recognize the danger of what was happening with their children and to ask for help or take other protective action before this escalated into serious physical or sexual harm:

> Although I wasn't going to hit my children, I was doing the same sorts of things to them that had been done to me. I thought: 'I need help – I'm not going to repeat this pattern, I need someone to help with this.' (Alice – 04)

> What happened when I had my son was after I had him I was aware of sexual feelings with him. And then everything goes black – I cut off my sexuality to protect him. (Sarah – 10)

> I was starting to have very negative feelings against (daughter). She was five, now at this point. And it got to the point – I must have been quite psychotic – because I felt she was plotting against me. That if I didn't get rid of her, she would get rid of me. So I was admitted to hospital that day. (Sonya – 33)

Not knowing the basic skills of being an effective parent stems from lack of positive models and experiences as a child. Eleanor contrasted herself as a child and her own eleven-year-old daughter:

> This is what I find hard now, I suppose, is that I never had a parent at (own daughter's) age. At (daughter's) age I was looking after four children. There was no one at home – they'd all cleared off and I was bringing them up! So how do you become a parent when you've never had one – you've never had a role model have you? (Eleanor – 45)

Fears of abusing children are reinforced by awareness of the popular notion of inter-generational transmission of abuse – the suggestion that abused parents are highly likely to abuse their own children. Many participants felt angry and upset by the implication or direct suggestion that because they had been abused they would inevitably abuse their own or other children:

> And one thing that really annoys me is that people say if it happened to you then you're going to do it to somebody else. But I've known, ever since it happened to me, I would never do it to somebody else. I don't have much to do with children, I can't handle them, I can't cope with them. But I would never do anything to harm them. Because I know what it does to you, and you just shouldn't have to live that way. (Mary – 53)

> A really big area is having your own kids afterwards and worrying about that you might do it to them. Because you read all these things – about that if it happened to you so you might do it to others. It's a risk of course, but you don't have to repeat the things that have been done to you. We're not so passive – I don't have to give in to fate, you know. (Soraya – 52)

> The reason why I haven't abused a child and won't abuse a child is that I've found the support that I need to deal with it. (Sophia – 64)

Others can be affected by this notion in a different way, as it touches pre-existing fears that they might have a propensity to re-enact their own abuse with children. Jamie remembered such anxieties:

> I think I did have those sorts of fears. Because I work with young people anyway, and because I'm male. And I have wondered, yes. Because when I come to think about my own family and I think about my father, then I start to think: 'Well, what about his father? Was he doing it? What about his father?' And: 'How far back does it go?' And: 'Will it come to me? Is there, like, a bad seed passed down?' (Jamie – 12)

He had reflected deeply in therapy on the processes which may lead some abused people to abuse others and factors which prevent this:

> From what I've learned about adults who do abuse, after having been themselves abused, it can be to do with distorted perceptions that they have about how to express affection or love towards children. Because that's been expressed in a particular way, they perpetuate that. Or, that they themselves as children were abused and not valued – made to feel worthless. And so now it's their turn to do the same, you know: 'It happened to me, so I can do it as well.' That sort of thing.
>
> But as to why they don't – I have been thinking about this. What I actually think is that if people had been getting help for it, have been put in touch with their feelings as children being abused, it would be unthinkable. Because they would recognize what an effect it had had on them. And so, even if they were tempted or in a situation where it could happen, shall I say, it would be unthinkable. (Jamie – 12)

While childhood abuse experiences can be a contributory factor in parents abusing their children, many adults who were abused as children are very alert to this possibility and take determined steps to be non-abusive parents. Because of such concerns, one participant had gone so far as to make a firm decision never to have children.

There is a significant popular misconception about the inter-generational transmission of child abuse. Reviews of research (Egeland 1988; Kaufman and Zigler 1987; Oliver 1993; Steele and Pollack 1968) and clinical experience (Dale et al. 1986a; Dale and Fellows 1997) indicate that high proportions of adults who seriously abuse their own children were themselves abused in childhood. However, this correlation does not hold in reverse: it is not the case that high proportions of adults who were abused as children will abuse their own children. The small number of relevant studies estimate that approximately 30% of abused children will eventually become abusing parents (Kaufman and Zigler 1987; Oliver 1993).

Given sufficient motivation, problems in parenting is an area where significant positive changes are possible. This had been a central focus of therapy for Veronica:

When my little girl was small I was always very, very tense. I tried to bottle everything up and then something would happen and I would go completely bonkers – which is the way my life was. And that had an effect on my daughter. It made her frightened and I didn't realize that she was frightened of me. And I understand, too, now the difference between being strict or firm, and being cruel. That's what I had to find out. That's what the therapy was about.

I went along for therapy and firstly, it helped me to understand that I hadn't imagined it and it was true – I had had a rotten childhood. And secondly, I wanted to break the cycle. I knew that there was something not right with my relationship with my daughter and my children. And I knew that it was to do with my upbringing. And the last thing I wanted to be was like my mother. And I knew I *was* like her. And I also know that it is said that the abused go on to become abusers and I'd never been able to understand that. But I hadn't got a blueprint to go by. I'd rejected the one that I'd been given and I didn't have another one. (Veronica – 23)

In contrast, Katie believed some benefit had been derived from her own abuse, in that this had made her determined to be an excellent parent:

I think that despite all the weaknesses, and all the doubts, you're also left with a lot of strengths. It is very important to look at actually what kind of person it makes you in the end. I mean, I think I've become a wonderful mother, because I've never had any mothering and proper fathering. I think I've become a very good Mum – to make sure that I didn't repeat any of the patterns that were in my own life. (Katie – 32)

Relationships with abusers and families of origin

The research generated many stories of significant changes which had been made over time in perceptions of and relationships with abusers and other family members. Often this involved taking steps to communicate about the abuse and its effects to abusers and others. One theme of 'survivor' literature in the 1980s emphasized the merits of confrontation and severance of contact with abusers. Testimonies of some people who have followed this path indicate that this can be one way of revising family relationships which leaves them feeling safer, more confident, and free to get on with their lives.

Mary described such an experience as a major turning point in her life. This had involved the planned public confrontation in a family gathering of the brother who had sexually abused her between the ages of ten to fourteen. In therapy she had been encouraged to carefully rehearse the confrontation:

When I actually came out with it, his face was absolutely – complete shock that I'd actually got the guts to come out with that, you know, in front of three other people. It was funny because he just said: 'Well, I don't feel well.' And I said: 'I don't care how you feel – I haven't felt well for twenty years because of you.' And he said: 'I've got a bad stomach', or something. And I said: 'Well, I hope you die.' And afterwards I thought: 'God! What a terrible thing to say.' But then I thought: 'Well, I really do – because he has given me so much grief.' (Mary – 55)

Part of the preparation had been for Mary to tell her mother beforehand. The outcome of this was unexpected:

And another thing that the counsellor made me do is go and tell my Mum. And God knows how I told her, but I did. I got the strength from somewhere and I just, kind of, came straight out with it. And from what she said I realized that she knew anyway – and that made me very, very angry. And I still haven't forgiven her for that. (Mary – 55)

Mary received a great deal of support from a number of her other siblings who believed her account. It was clearly therapeutic for her to be publicly heard, to have the reality of the abuse and its effects acknowledged, and to experience some satisfaction through the humiliation of her brother. She stressed the positive impact of the confrontation for her:

Oh God, yes! I would tell anybody who had it done to them, to do it. I just felt like I was on Cloud Nine. I was just unbelievably happy about the situation, because I felt that I'd got my revenge on him. And just the fact that I'd told him, as well, that all the family knew. That also had a big impact on him. But it was just sheer – like a complete weight off my shoulders – it was just unbelievable. I would never have done it on my own, you know, without the counselling. (Mary – 55)

However, being in the presence of abusers and other key family members can exert strong unexpected pressure to behave according to old patterns. Recognition of her susceptibility to such dynamics led Sue to confront and sever contact with her family:

My father was really repeating his old behaviour patterns with me as an adult and fully expecting that if he treated me as a child, I would behave as a child. I haven't seen my father for five or six years now – that was a major row. I actually confronted him. One of his things in life is appearing terribly respectable. I don't know what the neighbours made of me slamming out, screaming abuse at him, and marching off to the station – just no going back whatsoever. I'd love to know how he explained that one! (Sue – 27)

While these two examples felt very positive for Mary and Sue, confrontation and severing contact is not a style of communication or outcome which feels comfortable and appropriate for all people. Others were interested in the possibility of opening up a dialogue with their abusers and other family members about the abuse. Often this was disappointing. Attempts at more honest communication may follow long periods of maintaining relationships while adaptively 'pretending' that everything is OK. Ultimately such facades can become unsustainable:

> There's no way I could keep up a relationship with my father, just for appearances sake. I feel as if, ever since I've come out into the open about it – I feel as though I've totally cut the umbilical cord. And I feel that I've become more of a person in my own right. If he were to acknowledge what he did, then there might be some sort of meeting point. But all the time he's denying what he did – and my mother believes him and thinks that I'm making it up – then there's no way. I've no guilt about that. (Katie – 32)

Establishing some sort of meeting point is frustratingly difficult when attempts are continually met with denial or minimization of the abuse and its effects. When there is hope for dialogue to gain understanding of abusers' perspectives and motivations, denial was the predominant feature of abusers' responses which increased frustration and the likelihood of ultimate estrangement. Eleanor described attempting to communicate with her mother who had sexually abused her:

> Yes, I think it was very hard. And that's another thing when at that point I felt therapy wasn't helping. Because I felt I'd built up a relationship with my Mum and then one day I sat and threw everything at her about my childhood. And I said to her: 'That's why I don't want you in my life and don't want you around.' And she used to deny everything that had happened. And I said to her: 'That makes it even harder.' Because, all the time she was denying it, I felt as if I was mad – as if really it was all in my mind. And I said: 'You don't realize that because you're denying it you're making it harder for me.' (Eleanor – 45)

In the face of similar denial, Claire also eventually ceased contact with her father:

> The main abuser was my father and I just don't see him anymore. I don't maintain any contact with him. I confronted him, tried to talk to him about it, and we did have some kind of conversation. But he's basically in denial of it. And I know that something's happened and if he doesn't want to accept that then I don't want to associate myself with him. (Claire – 57)

These were painful decisions and people were sometimes surprised by the impact of the subsequent feelings of loss and grieving which they faced. Such loss could either be in relation to real aspects of the actual person (especially when the relationship had involved ambivalent feelings), or a profound sense of disappointment about what could have been – but never was:

> My Mum had done so many things to abuse – and my father, but in a different type of way. They'd done so much. Yet I still wanted them in my life. And I

think, especially with my mother, I think what it was – I wanted a Mum. I'd never had a mother and I think that you just hope that some day that you'll have your Mum. (Eleanor – 45)

Following a particularly poignant response to her confrontation of her father, Sarah found the process of grieving opened up an unexpected direction:

My parents were divorced as a child and I didn't see him until my early thirties, late twenties. He lived in (abroad). I then had a period of relationship with him, and then remembered. And I confronted him by letter and there was this massive denial and then no more contact. So, the shocking thing is, that he committed suicide in a very horrific way.

So up until then, I don't know, I tried to ignore his existence really. I had the anger and then I ignored his existence. And I had always said – because I practice Judaism – that I would never sit Shiva – sit in mourning for him . . . I decided that I wanted to, and just one day the ritual of really mourning for his soul. And also for me. It felt really important. It made some closure. So that's what I did and I think it was letting go of some of my anger and desire for revenge. (Sarah – 10)

Mary found that her perspectives unexpectedly changed following a confrontation:

It had been a pretend relationship always. I mean, within the family, it was always known that I was his favourite – that he thought I was marvellous. And it was always a family thing that he was fond of me, and I always had to pretend that I liked him. I didn't. I hated him. As a child, anyway, I hated him.

I've actually confronted my father, before he died. He died only a couple of years ago. And just because I wanted to get a few facts straight in my head to make sure I wasn't – I wasn't enlarging a whole lot of stuff. I wanted to make sure I was clear. And so that was important for me. That was an important stage I had to go through in actually making things – making things OK with him really. I think it was very good for both of us. It certainly was for me. And I think for him.

Because he actually said there wasn't a day went by when he didn't feel guilty about it. Certainly it was good for me to hear that. And I think it was good for him to have been able to actually admit to that. I also felt it important that I had to let him know that it was OK now. Because I just felt sorry for him. I actually had to go through that with him and say 'Look, I like you now. In fact I can love you now because I understand you and I've worked through all this' – and everything. And actually go on to that stage of the process. (Mary – 43)

After many years of estrangement from her father, Jean recalled a deathbed reconciliation:

I had never wanted to discuss the abuse with my father, but before he died he became very depressed. Some months before his death he told me he was having flashbacks to the 'bestial' things he had done during the war years. I was caught off my guard and just said: 'I know, Dad.' We looked at each other for a moment and just nodded to each other. It looks so little on paper, but feels so important for me. (Jean – 36)

Roles of mothers

From many of the interview excerpts throughout this book it will already be apparent that participants had very strong feelings about their mothers. In the child abuse literature there have been longstanding theoretical divisions between psychodynamic, systemic and feminist theories about the causes of abusing behaviour, and the roles and dynamics within families where abuse takes place. For example, beliefs vary about the roles that mothers play in protecting – or failing to protect – children who are being abused by males; and the extent to which females sexually abuse children. Two studies from a feminist perspective concluded that mothers were either ignorant of sexual abuse occurring to their children or powerless to prevent it from continuing (Hooper 1992; Humphreys 1990).

In this study, however, a broader picture emerged from the retrospective recollections of adults abused as children in relation to the behaviour and family roles of their mothers. The following sequence of interview excerpts illustrates the range of respondents' experiences of mothers:

It's only because I realize that she'd abused me, that I realize why I had sexual feelings towards her, very strong ones. If your mother had sex with you, then you're bonded with her in a sexual way, and you're not able to relate to other people intimately. (Carol – 17)

And when he was in my bedroom, what was my mother doing? My mother had said – because I'd tried to have some of these things out with her – she said: 'Oh, I suspected something was going on.' It takes, sometimes, a long time for things – to have an impact on me. And I thought: 'God, she's *known*!' She might be his collaborator, or she might be so weak that she can't do anything about it. But at the end of the day she was my mother and she was supposed to protect me and she didn't do that. (Katie – 32)

Although she was allowing it to happen, I never realized how much involved she was. I never used to cry, even as a kid, I never cried. Even when I was being beaten and that, I never cried. My Mum said recently: 'It was as if it was a battle of wills – like, in the end: "You will cry!" ' And I'd be: 'You're not going to make me cry.' (Eleanor – 45)

When my Dad tried to strangle me, my mother put a scarf around my neck and told me not to tell anybody. If anybody asked about the scarf about my neck I was to say I had a sore throat. And I didn't tell anybody until I was thirty. (Sarah – 30)

You see, what she's presenting is that she feels so betrayed. She felt that she was *special* to her dad. She felt that she was everything to him, that he really,

really loved her better than anyone else in the world. That has been totally and utterly devastated. Because – well, she knows now that what went on was wrong. He used to tell her that it wasn't wrong – that it was society who had it wrong: 'Society was ridiculous and it was a perfectly natural thing for a Daddy to do to a little girl he loved.' And some of it was nasty stuff. But she now knows that he also was doing it to her sister. He did it to two of her cousins, and, she's just discovered, he did it to someone else as well. And so there's that sort of total betrayal of: 'Well, I did it because I was special to him, and I did it because that was what you do with someone you love. And I did it because if I didn't do it – he was in a very bad mood. And I did it because Mum told me to go to his room because: "You could always make him in a better mood, dear." ' (Jane – 12)

The sample involved a surprising proportion of women who reported having been sexually abused by their mothers: 25% who reported a history of sexual abuse recorded mothers as being involved. Of the sample of forty-seven interview participants who completed the questionnaire in relation to their own childhood abuse, thirty-six reported sexual abuse; twenty-three reported physical abuse; thirty-five reported emotional abuse; and fifteen neglect. Of the thirty-six reporting sexual abuse, fifteen gave fathers as the perpetrator; fourteen gave 'other family males'; and nine reported mothers as the perpetrator (singly or jointly with others). The extent and nature of female sexual abuse of children has also been reported and discussed in detail by Elliot (1993).

Searching for understanding

The search for the essence of meaning underlying existence and the vagaries of experience, and the development of a consistent sense of personal identity, is a core component of the human condition which has occupied philosophical, religious and other scholars for centuries (Frankl 1992). It also occupies the attention of many clients in therapy. Developing ways of making some sense of experiences, especially those involving bereavement, pain, trauma, abuse and loss, is invariably a central part of therapeutic exploration, recovery, resolution and growth. For abused clients, specific questions are asked and meanings sought in respect of their abuse: 'Why?' 'Why me?' 'Why didn't people protect me?'

Effective therapy often focuses on helping clients to reassess whether existing perspectives are the most helpful ways of interpreting past and present events and relationships:

The only way of finding out 'Why?' is to experience the feelings and to re-live things so that I remembered what it felt like. I had a key memory of my mother beating me very viciously when I was seven years old. I remember resenting it particularly, you know, thinking it was grossly unfair.

However, there was another feeling at a much deeper level than that which might sound puzzling to people where I agreed with her. Where I felt she was an angel really, and she was completely justified in beating me up. And I had to reach those unexpected feelings that were underneath the other ones, that were preventing them being worked through – then there might be another feeling at an even deeper level.

I mean, first of all you don't want to face the fact that you weren't loved by your mother, or that you hated your mother – that's difficult to face. But then, there was another level of feelings where you feel that she was probably right and you were no good – you don't want to face that either. (Mary – 31)

Mary emphasized that it was vital to the ultimate effectiveness of the therapy that these thoughts and feelings could be acknowledged, explored and respected, rather than being challenged or contradicted:

I don't know what would have happened to me if I hadn't seen her. She helped me by just being there, you know, being there three times a week. To listen to things and *listen* to what my life was really like for me at a deep level which, of course, nobody had done before. And she was also able to probe into terrible things that had happened as a child which unfortunately tended to repeat themselves with my son. She was taking me on a terrifying voyage of exploration and it was very horrifying, very terrifying you know. It was almost like going really mad, like a sort of psychotic experience. But it was absolutely essential. (Mary – 31)

Focusing on understanding may sometimes involve therapists introducing alternative concepts for clients to consider. In the wake of the events described in Chapter 6, Esme had found a new therapist and felt that important progress was now being made:

Part of my relationship with my present therapist is one of learning concepts that I did not learn as a child. Learning how to relate to others on more than a superficial way is something I never did as a child and therefore is something I don't know how to do as an adult. By a process of re-learning, whilst maintaining boundaries, I can then transfer this knowledge to those I choose to be closer to in the wider world. I will then become part of the human race rather than living alongside it. (Esme – 42)

It is important that concepts introduced by therapists are provided tentatively as 'food for thought' to be considered – and then either assimilated or rejected. Therapists need to take care not to attempt, consciously or unconsciously, to superimpose their own favoured theories, or perspectives generalized from personal experiences, onto their clients. To do so can create dissonance, dissatisfaction and potential harm.

Resolution

What do I mean by the word 'resolved'? They're taking a pathway which is the right way for them. (Sue – 54)

My criteria for somebody having healed their abuse is that some gentleness has come into their life. That they're on the way to being able to have intimacy with love. (Abida – 09)

Many clients and therapists talk of the potential for abuse experiences to be 'resolved'. I took the opportunity to explore with a number of participants exactly what they meant by this notion. What exactly does 'resolution' involve? What part can therapy play in helping clients move towards 'resolution'? To what extent can childhood abuse experiences be 'resolved'? Disparate views exist regarding these questions. This diversity of opinion underlines a key message of this book regarding the inappropriateness of a single categorization of child abuse, and of construing adults who were abused as children as a homogeneous group with identical perspectives and needs.

Developing a level of understanding of abusers' reasons for abusing was crucial for participants who felt that resolution could involve forgiveness and reconciliation. When this occurs, two factors are involved: recognition that the abusers had themselves been abused; and an acknowledgment that the relationship had involved good elements as well as abuse:

> I could see him as a real person with all his good and his bad sides. Because he had a lot of very nice things about him. But I wouldn't have been able to see the positive or feel the positive part – because of the contamination of the bad side. But I do think that's something one needs to come to after you've exorcized, so to speak, the negative. If you do that too soon, you actually deny the negative. I believe the process has to go in that order. (Mary – 43)

The potential for the development of forgiveness by means of greater understanding posed a particularly poignant dilemma for Sophia:

> I suppose I take a historical view – looking at their childhoods. I know a fair bit about my mother and stepmother's childhoods which were both miserable and they were probably abused. Certainly neglected. I struggle quite a lot between feeling anger towards them and compassion for them. Their own pain must be *enormous* to do that. And it's not my responsibility to heal them but I do feel compassion for them sometimes.
>
> And then I just feel this absolute rage: '*Why?*' It doesn't matter what was wrong with them, what was wrong with their lives, I'm left with it. (Sophia – 64)

Resolution involving understanding and forgiveness is likely to be the culmination of an ambivalent and painful struggle. Therapists should not attempt to promote, accelerate or impose the notion of forgiveness. If it is to happen, it will occur in its own time:

> Part of me likes to think that I will forgive them. Another part of me likes to think that I won't because quite often in the past I've tried to brush it under the carpet by forgiving. And it hasn't been very genuine. (Sophia – 64)

> I recognize with my mother that I'm pretty certain that she was severely abused herself in her childhood. I've got some photographs of her when she's three or four. And it certainly was revealed to me intuitively that she was

desperately hurt and my heart goes out to her now. Because I've had the benefit of very, very sophisticated help. I've spent £15,000 over the years on my own therapy. But I don't begrudge it because I'm alive, I'm able to love – give and receive love. I'm able to have joy in my life because I've had all this help. Now she never had the chance of that help. She's coming toward the end of her life now and I'm very pleased that I can have a friendship with her now. (Abida – 09)

In the midst of this discussion, the strong feelings of many abused people against the notion of forgiveness should not be lost sight of. Sarah made this point well:

I have real problems with people who feel forgiveness is necessary for healing. I don't think it is. And I think there are some things beyond our forgiveness, and sexual abuse of children happens to be one of them. (Sarah – 10)

Reflecting on forgiveness often involves spiritual questions and dilemmas. Beth, a committed Christian, struggled with an incongruity between her religious beliefs and her felt inner experiences. She had specifically sought a Christian counsellor. However, the combined influence of the counsellor's acknowledged inexperience with abused people and her views about forgiveness created a strong negative effect:

I now realize that she wanted a happy resolution. There was always very much a sense of needing to bring in forgiveness and understanding and tolerance. (Beth – 16)

Progress ultimately lay in recognizing that, despite her own committed Christianity, she needed to resist (at least at this stage) the counsellor's emphasis on forgiveness – as being either inappropriate or premature. Instead, with her third counsellor, she was increasingly able to accept and express the reality of her angry, unforgiving feelings and to accept that, in the circumstances, these were not incompatible with her faith:

I still get very hung up on the idea of whether or not I need to forgive my brothers and quite what that entails and how I'll know when I've got there. But I think that the idea of a return to a normal happy family status has gone completely out of the window – this is not realistic. Certainly one of the things that's happened is that I have had to view my family very objectively and my role within it. I suppose the question is: 'What is Christian? And what's not Christian?

I've gone away from the idea of feeling that everybody should be nice to one another, and that all that this world needs is for everyone to be nice to one another and everything will be OK. I have moved on to the idea that really what's important is being nice to yourself and finding out what your own needs are. It's a real turn round in terms of outlook, but I think it's still very much a Christian one. (Beth – 16)

Another interesting perspective involves people who develop various forms of spiritual awareness which they see as a positive consequence of their abuse:

I believe that I've been led into a spiritual dimension that I never would have dreamt possible without the experiences I've had. So I believe that everything that I've had in my life has been tremendously helpful. So for me, I'm a Transcender. But a lot of therapists are still between Victim and Survivor mode in their view of themselves. (Abida – 09)

Both Grace and Rose had come to believe that their abuse experiences had in some ways been deserved:

When you start actually seeing your life in terms of your soul rather than just this one physical life here and now, then all sorts of things can come in that don't have any space or relevance in day-to-day living. I mean, God knows I've been through forgiving my mother more times than I can remember. But what's happened to me, what I've begun to perceive is that without even addressing it I suddenly begin to realize that I just don't have the resentment towards her anymore. I've accepted much more that she did what she did or didn't do and that's part of her life's plan.

My whole way of being is to – well to put it in simple terms: bring me closer to God – or what one perceives as God. I let go of everything which stops me being that loving being that I know I can be. And, you know, I've had to go through this for a reason. To make up for whatever I've done before. Even if it isn't to make up for something I've already done, it's to teach me something and that's what's important to me. When I really learn what I need to learn out of the situation, then it seems to me that forgiveness is an automatic response to that – it becomes an integral part of it. (Grace – 63)

For Rose, turning to Buddhism had a major effect on the way she understood her abuse and responsibility for it:

The Buddhist philosophy – just appealed to me because we take sole responsibility for our actions. We don't blame our parents or partner, siblings or neighbour, people at work. We take full responsibility for our actions, and as a result, the causes and effects are 'reap what you sow', if you like. I was a victim of victims. The Buddhist point of view – we believe in reincarnation. And everybody is put in a situation they've got to learn to handle. (Rose – 20)

Thinking about ways of understanding and possible forgiveness is inherently linked with reflections upon responsibility for abuse. The dominant notion that children are never responsible for the abuse they experience at the hands of adults is indisputably appropriate in social and legal terms. Jane passionately underlined the principle that children never have any responsibility for abuse:

I feel very strongly that the abused person, be it male or female, was *not* to blame for what happened. And that, until they fully and wholly take that on board then they're not going to get better, they're not going to get through it, they're not going to come to terms with it. No, I'm not having any responsibilities put on them – whether they were sexually aroused, whether they were orgasmic – whatever they were.

I had one (client) who said: 'It was definitely my fault because I walked around in my bra and pants and my father just couldn't resist – he couldn't stop himself.' Well: I walked round in my bra and pants – my dad managed to stop himself. For goodness sake! What's that saying about men? That's ridiculous. My boys walk around in their boxer shorts – they are both beautiful handsome young men. Am I supposed to set upon them? Bloody ridiculous! Absolutely ridiculous! (Jane – 24)

From this perspective a firm stance is taken that adults who do feel responsible are reflecting distorted beliefs about responsibility which are likely to have been assimilated from their childhood environments. However, clients often adhere to a ruthless double standard on this issue: they insist that they would not in any way hold any other child in similar circumstances to blame to any extent whatsoever – but maintain that this does not explain or expulcate their own particular behaviour as a child. In these situations therapy can help clients to shed burdens of responsibility by counter-balancing such beliefs and encouraging them to externalize self-blaming tendencies onto their abusers. The maxim 'It wasn't your fault' can be helpful when clients have been unable to conceive of the notion that responsibility for anything in their childhoods may lie anywhere outside of their own self-perceived badness and deservingness of abuse.

However, the idiosyncratic interpretations of some adults who were abused as children are not always as straightforward as this. Notwithstanding the socially sanctioned 'children are never responsible' axiom, this does not preclude deeply personal 'What part did I play in it?' questioning and searching for understanding. Consequently, this highlights the importance in therapy of recognizing and understanding clients' potential ambivalence about the nature of the abusive relationship. For some people, not all experiences with the abuser or all aspects of the abuse are necessarily experienced or construed in a totally negative or powerless way:

I think in the culture that we've been through in abuse talk, it's not acceptable to regard the client as having any responsibility in the process at all. One of my concerns about abuse therapy is that there seems to be, in some people's minds, a belief that what you have to do is convince the victim that they were somehow in no way responsible for what happened and that it's somehow *all* the other person's fault. And that's very gratifying to the therapist and very naively attractive, but it flies in the face of any idea of integrating the bad and the good in a person. And if we learn anything from the analysts, I think it's that one of the mechanisms we use is splitting. And that's a prime example of therapy confirming and reinforcing splitting which, it seems to me, is wholly unhelpful.

But, if you are in the stereotypic example, a girl who was abused by her father, the fact is that the person who abused you is still your father – and you only get one of them. And I think to work as a therapist to facilitate that person seeing only bad in one of their parents is very unhelpful. It seems to me the desirable outcome of therapy is that the rage and the disgust is fully experienced and directed at the person who did it, and then, that what lies behind that is explored – usually the yearning for a 'good father'. (Robert – 07)

Identifying the potential therapeutic importance of this perspective does not involve minimizing the responsibility of abusers, nor does it condone child abuse. It does not resurrect victim-blaming stances that children are responsible for abuse, nor does it support paedophile beliefs that sex with children is justifiable, because in certain circumstances children will respond to and even seek out sexualized affection. However, it does recognize that abused people have many ways of making sense of their experiences and that resolution stems from a quest for carefully considered congruent meanings. Therapy that routinely pushes towards an externalization of all responsibility and segments relationships into watertight categories of victims and abusers (sanctifying the former and demonizing the latter) can miss the mark for people who experienced degrees of recognition, care and love within such relationships, and who may still miss the person concerned.

THE MEMORY CONTROVERSY

9

Childhood Abuse Memories:
Theory and Research

In Part Three our attention turns to the controversial topic of the nature and accuracy of adult memories of childhood abuse. This controversy has a long social history and is evocative of debates and disputes which occurred in European psychotherapeutic practice over a century ago. As noted in Chapter 1, for a significant part of the twentieth century there was little social recognition of the reality of child sexual abuse; during the 1980s and 1990s there was an explosion of reported cases. One type of sexual abuse memory has raised particular controversy: those situations where in adult life people 'recover' memories of abuse of which they were previously unaware. So called 'massive repression' or 'decades delayed discoveries' came to be reported extensively in 'survivor' self-help manuals and many clinical publications. One viewpoint holds that this reflects a true representation of a previously hidden phenomenon. Another argues that it is a manifestation of a process of social contagion through which unhappy and very suggestible people come to believe wrongly that they were abused as children.

In this chapter I will describe some of the relevant theoretical and research material which provides the context for these ongoing disputes about the nature of child abuse memories. This includes discussion of:

- general memory processes;
- traumatic/abuse memory processes;
- prevalence studies of 'recovered' memories;
- corroboration studies;
- studies of therapists' attitudes regarding abuse memories;
- 'False Memory Syndrome'.

In Chapter 11 I will present illustrations and analysis of the abuse memory experiences of the participants in this study and discuss ways in which clients and therapists make sense of these memories.

Memory – basic theory and research

A great deal of consensual knowledge regarding normal and abnormal functioning of memory has developed from a long history of memory research, although significant controversies and many mysteries remain. Various theories have evolved regarding different types of memory processing. One common distinction is between the notion of short-term versus long-term memory, dating back to the work of William James in 1890. James noted the extent to which immediate sensations quickly evaporate and are then unavailable for recall. From this it is accepted that the human mind is incapable of registering and retaining all that it perceives and that long-term memory of most ongoing sensation is not developed. Consequently, only a small proportion of what is experienced is available for later recall.

Much theoretical and experimental work has been undertaken to understand processes of remembering and forgetting. It is generally agreed that this is a multistage process involving mechanisms of attention, perception, encoding, storage and retrieval. Remembering involves registering and attributing meaning to an experience in relation to existing cognitive schematas (categories of prior experience). Memory is facilitated by rehearsal such as reflecting upon an experience and discussing it with others. Without rehearsal and meaning attribution it is more likely that an experience will be subject to the normal process of forgetting. This theory is important in the context of discussions of child abuse memories as, on this basis, the greater the significance of meaning ascribed to a perceived event of abuse, the more likely that it will be repeatedly thought about and remembered.

Memory processes differ in relation to varied developmental needs, tasks and challenges. Different processes are at work in: remembering how to ride a bike; being able to recall the name of your favourite (or most horrible) primary school teacher; and remembering a bank PIN number. Subcategories of memory functioning are known as:

- *procedural memory* which is concerned with learning and remembering the skills and habits of 'how' to do things (like learning language and how to ride a bike);
- *semantic memory* which involves the accumulation and remembering of general information and knowledge about the world;
- *autobiographical memory* (also often referred to as episodic/narrative/ declarative memory) which relates to memories of personal experiences throughout life.

In trying to understand the phenomenon of memories of childhood abuse, the autobiographical memory processes are of most significance. Over generations autobiographical memory functioning has attracted descriptive contemporary metaphors such as 'flashbulb' memories; memory systems related to filing cabinets; videotapes and computers. These ideas have influenced popular beliefs about how memory operates – particularly the common misconception that memory for events is preserved pristine and intact, subject to recall in pure and unadulterated form. Few memory scientists would endorse such notions. The prevailing research over many decades since the seminal work of Bartlett (1932) supports the view that human memory for autobiographical events is a process which involves an interplay of reproduction and reconstruction. Reconstruction is subject to many influences which promote fallibility and inaccuracy, especially regarding the details (more so than the core elements) of autobiographical events. A number of key encoding, storage and retrieval factors affect autobiographical memory functioning.

Normal forgetting

As previously noted, we forget a great deal more than we remember. It is impossible for human organisms to attend to, perceive, encode and process the millions of multidimensional experiences which constantly bombard us. Most experiences are forgotten. Salient experiences (either of a positive or negative nature) and experiences which are repeated are more likely to be remembered. Most memories will decay over time, especially in relation to the accuracy of peripheral details (and sometimes significant components) of events and experiences.

Infantile amnesia

The developmental process of brain maturation (particularly the hippocampus) results in the vast majority of people not being able genuinely to remember any autobiographical event before the age of approximately two to three years. The age of offset of infantile amnesia remains debatable and some researchers suggest that three or even four years of age is more common. There is almost unanimous consensus among cognitive memory researchers that no experience can be genuinely and accurately remembered prior to the first birthday.

One study of normal events, for example, demonstrated that very few people remember anything about the birth of a sibling if they were less than four years old at the time (Sheingold and Tenney 1982). This does not mean that people do not sincerely believe that they can remember experiences in the first year of life. However, such 'memories' are likely to be autobiographical reconstructions derived from stories to which the person has been exposed while growing up, rather than actual memory.

Source monitoring confusion

Beyond the period of infantile amnesia it can be difficult to discriminate between historical events as they happened and subsequent memories, reconstructions and assimilation of stories which have been told about such events. Also, with regard to similar events that have been repeatedly experienced, it is common for a generic memory of the 'type' or 'schema' of experience to develop, which results in a reduced ability to discriminate between recollections and reconstructions of specific events and details. This often produces confusion about specific details of individual events due to interference from the many other similar events experienced.

Motivated forgetting

Active attempts to forget information can lead to reduced conscious awareness of that information, a process also referred to as 'directed forgetting'. This involves a deliberate psychological act of disavowal – literally putting memory of an event 'out of mind' (Cohler 1994). This differs from the popular notion of repression as a disavowed memory would be available for recall (if this choice was made), whereas a truly 'repressed' memory would not. This is an important distinction as will be seen later in this chapter in the discussion of repression, dissociation and the research relating to base rates of 'recovered' memories of sexual abuse.

The effect of mood

Research indicates that mood states have a significant impact on memory functioning. For example, mood affects concentration, which in turn affects processing of memories. Depression often results in a predominant awareness of negative historical experiences and a disproportionate lack of recall of positive experiences. Mood states also affect the rehearsal and consolidation of memories in that people tend to spend more time ruminating over emotionally significant events. Such rehearsal is likely to mitigate against forgetting negatively construed experiences. The ways in which memories are reinterpreted (either positively or negatively) are also influenced by mood states. These reinterpretations can serve as cues for the retrieval of further associated memories.

State-dependent memories

It has long been known that the likelihood of retrieving a memory is enhanced when a person is in a similar state (for example, place or emotion) to the circumstances of the original event (Tulving and Thompson 1973). This principle is known as 'encoding specificity'. The similarity of context provides the necessary cueing to increase the likelihood that associated material is recalled.

Organic and psychiatric conditions

A great deal of research has been undertaken regarding the normal and abnormal neurophysiological functioning of the brain with respect to memory. Memory impairment is a feature of many psychiatric conditions including depression, alcoholism, addictions, epilepsy, fugues and degenerative conditions (Kopelman 1997).

Suggestibility effects

Information received following an event (post-event suggestion) can strongly influence memories about events, especially regarding peripheral details. The impact of suggestibility is heightened by the following factors:

- increased passage of time between the event and the suggestion;
- the perceived authority/status of the source of the misleading information;
- the plausibility of the suggestion;
- repetition of the suggestion;
- high hypnotizability of the 'rememberer' (for example, proneness to fantasy, willingness to suspend critical judgement and to accept logical incongruities);
- use of deliberately suggestive techniques (such as hypnosis, sodium amytal injections, directed reading and guided imagery).

These factors are well-known influences on general remembering and forgetting of personal experiences and information. We will now consider the argument and evidence which proposes that special memory processes exist in relation to the processing of traumatic experiences.

The impact of trauma on memories

There is a long psychosocial history dating back to Freud and Janet at the end of the nineteenth century which suggests that there is something inherently different about traumatic memories in general, and child sexual abuse memories in particular, which makes them susceptible to becoming unavailable to a person's conscious awareness for long periods of time. However, the dominant view from research holds that the most common reaction to traumatic events is one of over-intrusive recollections, rather than absence of recollection (Lindsay and Read 1995).

Notable exceptions to this view are expressed by Terr (1991), Freyd (1996) and van der Kolk (1994). Terr claimed that multiple experiences of sexual abuse are more likely to become totally placed outside conscious awareness than single experiences (Terr 1991). This theory has been criticized on the grounds that it is unusual for victims of other traumas (for example, combat, concentration camps, torture or rape) to report extended periods of total amnesia for such experiences with recall at a much later time in life. Freyd hypothesized that memories of sexual abuse which culminate in betrayal by the abuser and other family members ('betrayal trauma') are particularly prone to be lost. Van der Kolk (1994) and colleagues have argued that there exists a separate memory processing system for traumatic memories (so-called 'body memories') which bypass normal memory functioning.

In opposition to these theories, strong voices within the discipline of experimental cognitive psychology insist that the normal processes of memory and normal forgetting are sufficient to explain 'forgotten' episodes of trauma (Ceci and Loftus 1994; Lindsay and Read 1995; Loftus 1993; Loftus et al. 1994a).

Because of the prominence and impact on psychotherapy practice of theories which conceptualize trauma as invoking alternate memory processing procedures, we will now consider these in more detail. There are two groups of theories: those involving psychological concepts (for example, repression and dissociation) and those which stem from psycho-biological research (for example, PTSD).

Psychological theories

REPRESSION The notion that awareness of unbearable instincts or traumatic experiences can be blocked out by being placed in an uncon-scious compartment of the mind via a mechanism of 'repression' has had enormous influence on psychotherapy. The belief that extensive sexual abuse can result in massive repression, and that 'repressed' memories need to be 'recovered' as part of the process of healing and 'recovery', is both influential and controversial.

The term 'repression' causes much confusion as it is understood (and misunderstood) in different ways. The original Freudian concept was that this mechanism is involuntary and (while continuing to exert an unconscious influence on thoughts, feelings and behaviour) repressed material can never, by definition, become conscious. Another view is that 'repressed' material can become available via psychoanalytic techniques and therefore the influence of such material can be diminished (Cohler 1994).

Debates about the mechanism and function of 'repression' are best understood in the social–historical and personal contexts of Freud's original formulation of the theory. A number of psychosocial historians (Crews 1995; Webster 1995) have presented powerful critiques of the speculative, unscientific and allegedly somewhat fraudulent processes by which Freud developed, revised and established his original psycho-analytic theories. Critics quote from Freud's own writing (particularly his illuminating private correspondence) to argue that the small sample of patients from which the 'seduction theory' was derived were highly unlikely to have spontaneously 'disclosed' histories of sexual abuse in psychoanalytic sessions in the way that he reported. Instead, in accord-ance with his theoretical preconception, Freud inculcated such beliefs in his vulnerable female patients despite their protestations (Bowers and Farvolden 1996; Crews 1995; Powell and Boer 1994; Webster 1995). This is a major revision to the influential theory propounded by Masson (1985) and Miller (1983) that Freud had initially uncovered the 'truth' about the childhood sexual abuse origins of adult hysteria (the 'seduction theory'), but recoiled from the social implications of his discovery, substituting the fantasy wish fulfilment ('Oedipal' theory) alternative.

Following the conclusion of Holmes (1990) that fifty years of empirical research have failed to demonstrate the existence of a process of repression, many have argued that the concept should be abandoned altogether. However, because a robustly reported clinical phenomenon cannot be demonstrated in a laboratory, this does not mean that all accounts should necessarily be dismissed as being erroneous or fantasy. Though it does imply caution about the interpretation of such experi-ences in situations where the interests of others could be compromised, for example, legal proceedings. As with other sensitive and subjective areas of human experiencing, absence of proof is not proof of absence.

Subsequent to the review by Holmes (1990), Brewin (1997) has de-scribed the extent of memory research on active inhibitory processes in remembering (which is equivalent to some definitions of repression). From this, Brewin (1997) contends that there may be rather more empirical confirmation of repression from laboratories than is evident in the oft-quoted conclusion of Holmes (1990).

DISSOCIATION   Dissociation is a concept with a historical pedigree equal to the psychoanalytic notion of repression. This dates back to Janet's description at the end of the last century of a process of mental splitting (dual consciousness) which shields the personality from intense distress (Janet 1889). This theory holds that traumatic events which threaten to overwhelm the personality cause the mind to divide, result-ing in one 'part' holding the memory which is not conscious to the other 'part'.

One commonly held distinction between repression and dissociation is that the former involves a motivated defensive act which places a normally encoded memory of a traumatic event out of conscious aware-ness – a normally formed memory becomes unavailable. Theories of dissociation hold that when traumatic events are intensely threatening to the integrity of the personality, they are not processed in the same way as other memories (Bowman and Mertz 1996; Terr 1994; van der Kolk 1994).

Instead, the biological impact of extreme stress results in a failure of encoding of the experience – a memory is not formed in a normal way and remains fragmented. Unlike repression, which can be viewed as a failure of retrieval, dissociation involves a failure of encoding.

Some clinicians and researchers have proposed that separate 'somatic' (body) memory systems operate to process memories of trauma (van der Kolk and Fisler 1995; van der Kolk and van der Hart 1991). Unlike the constructive–reconstructive nature of post infantile amnesia auto-biographical memory processing, it is suggested that traumatic memories comprised of fragmented 'flashbulb' visual images and physical sensations are stored out of conscious awareness in relatively 'pure' form as sensorimotor memories. Retrieval of such memories is often spontaneously and unexpectedly cued, taking the form of physical sensations, visual images (often described as 'flashbacks') and a sense of re-experiencing the traumatic event.

While these experiences are often described, researchers continue to disagree about the existence of a separate processing system for traumatic memories and the veracity of memories which are recovered in this way (Conway 1997; Pezdek and Banks 1996).

Although major theoretical and diagnostic difficulties remain, the category of dissociative disorders has gained a stronger empirical foothold than repression. It has been adopted by mainstream psychiatry and is encapsulated in the official nomenclature of the American Psychiatric Association, the *Diagnostic and Statistical Manual of Mental Disorders* – the psychiatrists' 'Burgundy Bible' (APA 1994). Dissociation is currently defined as a 'disruption in the usually integrated functions of consciousness, memory, identity, or perception of the environment' (APA 1994: 477).

In the DSM-IV (1994) there are five specified dissociative disorders:

- *Dissociative Amnesia* is characterized by an inability to recall personal information, usually of a traumatic or stressful nature, that is too extensive to be explained by ordinary forgetfulness.
- *Dissociative Fugue* is characterized by sudden, unexpected travel away from home or one's customary place of work, accompanied by an inability to recall one's past and confusion about personal identity or the assumption of a new identity.
- *Dissociative Identity Disorder* (formerly Multiple Personality Disorder) is characterized by the presence of two or more distinct identities or personality states that recurrently take control of the individual's behaviour accompanied by an inability to recall important personal information that is too extensive to be explained by ordinary forgetfulness.
- *Depersonalization Disorder* is characterized by a persistent or recurrent feeling of being detached from one's mental processes or body that is accompanied by intact reality testing.
- *Dissociative Disorder Not Otherwise Specified (DDNOS)* is included for coding disorders in which the predominant feature is a dissociative symptom, but

that do not meet the criteria for any specific Dissociative Disorder. (APA 1994: 477)

In the DSM-IV each of these conditions is explicated in much more detail under headings relating to: Diagnostic Features; Associated Features and Disorders; Specific Cultural Features; Prevalence; Course; Differential Diagnosis. They are not, therefore, terms to be used casually or ascribed to clients by therapists who do not have appropriate diagnostic training.

It is a formidable challenge to generate agreed, valid, reliable and culturally sensitive diagnostic criteria of mental disorders (Goldberg and Huxley 1992). The DSM is a culturally and temporally evolving nomenclature which is the product of ongoing subcommittees of the American Psychiatric Association and represents the best consensual views that these committees can reach about current categorization of psychiatric conditions. Over the past four decades subsequent editions of the DSM have reflected significant changes in the conceptualization of many psychiatric disorders. These changes are often indicative of changing social attitudes (for example, the removal of homosexuality as a psychiatric disorder).

The influence of cultural construction is also evident in relation to the controversial notion of 'Multiple Personality Disorder' (as defined in the DSM-111, 1980). The diagnostic criteria of MPD were significantly revised in DSM 111-R (1987) and the condition itself was relabelled in DSM-IV (1994) as 'Dissociative Identity Disorder' (DID). These changes illustrate ongoing disputes about the nature of MPD/DID, particularly in relation to the role of cultural influence. Social anthropologists (for example, Kenny 1986, 1997; Mulhern 1994, 1997) have studied the historical ebb and flow of MPD over the past century, concluding that fashionable and contagious responses to personal and social distress lie at the heart of the phenomenon.

This is a significant controversy in relation to adults who were abused as children, as there is a firm belief among therapists who are proponents of MPD/DID that this condition is invariably the consequence of severe childhood abuse. A sceptical view sees MPD/DID predominantly as an iatrogenic (therapist-created) condition whereby therapists indoctrinate highly suggestible and compliant clients into this belief system (Piper 1997).

Psychobiological theories

Psychobiological effects on memories of the experience of trauma have been studied extensively in relation to the DSM diagnosis of Post-traumatic Stress Disorder (PTSD). Ceci and Loftus (1994) note that there is a fundamental difference of opinion between researchers in relation to the impact of stress and trauma on memory. One view holds that experience of high levels of stress during an event consolidates memory for the event, while another argues that high stress levels can interfere with memory formation and subsequent retrieval.

Research highlights that PTSD is by no means an inevitable response to severe stress or trauma. This finding has provoked further study of the intervening factors which mediate the development (or not) of PTSD. A number of factors (pre, during and post trauma) are associated with increased likelihood of subsequent development of PTSD (van der Kolk 1994; Yehuda and Harvey 1997):

- severity of the trauma;
- existing psychiatric conditions;
- levels of social support;
- history of previous stress/trauma;
- subsequent exposure to stress/trauma;
- history of behavioural and psychological problems;
- a lower IQ.

In addition, research has identified specific and distinct neurochemical reactions in people who have experienced severe trauma who then develop PTSD compared with those who do not (Yehuda and Harvey 1997). This research highlights the mutual influence of biological factors on behaviour, of environment and experience on neurobiology – an interaction which has specific implications for the processing of memories of trauma (Conway 1977; O'Carroll 1997).

Prevalence of 'recovered' memories of childhood abuse

Base rate studies

It is important to place into perspective the proportions of people who were abused as children who experience recovered memories, as opposed to those who have always had continuous awareness of abuse. A number of studies have explored the baseline of recovered memories of abuse. However, there are major methodological challenges in such research and continuing differences of opinion about interpretation of data and conclusions that are drawn.

Pope and Hudson (1995), who are highly sceptical about the phenomenon of recovered memories, argued that strict methodological criteria are required in such studies. They wished to exclude self-reports and case studies from therapists which they saw as self-validating and anecdotal. Pope and Hudson (1995) proposed that scientifically acceptable studies of 'recovered memories' should include:

- explicit confirmatory evidence that the abuse had actually occurred;
- demonstrate that there had been a period of actual amnesia for the abuse that exceeds ordinary forgetting.

On this basis they stated that they had only been able to find four relevant studies: those by Briere and Conte (1993); Herman and Schatzow (1987); Loftus et al. (1994b); Williams (1994). These four studies will now be described briefly.

HERMAN AND SCHATZOW (1987)   The authors reported that in a clinical sample of fifty-three incest survivors, 28% had experienced a period of full amnesia for sexual abuse and 36% a period of partial amnesia: a combined figure of 64% for some degree of amnesia. This study is vulnerable to criticism as the participants had been clients in the abuse 'survivor' group run by Herman and Schatzow themselves. It is not clear what evidence was used to substantiate claims that 'recovered' abuse memories had been corroborated. Illustrative examples in the published report are composites of cases rather than actual case material.

BRIERE AND CONTE (1993)   The authors provided data from a clinical sample of 450 people who were receiving therapy related to childhood abuse. Some degree of amnesia for the abuse was recorded for 59% of the respondents. This study (and the criticisms of it) highlight how difficult it is to formulate simple and unambiguous questions in the conceptually complex area of asking about memory for forgetting a memory (Loftus 1993).

LOFTUS ET AL. (1994)   The authors surveyed a clinical sample of 105 women in a substance abuse treatment programme. Of the 52% who reported a history of child abuse, 19% recorded a period of time of total amnesia for the abuse; 12% a period of partial amnesia: a combined some degree of amnesia rate of 31%. The results of this study may have surprised the senior author, Elizabeth Loftus, who is an internationally prominent memory researcher and critic of the notion of 'recovered' memories of abuse (and the impact of therapy upon them).

From this study Loftus found herself in the position of having made a significant contribution to the growing research which attests that a psychological process exists whereby some abused people experience periods of time when they are unaware of such abuse, only to 'recover' the memories later in life. The published report reads as though Loftus was uncomfortable with this finding, tailing off into a final half-hearted statement that 'always remembering abuse is more common than forgetting it' (Loftus et al. 1994b: 82). Pope and Hudson (1995) also pass quickly over this study in their critical review.

WILLIAMS (1994)   This is the fourth study referred to by Pope and Hudson (1995). Responding to methodological criticisms about retrospective self-report studies, Williams interviewed 129 women for whom there were hospital records of sexual abuse when they were children.

These records constitute contemporaneous documentation of childhood sexual abuse (the index abuse), satisfying the first of Pope and Hudson's criteria. The interviews with the women, seventeen years on, explored what proportion would not remember the documented abuse.

Of the participants 38% did not report the index abuse to the research interviewer; 32% said that they had never been abused; 2% said that they had fabricated the allegations of abuse. Unfortunately, it is not possible to tell how many of the 38% who did not report their abuse in the research interview did not remember the abuse; or, for whatever reason, chose not to disclose this. Because of this uncertainty Pope and Hudson (1995) commented that it would be hazardous to conclude that the non-reporters were amnesic.

From their review of these four studies – emphasizing the methodological difficulties – Pope and Hudson concluded: 'present evidence is insufficient to permit the conclusion that individuals can "repress" memories of childhood sexual abuse' (1995: 126). These studies, however, were initial attempts to explore more systematically a controversial subjective phenomenon which previously had mostly been described only in case studies. While they suffer from acknowledged methodological problems, these problems do not necessarily mean that the findings are erroneous (Scheflin and Brown 1996).

In this complex subjective area of human experiencing it is exceedingly difficult to design perfect studies. Since Pope and Hudson's dismissive review, further studies have accumulated, utilizing different methodologies, which reinforce that some people consistently report periods of amnesia for abuse experiences. Scheflin and Brown (1996) reviewed twenty-five studies, noting that every one to some degree supported the existence of the phenomenon of dissociative amnesia for childhood abuse.

The twenty-five studies used divergent methodology (which ameliorates some of the methodological shortfalls of individual studies) and gathered data from five sources:

- community samples (Elliot 1997; Elliot and Briere 1995);
- clinical samples (Briere and Conte 1993; Cameron 1996; Herman and Schatzow 1987; Loftus et al. 1994b; Roe and Schwartz 1996);
- therapists' observations of clients (Andrews 1997; Andrews et al. 1995; Polusny and Follette 1996; Pope and Tabachnick 1995);
- therapists' personal experiences (Feldman-Summers and Pope 1994);
- longitudinal studies (Femina et al. 1990; Widom and Shephard 1996; Williams 1994).

Across these twenty-five studies reported rates for amnesic experiences were as follows:

- *Total amnesia*: ranged from 4.5% (Goodman et al. 1995) to 68% (Kluft 1995).
- *Partial amnesia*: ranged from 45% (Goodman et al. 1995) to 12% (Loftus et al. 1994b).
- *Combinations of total and partial amnesia*: ranged from 31% (Loftus et al. 1994b) to 77% (Roe and Schwartz 1996).

On this basis, Scheflin and Brown (1996) commented that the conclusions of Pope and Hudson (1995) were no longer warranted:

> Most scientific studies can be criticized for methodological weaknesses, but such design limitations should not obscure the fact that the data reported across *every one* of the 25 studies demonstrates that either partial or full abuse-specific amnesia, either for single incidents of childhood sexual abuse or across multiple incidents of childhood sexual abuse, is a robust finding . . . these studies, when placed together, meet the test of science – namely, that the finding holds up across quite a number of independent experiments, each with different samples, each assessing the target variables in a variety of different ways, and each arriving at a similar conclusion . . . the great preponderance of evidence strongly suggests that at least some subpopulation of sexually abused survivors experience a period of full or partial amnesia for the abuse. (Scheflin and Brown 1996: 178–9, original emphasis)

There is a growing general acceptance that the phenomenon exists whereby some people lose conscious awareness, for a significant period of time, of some or all memories of abuse to which they were subjected as children. It is also becoming generally accepted that some people experience the 'recovery' of such memories – and that the content of the 'recovered' memories may be true, false, or combinations of both. Significant disputes continue as to the extent of amnesic experiences, the mechanisms through which they occur and what constitutes acceptable corroborative evidence of the accuracy of recovered memories (Read and Lindsay 1997).

We will now reflect upon research that focuses on evaluating the veracity of 'recovered' memories of childhood abuse.

Corroboration studies

There is an important developing literature that addresses the question of to what extent self-reported recovered memories may be corroborated and what forms of corroboration can be considered to be reliable (Andrews 1997; Dalenberg 1996; Schooler 1994; Schooler et al. 1997). It is vitally important to improve ways of establishing to what extent the abuse content of 'recovered' memories is literally accurate. As with the base rate research, this is methodologically problematic. Given the inherent secret and often undiscovered nature of much sexual abuse, the absence of independent corroboration is by definition commonly part of the abuse context. On this basis it is not logical to argue that absence of corroboration implies that the memories are false. Also, to assume that recovered memories are inherently untrue in the absence of supporting external corroboration (Ofshe and Watters 1994; Wakefield and Underwager 1992) reflects an unjustified belief that these memories are of a different categorical form than general autobiographical memories. As Brewin and Andrews pointed out:

> There is a basic integrity to autobiographical memory, even though there may be individual errors and biases of a minor nature. No data suggest that this integrity does not extend to reports of childhood trauma . . . Given our knowledge of the integrity of autobiographical memory referred to above, and of the various strengths and weaknesses of experimental data, we may question why recovered memories have to be assumed to be false and proven to be true. It would seem strange to assume that ordinary memories were false unless proven otherwise, and there is no statement of the grounds on which recovered memories are believed to be different from ordinary memories. (Brewin and Andrews 1997: 196–7)

A number of preliminary studies have begun to explore the possibility of obtaining some form of corroboration (or not) regarding the accuracy of 'recovered' memories of child abuse. In addition to two detailed case studies involving the corroboration of recovered traumatic memories (Bendiksen 1996; Davies and Robertson 1996), the reported studies in this area are:

- Feldman-Summers and Pope (1994) who surveyed a sample of US psychologists regarding their personal abuse memory experiences.
- Andrews (1997) who surveyed a sample of UK psychologists regarding their patients' abuse/trauma memory experiences.
- Schooler (1994) and Schooler et al. (1997) who analysed corroborative material in four case studies.
- Dalenberg (1996) who investigated the accuracy of abuse-memories recovered in therapy.

We will now consider briefly the relevant features and conclusions from these four studies.

FELDMAN-SUMMERS AND POPE (1994) The authors surveyed a national (USA) sample of 330 psychologists (185 female, 145 male). Postal questionnaires asked whether respondents had been abused as children and, if so, whether they had ever forgotten some or all of the abuse. Of the sample 24% (79 people) reported that they had been sexually or physically abused as children. Of these, 40% (32 people) responded that they had experienced a period of partial or complete amnesia for this; and 47% (15 people) reported that they had obtained some form of corroboration of the abuse. The most commonly reported forms of corroboration were: confirmation from somebody else who knew about the abuse (5 cases); someone else reporting abuse by the same perpetrator (5 cases); and the abuser acknowledging some or all of the abuse (5 cases).

ANDREWS (1997)   The author studied a sample of 100 psychologists in the UK who reported having recently worked with clients who had recovered memories of child sexual abuse or other trauma, either during or prior to therapy. The 100 therapists described 671 clients with recovered memories (47% involved sexual abuse; 39% other forms of trauma; 14% combinations of both). Therapists' views on the experiences of 217 of these clients were elicited in detailed telephone interviews. These focused on the abuse and other trauma memory phenomena described in therapy by the clients and the extent and ways in which the memories could be corroborated. Ratings were made by the researchers from the comments of the therapists in the interviews as to the degree of amnesia experienced by the clients prior to recovery of the memories. On this basis, 56% of recovered memories were classified as being from total amnesia, and 34% from a state of partial amnesia.

A similar rating process was used to assess degrees of corroboration for the recovered memories. Some form of corroboration was reported in 40% of the cases (86 clients). The most common forms of corroboration were: 'client reported that someone else had also claimed abuse by the same person' (20% – 43 clients); and 'someone else confirmed that the traumatic event had occurred' (17% – 37 clients). Official confirmatory records were reported in 8% of cases (17 clients); and confessions by an abuser in 6% (13 clients). In seven cases the therapist reported that he/she had seen corroborative evidence.

The reported corroboration rate of 40% is in line with the findings of Feldman-Summers and Pope (1994) obtained directly from an abused sample. The corroboration figures must, however, be viewed with some caution. They stem from a chain involving: researchers' ratings – of therapists' records – of clients' self-reports. Also, corroboration itself is a concept about which there is no general agreement regarding adequate and acceptable criteria. While the few reported cases of 'confession by the abuser' may be considered to be a conclusive indicator of corroboration, some critics would nevertheless point to the possibility of false confessions (Ofshe 1989). The criterion reported by Feldman-Summers and Pope (1994) and Andrews (1997) of: 'someone else claimed abuse by the same person' raises even greater potential challenge as to its corroborative validity, bearing in mind the undoubted possibilities of fabrication and collusive or coincidental false allegations.

While Feldman-Summers and Pope (1994) and Andrews (1997) have provided important sensitizing information about the extent of potential corroboration, studies by Schooler and Dalenberg have begun to examine in more detail examples of reported corroboration, including interviews with significant others in the lives of the person with the recovered memory.

SCHOOLER (1994), SCHOOLER ET AL. (1997) The authors described the methodological challenges in corroboration research in that studies ideally need to be able to demonstrate:

- the reality of the forgotten event;
- the reality of the forgetting;
- the reality of the remembering.

Four case studies are presented which illustrate phenomena associated with reports of recovered abuse memories where there is some form of corroboration. In all four cases, Schooler noted that it was not possible to obtain 'absolutely incontrovertible' corroboration. However, the researchers felt that they had found, in each case, 'reasonably compelling independent sources of support that some type of abuse did occur' (Schooler et al. 1997: 383).

In all four cases, memory recovery was characterized by vivid memories suddenly and unexpectedly coming out of nowhere, accompanied by a rush of emotion – phenomena similar to that described in PTSD 'flashbacks' and moments of cognitive insight. A second important factor is that all four people reported a deep sense of shame about their abuse experiences. Schooler speculates that the experience of intense shame may precipitate self-defence mechanisms which enhance memory distortions and forgetting. A third significant factor was that two people appeared to have forgotten that they had discussed the (recovered memory) events with others – during a time when they believed that they had forgotten the events. This is a potentially significant process whereby people may underestimate the extent to which they had previously been aware of events that they now consider they had forgotten. The memory error is forgetting that they had actually known – as evidenced by not remembering that they had told other people in the past about the events.

DALENBERG (1996, 1997) The author studied the extent to which corroboration could be obtained in relation to the recovered abuse memories of seventeen of her ex-psychotherapy patients. These patients fitted the following criteria:

- They had always been aware of some of their abuse (sexual or physical) by their fathers.
- In therapy they had recovered a 'substantial percentage' of further memories.
- They were not involved in the 'survivor' self-help movement.
- Their parents were not connected with the False Memory Syndrome Foundation.

- Their fathers (and significant others) agreed to be interviewed in relation to the abuse memories.

As all of the therapy sessions had been taperecorded, it was possible to analyse transcripts to identify the process of recovery of abuse memories as this occurred in therapy sessions. Of all the memories documented from the therapy transcripts, it was possible to obtain confirming or disconfirming evidence for approximately 70% of them. There was no difference in confirmed accuracy between the continuous and recovered memories and overall approximately 75% of the total memories were accurate.

A memory was regarded as confirmed if the father confessed to the event during the research interview; an eyewitness confirmed knowledge of the event during an interview; or if there was medical or photographic evidence. Of the seventeen cases, Dalenberg found confirming evidence in ten of them (seven confessions, two medical evidence, one eyewitness sibling). In five other cases corroborative evidence was weaker and could only be considered to be supportive or circumstantial. In the remaining two cases the accuracy of the abuse memory was positively disconfirmed.

This study is important both in respect of its conclusions and the methodology employed (especially the use of interviews with alleged abusers and eyewitnesses) to search for the presence of confirming or disconfirming evidence. It provides supportive evidence for the existence of 'true' and 'false' recovered memories of abuse.

Studies of therapists' attitudes regarding abuse memories

Led by concerns that the suggestive influence of therapists could create 'false memories' of abuse, attempts have been made to establish the nature of therapists' beliefs and practices regarding traumatic amnesia and 'memory recovery' techniques. The most pertinent studies are those by the British Psychological Society (1995), Poole et al. (1995), Polusny and Follette (1996) and Yapko (1993). We will now consider some key findings and discussion points from these studies.

The earliest study was conducted by Yapko (1993) who obtained questionnaire data from 869 psychotherapists in the USA that attended a range of psychotherapy (hypnosis and family therapy) conferences. Yapko (a practising hypnotherapist himself) was interested in the use (and misuse) of hypnosis and therapists' beliefs about the accuracy of memories 'recovered' by hypnosis. Yapko reported serious errors in beliefs about memory in a significant proportion of his respondents. For example, of the 869 therapist participants:

- Eighteen per cent believed that 'people cannot lie when in hypnosis'.

- Forty-seven per cent believed that 'psychotherapists can have greater faith in details of a traumatic event when obtained hypnotically than otherwise'.
- Thirty-one per cent believed that 'when someone has a memory of a trauma while in hypnosis, it objectively must actually have occurred'.
- Fifty-four per cent believed that 'hypnosis can be used to recover memories of actual events as far back as birth'.
- Twenty-eight per cent believed that 'hypnosis can be used to recover accurate memories of past lives'.

Yapko stressed that such views are substantially ill-founded and are not compatible with established research. However, it is interesting that 79% of the therapists also agreed that 'it is possible to suggest false memories to someone who then incorporates them as true memories' – a view which Yapko endorses. While these respondents were significantly biased in favour of a convenience sample of psychotherapists with hypnotherapy and family therapy orientations (which, of course, limits the generalizability of the findings across psychotherapy), this research nevertheless signals concerns about therapists' misconceptions which have significant implications for practice and training.

Poole et al. (1995) undertook national questionnaire surveys in the USA and UK of randomly sampled clinical psychologists to explore what proportion used what they classified as 'memory recovery' techniques. They characterized such techniques as: 'hypnosis, guided imagery, "bibliography" with popular books, "journalling" exercises, interpretations of "body memories" ' (p. 427). Of a total of 202 respondents, 71% reported using at least one such technique to assist clients to remember childhood sexual abuse; and 25% reported a combined set of beliefs and therapeutic practices which led the authors to classify them as 'memory focused' therapists.

Unfortunately, it is not clear from the published paper whether the use of such techniques, as reported, covered work across the whole spectrum of abuse memories. This is important as these techniques could be used with clients who have continuous memories (for example, to promote emotional connection); clients who have partial memories (to promote greater clarity); and with clients who have no recall at all. Pope (1996) also noted that many of the activities characterized by Poole et al. (1995) as 'memory recovery' techniques are also used by some therapists for purposes other than memory recovery. However, notwithstanding these observations, the findings of Poole et al. (1995) support the warning of Lindsay and Read (1994, 1995) that while only a small proportion of therapists may be inappropriately using 'memory recovery therapies', this could still result overall in significant harm being caused to clients and their families on a 'non-trivial' scale.

The research of Poole et al. (1995) has been used (perhaps in ways the authors never envisaged and may not support) in publications by 'False Memory' pressure groups and their supporters. For example, Pendergrast (1995: 491) transformed the more circumspect conclusions of the authors into: '25% of doctoral level therapists constitute True Believers' – a 'True Believer' being the contemptuous term reserved for those who do not subscribe to 'False Memory Syndrome' doctrine without question.

In fact, the conclusions of Poole et al. (1995) reflected a more complex picture:

> In our sample, only a minority of clinicians indicated a strong focus on helping clients recover suspected memories of CSA. However, this translates into a large number of practitioners . . . our results are inconsistent with the idea that a large percentage of psychotherapists have a single-minded focus on getting their clients to remember CSA. (Poole et al. 1995: 8, 435)

Like Yapko (1993), the authors also noted that a significant majority (91%) of practitioners were highly alert to the possibility that people can erroneously come to believe that they have been sexually abused. From this they made the prescient observation: 'We believe that the therapeutic community is in a state of transition, in which enthusiasm for memory recovery techniques is giving way to concerns about their potentially suggestive nature' (Poole et al. 1995: 435).

In the British Psychological Society (1995) study, a total of 4,005 questionnaires were sent out to clinical and counselling psychology members of the society. Of these, 27% were returned, which reduced to a sample of 810 respondents who met the inclusion criteria – that they worked with adult clients over the age of 18 (psychotic disorders excluded). Results included the following:

- Approximately one-third (31%) of practitioners reported that they knew of clients who had experienced the recovery of abuse memories prior to any therapy.
- Fifty-eight per cent had experienced clients recovering further memories of abuse while in therapy.
- Twenty-three per cent had experienced clients recovering memories of abuse for the first time while in therapy with them.

Therapists' beliefs in the accuracy of such memories were as follows:

- Fifty-three per cent – sometimes accurate.
- Thirty-eight per cent – usually accurate.
- Six per cent – always accurate.
- Three per cent – never accurate.

Two-thirds of the therapists believed that false memories of abuse were possible (one in seven of the therapists had experienced this with clients); and one-third did not believe that false memories of abuse occurred.

Like the studies of Yapko (1993) and Poole et al. (1995) in the USA, these findings of the only British exploration of the question so far do not give support to claims that therapists (at least clinical psychologists) are unaware of the potential for erroneous recollections of childhood abuse. However, whether a figure of two-thirds believing in the possibility of false memories would have been recorded prior to the topical controversy must be open to doubt and may indicate the effectiveness of the 'False Memory' pressure group campaign. Also, it is not clear, given that the exploration was restricted to its own members, to what extent the views of the many other groups of therapists would replicate these findings. Comparative studies on this issue would be very valuable.

False Memory Syndrome

In the USA an important legal effect stemmed from the topical belief in high prevalence of 'repressed' memories of child abuse. Abuse 'survivors' successfully lobbied for statutes of limitations (the time period after an event following which it is normally not allowable to press criminal charges or sue for compensation) to be amended so that litigation could be brought against alleged abusers within a period of time following the remembering of abuse. High profile cases resulted and alleged abusers were jailed and financially penalized on the basis of 'recovered memory' testimony of 'survivors' and supportive expert witnesses. Many of these cases resulted in bitter court hearings with opposing experts stacked up on each side engaged in hostile and polarized 'memory wars'.

In response to the dramatic increase in the late 1980s and early 1990s of adults who accused their parents of childhood sexual abuse (on the basis of 'recovered' memories), a coalition of people who considered themselves to be falsely accused rapidly developed. This was led by the False Memory Syndrome Foundation (FMSF), which was established in the USA in 1992. The UK equivalent, the British False Memory Society (BFMS), was established in 1993. The FMSF was founded by two parents who felt aggrieved that their adult daughter had severed contact with them on the basis of recently acquired beliefs that she had been sexually abused as a child. The parents insisted that this was not so and that her erroneous beliefs were the consequence of her participation in 'memory recovery' therapy.

The sad and bitter story of this family became public knowledge as the mother published her account, at first anonymously as 'Jane Doe' in the journal *Issues in Child Abuse Accusations* (1991); and then personally in the *FMSF Newsletter* (P. Freyd 1992). By publicly portraying her as having 'False Memory Syndrome', the daughter (a professor of psychology) was effectively 'outed'. She responded with her own public account of abuse and other problems within her family (J. Freyd 1992), a perspective which was given support by her paternal uncle in a public letter.

The existence of such fervently held oppositional beliefs about family history and the tone of the exchanges illustrate vividly the intensity of complex feelings (anger, injustice, loss and despair) which are experienced on both sides. These feelings have fuelled a high profile media, scientific, legal and political controversy.

One of the first strategic moves of the founders of the FMSF was to establish a Scientific and Professional Advisory Board comprised of prominent and distinguished academics in the fields of psychology, psychiatry, sociology and social anthropology. The board provided a backdrop of scientific prestige against which the raw emotion of the 'falsely accused' parents was expressed for maximum public influence. A second early FMSF development via the Scientific Board was to delineate 'False Memory Syndrome':

> A condition in which a person's identity and interpersonal relationships are centred around a memory of traumatic experience which is objectively false but in which the person strongly believes. Note that the syndrome is not characterized by false memories as such. We all have memories that are inaccurate. Rather, the syndrome may be diagnosed when the memory is so deeply ingrained that it orients the individual's entire personality and lifestyle, in turn disrupting all sorts of other adaptive behaviours. The analogy to personality disorder is intentional. False Memory Syndrome is especially destructive because the person assiduously avoids confrontation with any evidence that might challenge the memory. Thus it takes on a life of its own, encapsulated, and resistant to correction. The person may become so focused on the memory that he or she may be effectively distracted from coping with the real problems in his or her life. (Kihlstrom 1994: 2)

While few would now dispute that a phenomenon of this sort can and does occur (and not only in relation to false beliefs about childhood abuse), others added dramatic emphasis:

> Accusations of child sexual abuse based on repressed memories that are decade delayed discoveries are running rampant – an epidemic is emerging. This is the mental health crisis of the decade – if not of the century! (Goldstein and Farmer 1992: 231)

The passion (and exaggeration) of such claims may be understandable given the personal pain of people directly affected. However, the Scientific and Advisory Board of the FMSF did not apply the same degree of rigorous scrutiny to material produced on behalf of the FMSF as it did to its primary target – the therapeutic community. This double standard was outlined in detail by Kenneth Pope in 1996 in an American Psychological Association award address. In a detailed critique of the theoretical and scientific fallibility of 'False Memory Syndrome', Pope pointed out the fundamental inappropriateness of portraying this reported phenomenon as a 'syndrome'. Syndrome status can only result from research which requires:

> Independent examination of the primary data and methodology used to establish the validity and reliability of a new psychological diagnosis, prior to its application to large numbers of people. (Pope 1996: 962)

The concept of 'False Memory Syndrome' was not derived from any research of this nature. A number of other significant points are raised by Pope which question the validity of FMS:

● How was it determined by those who formulated this 'syndrome' that in the cases upon which the research was based, the memories concerned were 'objectively false'?
● Having (somehow) determined that the memories were 'objectively false', how was it determined that they 'orient the individuals entire personality and lifestyle'?

These questions are particularly pertinent as cases of the 'syndrome' are invariably declared without the subject ever having contact with the person making this diagnosis. For any professional to make what amounts to a psychiatric or psychological diagnosis of someone without direct evaluation of the person concerned constitutes unethical professional practice.

Important exceptions to third-hand diagnoses are provided by the increasing number of first-hand reports of 'retractors'. These are people who state that they came to experience False Memory Syndrome (usually as a result of the influence of therapy), but who now believe that the memories were false, that they were not abused and that the false allegations have caused tremendous harm to themselves and their families. Detailed case examples of this growing phenomenon are given by Pendergrast (1995) and others appear in each edition of the *FMSF Newsletter*. These cases pose a number of important questions:

● To what extent are 'retractors' escapees from highly damaging therapy?
● To what extent can casualties of such therapy and their families reconcile?
● To what extent are 'retractors' people who have succumbed to family pressures to recant true accounts of abuse?
● What does future life hold in store for people in these circumstances?

There is an urgent need for research in these areas.

Membership of the FMSF and BFMS (and other similar organizations in Canada, New Zealand and the Netherlands) grew rapidly and provided much-needed information and support for distraught parents who believed that their children had been lost and their lives destroyed by the influence of 'memory recovery' therapy. New cases coming to the attention of such organizations peaked in 1994–5 and have decreased steadily subsequently. This suggests that the therapeutic community in general (although not entirely) has responded to the criticisms of cognitive memory researchers and the lobbying of the False Memory societies.

In fact these challenges to forms of therapy (usually characterized as 'recovered memory therapy' or variations on this) led by some of the well-known cognitive psychology researchers (Ceci and Loftus 1994; Lindsay and Read 1994, 1995; Loftus 1993; Neisser 1993; Weiskrantz 1995); and the highly effective pressure of the False Memory societies jolted the therapeutic community in the mid-1990s. There is increasing acceptance within this community (for example, Briere 1997; Courtois 1997) that certain forms (but by no means all) of therapy practised during the 1980s and 1990s were implicated in the generation of false beliefs and false memories of abuse. (There is ongoing concern that a similar damaging 'therapeutic' process is continuing in relation to many clients who are considered by therapists to have multiple personalities.)

As therapeutic approaches in this area are being corrected, a common ground between clinicians and memory researchers is emerging. Many influential cognitive memory researchers (who have previously expressed considerable scepticism) are coming to accept that the functioning of autobiographical memory systems (by mechanisms which remain uncertain) sometimes excludes memories of abuse and trauma from conscious awareness, only to be remembered/recovered in a reasonably accurate form at a later stage of life (Ceci and Loftus 1994; Lindsay and Briere 1977; Read and Lindsay 1997; Schooler et al. 1997).

There is also increasing agreement that other people (perhaps heavily influenced by child abuse material and/or forms of psychotherapy) may develop beliefs that a personal history of child abuse underlies their unhappiness – and that 'pseudo-memories' of abuse can emerge in accord with this new belief system. It is important in consideration of the 'False Memory Syndrome' controversy that the two separate phenomena of 'recovered' memories of abuse, as opposed to the adoption of false beliefs of abuse, are not confused or conflated. There is a significant difference between processes whereby new memories promote belief, as opposed to new beliefs promoting memories.

The complex theoretical and research material in this chapter provides the context for understanding the experiences of child abuse memories reported by participants in this study. In the next chapter we look in some detail at ways in which therapy clients describe their memories of abuse; and ways in which clients and therapists attempt to understand their accuracy and significance.

10

Experiences of Memories of Childhood Abuse

From the total number of fifty-three interviews in the study as a whole, thirty-seven included discussion of memories of abuse. These included twenty-five client and twelve therapist perspectives of abuse memory phenomenon. From these descriptions six types of memory experiences can be distilled:

1 *Continuous abuse memories*: the abuse has always been known about and the person has always interpreted the events as abuse.
2 *Disowned abuse memories*: knowledge of abuse is 'put out of mind' and not thought about on a daily basis for long periods of time.
3 *Partial abuse memories*: certain abuse events have always been remembered, but in adult life further unexpected and surprising incidents of abuse memories are remembered.
4 *Recovered abuse memories*: following complete non-awareness of abuse, in adult life unexpected incidents of abuse are remembered.
5 *Inaccurate abuse memories*: incidents of abuse are 'remembered', some of which are subsequently believed to be inaccurate in significant ways.
6 *False abuse memories*: new beliefs about a history of abuse develop that are illustrated by new 'memories' of abuse which are subsequently believed not to be true.

Table 10.1 shows the number of participants experiencing each of these six types of abuse memories. The sample is reduced to thirty-six as insufficient information was obtained from one participant to allocate the experiences described into a type. The overall total of abuse memory experiences is greater than thirty-six (and percentages greater than 100%) as five people's abuse memory experiences fell into different types according to the nature of the abuse and different abusers. For example, one person reported continuous memory for one incident of sexual abuse by a babysitter and recovered memories of sexual abuse by her natural mother and stepmother.

Table 10.1   *Abuse memory experiences by type*

Type of abuse memory experience	Numbers and percentage of participants reporting each type (N = 36)	
Continuous	9	(25%)
Disowned	16	(44.5%)
Partial	6	(16.5%)
Recovered	9	(25%)
Partially inaccurate	1	(2.5%)
False	1	(2.5%)

Looking at some of these types in combination it can be seen that:

- Almost 70% of this sample reported they had always had basic knowledge and continuous memory of their abuse (combination of types 1 and 2).
- Regardless of prior state of knowledge (that is, no previous knowledge or partial knowledge) of their abuse, nearly half of the participants (46.5%) reported that they have experienced the phenomenon of remembering new abuse memories.
- Almost one-third of participants (30%) reported that they had experienced unexpected memories of abuse from a state of having no prior knowledge or belief that they had been abused.
- One in six participants (16.5%) reported that they had remembered new memories of abuse from a state of prior partial knowledge.
- Two out of thirty-six respondents (5%) reported having experienced some form of inaccurate or false memory of abuse (one inaccurate and one false).

To illustrate these phenomena in more detail we will now turn again to material from the interview transcripts.

Six types of abuse memories

Continuous abuse memories

Abuse is described as always having been known about or remembered. The memories have always been interpreted as abuse. Nine of the thirty-six participants (25%) described this type of experience:

> I don't know how many times it happened but it happened quite frequently. I remember the kind of scenario, the room. I remember my bedroom. I remember the bathroom vividly, because it happened when I was in there. I remember it all so well. (Katie – 32)

> I'd always had conscious knowledge. Yes I had. And I'd intellectualized it. And I'd excused it. Because it was my father who abused me. And I'd literally researched into his life to see why he was the way he was. So in my mind, that

was all that mattered: 'OK. I've come to terms with it, and it wasn't affecting me and it didn't affect my life etc.' But it actually did. (Mary – 43)

If problems develop in later life for people in this category, they are likely to involve either or both: a delayed realization of the impact of the abuse; and emotionally intense re-experiencing of the events.

Disowned abuse memories

This is the experience where there is basic knowledge that abuse occurred but this awareness is described as having been deliberately 'put out of mind'. Sixteen of the thirty-six participants (44.5%) described having such experiences. The abuse history is not thought about at all, although such memories are likely to be available for recall as part of personal history. This does not mean that such people are happy, far from it. Participants describing this reaction were often deeply troubled and affected by a wide range of symptoms and problems (especially depression and relationship difficulties) which they had not associated with their abuse histories:

> Well, I'd always known that it had happened. It's not that I had completely blanked it out. But I'd also separated it so much from myself that it didn't invade my life. I mean, I didn't allow it to. Obviously it was affecting me, but I didn't ever allow it to come into my mind. (Eva – 57)

If problems develop in adult life, combinations of the following experiences occur: delayed realization of the impact of the abuse; retrospective reinterpretation of the events as abuse; and intensive emotional re-experiencing of the events. When disowned abuse memories do come to mind, this process is described more in terms of 'reconnecting' than 'remembering' and is often emotionally overwhelming. As noted in Chapter 6, these subsequent powerful emotional connections were often destabilizing factors that precipitated people into seeking psychotherapeutic help.

It is possible that some clinicians and researchers have conflated disowned memories with abuse memories recovered from a state of prior non-awareness, leading to overestimates of the prevalence of 'repressed' or 'dissociated' abuse memories.

Partial abuse memories

Certain abuse events are described as always having been known, but in adult life further unexpected and surprising abuse incidents are remembered. Six of the thirty-six participants (16.5%) described having such experiences:

> For me there's always been memories that I've had which just never left me. They are very clear. I knew they happened and they are concrete – I've never

doubted them. And then I started becoming aware that I was starting to get a lot of physical feelings, just very, very strong physical feelings. Feeling uncomfortable and feeling revulsion in my body and that started me thinking 'What's this all about?' But when I had a flashback, I knew. (Claire – 68)

I knew I'd had an unhappy childhood, but I didn't fully realize what it had done to me until much later. I think that's one of the worst aspects of it, that just when you think you might have dealt with something, you realize a lot more has happened. (Anna – 19)

Recovered abuse memories

Following complete non-awareness of abuse, in adult life unexpected and surprising Incidents of abuse are remembered. Nine of the thirty-six participants (25%) described having this experience:

It was horrendous actually. It happened very suddenly. Because I had been in ongoing therapy and, I think, it was the first year of my professional training. So I had, sort of, worked on several issues. And I was actually working on my sexuality which seemed to be very important to me. And I got some visual imagery which suggested danger: 'Don't look at this, don't investigate this.'

And that very quickly turned into a phallic symbol and it was like a cold shock really. And I just said to my therapist: 'I was abused – and it was my father.' And I knew in that instant that it was my father. And then I can only say that I went into trauma for a couple of weeks at least, it was horrific. My experience was of deep shock. Not the realization that I'd been sexually abused, but it was like my life was like a lie – who I'd thought I was, I wasn't. (Sarah – 10)

Inaccurate abuse memories

Incidents of abuse are remembered which are subsequently believed to be inaccurate in significant ways. One of the thirty-six participants (2.5%) described this experience. Carol reported over a period of four years, the spontaneous 'return' of extensive 'repressed' memories including sadistic sexual and physical abuse by both parents and siblings:

My parents – it turned out later on – were sadists. And I didn't know that you see. That's why it has taken me so long. Because I was sexually abused by my mother for ten years. But I was tortured by the whole family. And my father raped me, and my brother.

Over the first two years I didn't just get memories that were true. They were overlaid, unfortunately, with other things that didn't actually happen. And this was very confusing because I had a lot of memories of things that didn't happen. I got all these detailed memories of seeing him (father) being murdered which I spent weeks talking to (husband) about. Now this simply didn't happen. I didn't see anything – it's my mind trying to make sense of what happened. There were some really bizarre things that just didn't happen. It must have been my mind preparing me for what really happened, perhaps, or maybe it's your mind being terrified of what might happen. (Carol – 17)

Carol's initial reaction had been to believe strongly in the accuracy of all of her memories, as they seemed to be the 'missing information' which helped to make sense of the problems she had struggled with for a long time in her adult life. After a time, on this basis, she had confronted her parents and brother about the abuse which she had 'remembered' and had been met by firm denial and ostracism by the whole family. To her surprise, as the 'memories' continued to return, she found herself beginning to discriminate between events that she believed had happened and events which she became increasingly sceptical about. At the time of the research interview, she felt certain that the 'memories' which had returned had been an interwoven mixture of fact and fantasy.

False abuse memories

False memories and beliefs about abuse can temporarily develop which are subsequently believed not to be true. This was also a minor category in this study with only one participant (2.5%) describing this experience. Given the controversy surrounding the notion of 'False Memory Syndrome', it is important to understand what this phenomenon involves and to recognize that bad therapy can be heavily implicated in the genesis of these experiences. This is illustrated by the story of Amanda who described how she had initially sought therapeutic help with the desire to lose weight. She consulted a hypnotherapist who she felt had continually conjured up images and suggestions of abuse while Amanda was in a regressed hypnotic state. This culminated in a 'crescendo session' in which Amanda 'remembered' being sexually abused by her grandfather. She had then become totally preoccupied with beliefs and 'memories' of abuse to the point that:

> I was losing control and grip on reality – felt I was going insane.

The response of the hypnotherapist was reported as follows:

> She was really excited about it, like a missionary. She kept wanting to book me in for extra sessions at £12.50 a time. In a way I wanted to believe that I'd been abused. She was saying, 'I will give you a magic present of happiness if you believe me.' I lost control – I allowed it to happen with that woman. I allowed it to take place. I wanted to believe that I'd been abused. I was terrified of my grandfather dying. To believe that he'd abused me would stop me worrying about him dying. I don't think I will ever forgive myself for thinking those things about him. (Amanda – 67)

At the time of the interview Amanda remained extremely angry with the hypnotherapist whom she knew was still advertising her services in Yellow Pages. She still felt guilt-ridden about what she had believed about her grandfather and that she had told a number of people about the 'abuse'.

Phenomena of 'returning' memories

Remembering abuse is commonly described as involving combinations of dreams, somatic sensations, spontaneous regressive experiences and flashbacks. Dreams ranged from the vague, the symbolic, to the specific and presented phenomena which heralded a growing conscious awareness of childhood abuse:

> There was so much around in nightmare form of the abuse coming out that it was obvious that by this time what I needed to deal with. (Zoe – 11)

> The night before I had a dream and to my horror – this is not a fact – I dreamt that I was sexually abusing my daughter. And then I came down to the kitchen and it was just like, it was almost like the whole world had turned upside down. The whole kitchen kind of turned upside down. And it came to the front of my mind that I'd been sexually abused by my mother – and then the memories started and they haven't stopped for four years. (Carol – 17)

Sophia described the physical feelings that she experienced as part of the process of recovering further memories of abuse:

> There's a sort of precursor to remembering for me that is very difficult to describe. But I imagine it's similar to the way that some epileptics know before they're going to have a fit that there's a fit on the way – and I get a sense that there's a memory on the way. It's like a mild anxiety attack – a sort of heightened awareness of everything around me. And a need to get somewhere safe, a sense of trying to contain myself until I can allow it to happen.
>
> Sometimes it's a re-experiencing complete with all the feelings and the colours and smells and textures, and bodily sort of sensations. Other times it's really like watching it on a TV screen. Or sometimes, it feels like the memory sort of explodes in my mind's eye. (Sophia – 64)

Grace described a spontaneous regressive experience which presaged vague awareness of sexual abuse in addition to the physical abuse of which she had always been aware.

> *Grace*: I was dreaming quite prolifically and one particular dream I decided to work on my own. I did it in my room and I spontaneously regressed to a child. I knew that my father used to be quite heavy handed and we used to come in for a fair amount of good hidings. But what I went through in this spontaneous regression – I felt that the implication there for me was that there was more to it than just waiting to be smacked.
>
> *PD*: I'm interested in that experience – can you say a bit more about what actually happened in the regressive experience that made you think: 'Well, maybe there's more behind this?'
>
> *Grace*: Well, I remember I was sitting on my bed and I'd written the dream out and I was just looking at it. And it was actually a circular bed in the dream – so that was kind of odd, you know. I wasn't expecting anything unpleasant at all – except there were a couple of men bouncing up and down on the bed. So I tried the Gestalt exercise of being the bed. And then what

happened was that I had this overwhelming urge to get on the floor and I curled up like a baby. And then I just felt I could hear somebody coming – and that was very, very frightening. But I felt – as the sounds had got closer – I felt very much that I needed to protect my genital area more than anything else. And I just cried a lot and felt very fearful. And I was in quite a state for the rest of the day. And then I worked on it in the evening with my therapist friend. But she didn't want to acknowledge that there might be any abuse there. And she more or less talked me out of it.

PD: How did she do that?

Grace: She asked me why I thought that I might have been abused. And I said that I had this feeling that I had to protect myself down here. And there was just a lot of fear there. And, in fact, what I felt like was that all the men that I'd ever known in my life were all trying to get on top of me at once – and it was extremely disturbing. And she asked what was there in the background to suggest that my father might be involved. And the only things that really stood out in my mind that he did for me was to beat me and bath me. (Grace – 63)

Experiences of 'flashbacks' involved sudden, intense and disorientating incidents:

It was like watching a slide show. Suddenly, I mean, no matter where I was or what I was doing, suddenly another slide would come into focus – it's very unnerving. They were being triggered by bricks and mortar, they weren't just coming out of nowhere. Every street I walked down seemed to hold its own memories and set off its own slide show. (Beth – 16)

One participant differentiated various types of flashbacks:

I have three types: I sometimes have a very clear visual memory which is accompanied by no feeling at all – just a sort of cold kind of viewing of a scene. Then I have a total physical reaction, which is very violent – I convulse. The third type is just a sound – like explosions in my head – a sort of: 'Kaboom', and then a sort of fizzing noise.

I think I was beaten with some kind of a flexible thing, like a leather thing, or something. And I will hear a kind of: 'K'shish' noise, you know, suddenly. And that'll be it – it will just be gone. And I also hear voices. I hear a child scream sometimes. And I hear a voice if I'm asleep. Sometimes I'll just hear a voice saying my name by the bed, which instantly wakes me up. (Ragbag – 39)

Many of the people in this study who experienced the recovery of abuse memories had had significant exposure to abuse-related written material and therapeutic contexts in which abuse had a high profile. These influences have powerful impact, as the following examples illustrate. The impact on Ragbag of reading *The Courage to Heal* (Bass and Davis 1988) was dramatic:

I was going through it – it was like hearing myself speak. I took to underlining things – it's all covered in biro. And the next thing is you go into disbelief. And then I started having flashbacks. The first one was awful, because, you know, it was such a *shock!* You just don't know what happened. Sometimes my body remembers things that I don't, so I mean, I actually felt pain, and still do. After the initial two or three flashbacks they all kind of stopped. And that was horrible. Sort of like waiting for the next doodlebug to come – you don't know when or what. (Ragbag – 39)

Sue recalled the effect of reading a book by Alice Miller which had been given to her by a friend:

I can remember we were sitting downstairs, I'd read a bit of this book and I'd started getting really quite perturbed and very shaky and very frightened. And there was this bit about a mother masturbating her daughter and I just couldn't cope with that at all. I can remember just silencing up. And I knew that there were thoughts occurring to me and I couldn't quite get them straight in my mind. I was very, very confused – very frightened. It didn't take long for the remembrance to happen at that point. (Sue – 54)

At the time she experienced this incident as being very disturbing and unhelpful – to the extent that she actually burned the book. However, in retrospect, she felt it had ultimately been an important part of the process of remembering the sexual abuse by her mother. The experience also led her to seek further helpful therapy from her original therapist.

Of the people who described recovered memories from a state of complete prior non-awareness (one of whom subsequently came to the view that the memory was not true), four described the immediate trigger for these being some form of therapy:

I had forgotten my abuse. I remember how it came into my awareness – that was in the context of the therapy group for my Gestalt training. A man in the group said he was abused by his mum. And I remember my breathing got quite fast – I was unable to think. I wasn't able to get a kind of logical sense of what he was talking about – too much caught in my own response. And I remember symptoms feeling similar to a diabetic shock – I had shaky knees, no energy whatsoever. I had pins and needles all over the place. I could hardly raise my arm, felt extremely sick. It was massive, and at that stage there was a physical reaction with no cognitive connection – it hadn't clicked.

Then I had a dream, or it felt like a dream. There were bits and pieces of memory and images coming up. And I brought them to therapy the week after. That's the place where I talked about my first dream and I had a similar, smaller scale physical reaction. And I remember saying something like: 'Oh God – I wonder if something happened to me?' They continue to come. I start dreaming vividly, and they tend to be often about my mother, and what happened. And they feel so violent that I wake up screaming. (Christopher – 59)

Carol also had a very powerful reaction to her experiences in group therapy:

I've only discovered in the last two years that I was also abused when I was two. I was in the group – and there were other people in the group who'd been sexually abused so it was all part of the group culture. I started to hit the cushions and he said: 'Put your fists through the cushions.' And I put my fists between the cushions and I started to gag and I couldn't. I thought I was going to throw up, so I tried to get out of the room and I couldn't get out. And he said: 'It's OK, someone get a bowl, It's OK, You're not going out.'

And I went right back to when I was two – and I was sitting with my knees up to my chin. I was sitting on the floor and I could feel the cold lino and it was summer. And my Mum came up to me and said: 'What's the matter?' And I couldn't speak. I'd been sick and I could feel – I can almost feel it now – my dress was covered in vomit. But while I was feeling all that, I couldn't tell. The therapist was sitting right there with me, and the group was all there, but I couldn't say anything. It felt like I'd been back to different times in my life, different ages. And in my brain it just feels like a big brain wave change. (Carol – 14)

These examples pose questions about the influence of written abuse material and certain therapeutic approaches on clients' experiences of abuse memories. It is apparent that some respondents had encountered therapists with strong convictions that undisclosed child abuse lay behind their problems. However, it is important that not all therapists are negatively caricatured in this way. One respondent who experienced recovered memories of abuse stressed that this was not connected with any suggestions made by her therapist:

I actually described one memory which I'd been too abhorred to tell her before. She never put the idea into my head, I'm very clear about that. Because I'd started mentioning that to my mother and the first thing she did was blame my counsellor, and say that this was brainwashing. But, in fact, she was so careful not to do that. I mean, that's one of the reasons why I respect her so much. (Ragbag – 39)

As discussed in the last chapter, research is beginning to address the problematic issue of corroboration of recovered memories of abuse. In this study, two people described subsequent events which they considered as being corroborative of their recovered memories. Sarah had eventually confronted her father by letter about her new recollections of sexual abuse. She believed that the tacit acknowledgement of her mother, a childhood medical record and her father's subsequent suicide were indicative of the essential truth of the memories. A second participant had spoken with a relative after recovering memories of sexual abuse, who then described her similar experiences with the same person.

Without the benefit of robust external corroboration to assist reality testing, people rely on idiosyncratic subjective criteria to determine for themselves the veracity of such memories. There were four factors which inclined participants to believe in the essential accuracy of their recovered memories:

- a deeply intuitive experience of 'knowing' – where a newly realized history of abuse finally makes sense of long periods of confusion and painful problems in lives and relationships;
- the intensity and vividness of physiological, emotional and visual sensations;
- a sense of reliving the experience;
- the presence of era-appropriate contextual detail within dreams and flashbacks.

If you remember something, you remember all the physical circumstances – the room it happened in or where it was. And I think a phony memory would soon show up. I am not saying that it doesn't happen to people but I just think: 'How can it happen?' How can they rustle it up or are they just imagining it as you would imagine a popular story or something? It's certainly mystifying. Because a real memory is accompanied by physiological accompaniments, that's the thing – where you start going hot or cold or, there's some sort of emotion. (Mary – 31)

Instead of seeing something when you might go back and remember a situation – this memory was very much completely being transported back to that age again, and experiencing it the same way. (Claire – 68)

You get the most incredible details of things, images that you couldn't know about. I mean, I've had details of images that I know are related to the 1950s – like my sister having her hair plaits, and the ribbon going through her hair, things like that I know are related to the 50s. I mean, you couldn't make these things up – it wouldn't be possible. (Carol – 17)

However, despite the widespread nature of such beliefs, these ways of self-evaluating the accuracy of 'recovered' abuse memories cannot be relied upon to determine to what extent the memories are 'true' or not. The criteria outlined here – intuitive knowing, intensity and vividness, reliving and era-appropriate detail – are equally characteristic of strongly believed in, but erroneous, general memories. For example, intense levels of emotional re-experiencing have been shown to be associated with an extremely high degree of hypnotizability – a propensity which tends to include significant suggestibility, a suspension of critical judgement and lack of awareness of logical incongruities (Ganaway 1989; Spiegel 1974). Experimental research has also demonstrated that while richly elaborated memories are more likely to be believed by others (for example, jurors) there is no significant relationship between the amount of detail in a memory and its accuracy (Loftus 1993). Thus, despite the phenomeno-logical vividness (and convincingness to others on this basis), factors such as emotional intensity, sense of reliving and contextual detail do not in themselves provide reliable criteria that the recalled experiences are literally true (Lindsay and Read 1994).

Therapists' perspectives on abuse memories

Twenty-three participants had experience of providing therapy for clients who were abused as children. Thirteen of these interviews (six therapists and seven therapists-abused-as-children) included a focus on their views of abused clients' memory processes. The therapists had worked across the spectrum with clients who had always had continuous memories of abuse; those who reported they had been unaware of abuse until recalled in later life; and others who had a partial awareness. In this section we will illustrate and discuss the various ways in which therapists interpret and respond to experiences of abuse told to them by their clients.

Reference was often made to the historical context of social denial of child sexual abuse and the disservice and damage done to clients in the past by professionals tending not to believe accounts of abuse. All of the therapists felt that it was important for true memories of abuse to be believed and that not to believe them would be unhelpful and damaging. However, there are also risks involved in a stance which believes all accounts of abuse without question – perhaps as an overcompensation for the long period of social and therapeutic denial.

Therapists generally believed in the reality of a phenomenon referred to as 'repression', 'dissociation' or 'amnesia' by which whole or partial memories of abuse can be deleted from conscious awareness, to re-emerge in later life in a sudden or a gradual way. There were, however, significantly different opinions as to whether 'recovered' memories of abuse could necessarily be considered to be literally accurate. There were three general views which can be characterized as:

- those who have a strong inclination to believe without question;
- those who have an open mind about literal accuracy;
- those who stress the importance of 'narrative truths' and see the question of veracity as being largely irrelevant.

Believing without question (emphasized in much of the influential 'survivor' literature as 'validation') is an approach which is based on the belief that it is therapeutically beneficially to counter clients' tendencies to doubt their own feelings and memories of abuse. This approach is also associated with a much criticized assumption that 'repressed' memories of abuse are likely to lie behind extensive constellations of symptoms and problems, and that therapeutic techniques should provoke and then validate such memories. Whatever the prevalence of therapists with such beliefs in the UK (and they do exist – as clients in the study had encountered them), there is only one representative of this position in this study.

Dr S, a consultant psychiatrist in a privately funded psychiatric hospital, routinely used sodium amytal injections to facilitate patients' remembering and describing their abuse:

PD: How do you form a view as to whether what they remember is necessarily literally true?

Dr S: Well, I look for a number of things. First I look to see whether their experiences of what they've gone through and how they felt about it fits with various stereotypes that you have in your mind about how people feel about things. So, I look for that kind of psychological consistency. When they describe things to me, I am also looking for an emotional reaction that seems to be real and seems to be genuine – at some point. That might not come initially of course because they might just remember the facts before they can get in touch with the emotion.

I also will ultimately look to see whether they recover. If they recover because of work that I've done in that area, then I feel reasonably comfortable that the work that I've done has been valid and that they haven't recovered spontaneously. I mean, that's ultimate proof. I am also interested in historical consistency so that when I talk to them from one session to the next, they are giving me basically the same story. And that's interesting under injection because: I can inject people – they can give me a story – then outside the injection they can forget what's happened in the session and what they've told me. And I might not give them feedback. And I can inject them again, and I can ask them the same questions and I get the same answers. So I always get that kind of consistency.

I will also try to find more independent corroboration – and that's always very pleasing. I've had several patients in the last year who've recounted stories to me under injection – and we have had complete corroboration of their stories through other family members who they have not been in contact with for years. (Dr S – 08)

One controversial theory surrounding the non-remembrance of childhood abuse is that of dissociation. Dr S was a firm believer in this notion, and its extreme manifestation Multiple Personality Disorder (now officially known as Dissociative Identity Disorder). He detailed his understanding of this phenomenon:

Dr S: The people I treat who have been abused are people who, by and large, have forgotten the fact they've been abused. I have some patients who've remembered bits of their abuse and I've uncovered more of it. But the largest population of people I treat who've been abused have no recollection of that abuse. In general, what I'm finding is that, in that population of people, when you uncover the abuse – the abuse is far more extensive and far more severe than in those people that have remembered some of the abuse. That would explain, in theory, why their abuse has been completely forgotten because it has been so much more severe and extensive.

PD: What's your understanding of the process?

Dr S: Well, the memory of the abuse seems to be completely suppressed. The person can suppress the abuse almost from one episode of abuse to the next. So, I've treated people who might be raped in the morning and within five minutes of the rape have forgotten that it's occurred. They've split their consciousness. They've dissociated. . . .

PD: This issue of dissociation and memories is becoming increasingly controversial. What's the difference between someone who was abused who does dissociate as opposed to somebody who was abused who doesn't dissociate?

Dr S: I think a number of reasons. I think the severity of the abuse is one thing. I think the ultimate dissociation is Multiple Personality Disorder. And everyone I've treated who's had a Multiple Personality Disorder has been horrendously abused. If you have Multiple Personality Disorder then you have enormous holes in the person's memory as they switch from one personality to the other. I think in MPD you have gross suppression and that's linked with the most severe types of abuse.

I think other variables come in. So, for example, if you have one person who's suffering gross emotional deprivation at home and they are abused on top of that by, let's say, one of the parents, then they are more likely to forget than someone that has less of an emotional deprivation and is abused. The more emotional pain a person has in addition to the sexual abuse pain, the more likely they are to suppress the abuse. I think personality variables come in – I'm very struck with the fact that some of my patients just are naturally more courageous than others. And the more courageous ones tend to remember. (Dr S – 08)

Dr S routinely used sodium amytal injections to facilitate the recovery of dissociated abuse memories:

I use sodium amytal or briotyl methahexatone. And these people can feel intensely suicidal. You can inject a person six or seven times with, let's say, amylobarb, and uncover nothing significant. And they'll have no reaction to the amylobarb. Then you can inject them – I am thinking about a particular patient now – I injected him and he talked about his abuse. And the next morning – well, at five in the morning – I had an emergency call from his wife – because we did this as an outpatient – the majority is done as inpatients. And he was acutely suicidal: out of the blue he was acutely suicidal. And he didn't know why he was acutely suicidal. So that's another piece of evidence that you might have hit on an important area. (Dr S – 08)

Dr S conveys graphically a number of beliefs about abuse and therapeutic practices which are particularly controversial. The injection of drugs to promote abreactions – and the discovery of 'repressed' abuse is a practice which (since this interview took place) has been discouraged by the Royal College of Psychiatrists (Royal College of Psychiatrists 1997). In the case example described, Dr S seemed unaware of obvious concerns that this 'treatment' had precipitated his patient into an acutely suicidal state.

In contrast to Dr S, the views of all the other therapists about using any form of procedure or technique to facilitate recovery of 'repressed' or 'dissociated' memories were cautious. Therapists with hypnotherapy training agreed that hypnosis as a technique is not appropriate for 'uncovering' unconscious abuse material:

There's a whole question about the kind of reliability of memories under hypnosis. I wouldn't use hypnosis to try to help people get in touch with traumatic material. The likelihood is that if they are amnesic, they're amnesic for very good reasons. We need to pay attention to those reasons before this kind of content stuff is unleashed from them. It can be very destructive in fact. And my sense is that we have to be very attentive to what people can cope with at any particular time and work with that – rather than going fishing for material. (Nor – 35)

Therapists were sceptical about the literal accuracy of memories 'recovered' under hypnosis. The small number interviewed who also practised hypnotherapy were not in favour of using inductive hypnotic techniques to 'retrieve' memories, nor for clients to explore in a regressed state the content of 'repressed' trauma. Concerns were felt that 'one-off' memory retrieval sessions without the protection of a secure therapeutic relationship could be deeply re-traumatizing for clients. Such practices reinforce not uncommon beliefs among clients that hypnotherapy can 'prove' unequivocally whether abuse took place or not.

As a hypnotherapist, Mary was particularly concerned about the potential for memory distortions under hypnosis:

> *Mary*: My theory is that under hypnosis people can actually invent – because the imagination is fantastic. I mean, I can do it myself. I've got the most fantastic imagination – I can imagine anything you'd ask me to imagine.
> *PD*: Would you ever lose track as to the actual reality of that or not?
> *Mary*: No, no, I wouldn't. I developed my imagination through a self-preservation thing through childhood – being able to dissociate and being able to actually live in a fantasy world. But I was always aware of what was real and what wasn't.
> *PD*: Do you think it's ever the case that people do the dissociating in childhood, invent the fantasy world, and then are not clear as to what's fantasy and what's reality subsequently?
> *Mary*: I do. I do actually believe that happens. And that's why it's such a delicate situation. Because it's so important that people are not ignored and that people are believed. But it's also equally important that people aren't accused of something they haven't done. I think the most horrific idea that somebody could be accused of abusing somebody, and they haven't done it, is just as bad as somebody being abused. (Mary – 43)

Further perspectives on interpretation of the veracity of recovered abuse-memories were provided by Robert and David. Robert, a consultant psychiatrist/psychotherapist in a large city psychiatric hospital, explained his view of the literal accuracy dilemma:

> Well, I suppose my position is that I listen very carefully and believe nothing. Because I think that's the only safe position. If I believe everything that my client says is true, I've got to be the most gullible person around. On the other hand, I think that for a long time, the idea of wish fulfilment fantasies was actually an extremely destructive way of denial. I mean, the people who have taken Freud to task are quite right to do so.

So it seems to me that both ends of the spectrum are dangerous positions to take up: either that all patients are lying or that all patients are telling the truth. I suppose in any immediate individual situation, I get a feeling about how true I think this is. And as a working position, I tend to accept what people tell me as being their truth. Whether it's literally true, whether what they remember actually happened, I am more cautious about. (Robert – 07)

David, a consultant psychiatrist in a major teaching hospital, acknowledged that he was rather sceptical of 'recovered' memories of abuse. However, he recounted an example of a patient's experience that he did believe:

> *David*: I'm always highly suspicious of people who say they don't remember sexual abuse – but this chap had completely blotted any memory until he found himself telling his wife in a restaurant that he'd been abused by his mother. A lot of his memories came flooding back. And he was pretty disturbed by it and wanting some sort of therapy. He said he suddenly found himself almost depersonalized. He was on the ceiling looking at himself suddenly telling his wife he'd been sexually abused. And it was the first time that it had ever occurred to him that he had been.
> *PD*: As a psychiatrist, how do you interpret that process – when he's suddenly twenty-eight years later sat in a restaurant?
> *David*: I'm afraid I don't know. I suppose you can call it denial, repressed memory – I don't really particularly understand what the process is. That, to me, was the clearest example of someone who thoroughly had repressed a memory. There were no other psychiatric symptoms. I always worry about rather hysterical personalities. He was a very straightforward man who'd never had any psychiatric problems in his life – and an intelligent man. I believed him. I thought that the process had occurred – I think it's a fascinating process. (David – 66)

Despite his general scepticism, this experience had led David to accept that the phenomenon of spontaneous 'recovery' of accurate abuse memories is something that does occur in certain circumstances. The concreteness of the memories and his assessment of the man's personality were the key factors regarding his belief in this account.

There are certain situations where therapists were particularly inclined to raise a sceptical eyebrow about the literal accuracy of some 'recovered' abuse memories. Caution was most often felt in relation to clients who claim to have no previous knowledge at all of any abuse where, in addition, the scenario includes:

- the potential influence of psychiatric conditions;
- possible conscious or unconscious malicious or manipulative intent;
- the presence of increasingly bizarre and extreme content;
- the potential impact of suggestive influences such as certain forms of hypnosis.

This highlights the potential importance on occasions of therapists helping clients to test the reality of their memories and other experiences. However, the primary purpose and culture of a therapeutic session is precisely that: therapeutic and not an investigative or forensic inquiry. Therapeutic benefit stems from clients developing personal awareness and communicating their subjective experiences of themselves, their lives, their environment and their relationships; in order to feel understood and accepted by the therapist. Subjective experiencing is the core of conversations which occur in therapy. The culture of most therapeutic approaches (there are a few exceptions) facilitates expression and gradual understanding of subtle, complex and ambiguous experiencing. On this basis, few therapeutic models encourage challenging clients' subjective experiences and beliefs with contradictory assertions about 'reality' – without first having gained a good understanding of the client's cognitive and emotional processes and having developed an effective therapeutic relationship:

> Well that's quite difficult because I'm such a believing person. I've been brought up to trust and to believe what people tell me. But I think some of my work has broadened my horizons a bit. One of the things I was taught when I trained was you should believe everything that you're told and if the person comes in the next week and says something completely the opposite, you don't say: 'Last week you said the complete opposite' – You acknowledge that their reality has moved on. (Patricia – 61)

On this basis, whatever reservations a therapist might feel about certain aspects of a client's account of an experience or even their entire history, at the beginning stages of a therapeutic relationship it is vital that the client feels listened to, understood and accepted. Any communication at this stage of doubts about the client's story at best is likely to interfere and delay the establishment of rapport and at worst to provoke a negative response which may reinforce previous experiences of being misunderstood, not believed and not taken seriously. Therefore, to establish an effective therapeutic relationship requires, at least at the early stages, that the client's story is largely accepted at face value:

> I take the stance that if the client discloses that something happened when they were young, that I will accept that that is their reality. If later they tell me that this is pure fantasy, then I will be equally happy to accept that. But I really have to function on the basis of what they say to me is their reality. If they tell me that they think they imagined this, then that is what I would go along with. I may challenge them in a benign manner, I may ask them, for example, what leads them to think that this is their imagination and not the reality. But at no stage would I doubt their own perception of events. (Cliff – 05)

Even in settings where assessment and evaluation is part of the professional task, communicating understanding of the clients' subjective experience is an important part of an initial assessment:

> If we do not believe people when they come to us, we really have nowhere to start from. It is only in believing people that they will then trust us enough perhaps to disclose that the reality is something quite different. I have to keep a very open mind and be aware of, for example, when something may be a symbolic representation of something that occurred; or indeed, it may be a facet of a mental illness. That sometimes the person may enter into a fantasy world purely as a very defensive mechanism to protect themselves. (Cliff – 05)

> The first thing is that you won't get a sniff of abuse in your patients unless you build up a relationship of trust with them. A personal relationship – it has a personal as well as a professional dimension. You've got to be able to talk to your patients in some sense on the same level as they are – otherwise they won't disclose these intimate things to you. (Dr S – 08)

It is important to reiterate that all the therapists in this study believed in the reality and significance of childhood abuse. All believed that most clients who discuss childhood abuse were abused and that therapists must accept this to be helpful. Many pointed to the history in psychotherapy and other professions of the damage done to people by not believing their accounts of abuse. While the tendency of the therapists was to believe in the essential accuracy of recovered abuse memories, there are situations when significant doubts do arise.

Mike was unconvinced about 'memories' which suddenly returned and where clients expressed immediate strong belief in them:

> I think what raises my eyebrows is a sudden flash of, 'Ah, yes – I remember being in bed at four and suddenly seeing my father at the bottom of the bed.' Or suddenly remembering: 'Yes, my father was on top of me.' There's a sort of mismatch between the feeling and thinking. I don't think that it happens just like that. Also the desire for the client to cling on to that: 'Ah, right, that's it'! And therapists then say: 'Right, that's it – cling on to it. We've got something here – let's grasp it.' (Mike – 62)

Notwithstanding the exceptional example described earlier which he did believe, David's reservations remained about other sorts of 'recovered memory' phenomena:

> *David*: What worries me are the people who say because they feel very disturbed about their infancy or their young life, therefore they *must* have been abused. And yet they don't have a concrete memory of it. That always worries me because I do think that you can be led by a very powerful psychotherapist into thinking that maybe that happened too.
>
> I suppose children of two and three may not have a formed memory and we don't know what to do with that sort of situation – but I'm always worried when there isn't an actual memory. It's the thought that it *must* have occurred because they feel terribly bad about their childhood.
>
> *PD*: Do you think therapists are planting these sorts of notions that abuse must be the cause?

> *David*: I do. Actually. I wouldn't so strongly say that they are planting the notions but I do think it's flavour of the month – it's very fashionable. (David – 66)

Descriptions of bizarre and ritualistic abuse raised particular doubts. This was illustrated by one therapist who felt that her client's beliefs had been negatively influenced and reinforced by a previous therapist, who was well known for her interest in 'ritualistic' abuse. Catherine remembered her internal reaction when the client began adding bizarre and ritualistic elements to her abuse story:

> Sod this for a lark. (Catherine – 34)

Occasionally, a therapist may come to doubt a client's entire life story, including accounts of abuse. An illustration was given by Jane, a counsellor with strong views about child abuse and its effects, who was very concerned about the impact on abused people of not being believed. However, she described her single experience of having increasing doubts about a client's narrative:

> Well, I just don't know, do I – anymore than they do, in a way. I just work on the basis that I believe them. I've only had one client – I believed her until she then started to introduce more up-to-date stuff that was going on in her life. And it was like – everyone she came across from the postman to the lady in Marks and Spencers was getting at her.
>
> And I came to the conclusion in the end that she was actually ill. But she presented as very, very sane indeed. And so I was left recognizing how ill she was – psychotic I think. Well, I doubted the abuse. Now I could have been completely wrong – that the abuse was the reason she'd become so ill. But there were just too many things that she was telling me that were not believable – just plain ridiculous. That's the only one I've ever had like that. (Jane – 24)

The client's GP subsequently confirmed that there was a history and recurrence of a psychotic illness. Jane emphasized that her response was very much an exception to the many other abused clients with whom she had worked:

> Apart from that – I just do believe. I can't not believe: (a) it would be a pretty sick mind that made them up and (b) I'm sitting in the room with the raw emotion of these things: the disgust, the guilt, the facial expressions, the wringing of hands, the ripping of tissues, the crossing of legs, all the body language. As well as the total, total distress – and the blight it's having on their life. (Jane – 24)

Another example which also illustrates the importance of therapists keeping an open mind was provided by Mary:

> *Mary*: Some people just seem to remember quite straightforwardly without any difficulty and they seem to have things they can back it up with. The

ones that I think are difficult are when: 'I think I might have been abused but I'm not sure.' That situation's difficult. Because if somebody hates somebody enough and dislikes them enough – let's take for example: supposing a stepfather was really vindictive to a stepchild because he just didn't like them and was mean to them in an emotional sense, ignored them, neglected them, pushed them out – I believe that the child's pain could get translated into other sorts of abuse – especially under hypnosis.

PD: A person believing it happened but it didn't?

Mary: Yes, maybe. I'm not categorically saying Yes or No but I have a suspicion that that can happen. I had a client who before she came to see me had actually accused her father of abusing her. And she came to see me because she wanted to work through various things in her childhood. And when we really went through it really carefully I said: 'Are you sure – Do you think he did?' And she said: 'Well, I really don't know that he did.' And he'd left them when she was eight, and she'd been really angry and upset about it. She was furious with him. She really liked him. He was the only one in the family who read to her or gave her any attention. And she was literally livid.

Now through the sessions she expressed that anger. What really eventually came out of that was she said: 'I don't think he actually ever did anything to me.' And she admitted it – she said: 'I think I was just livid with him for having left me.' And she went and talked to him again about it and they talked it through. And he actually swore, he said: 'Look, I didn't. Yes, I was terrible to leave you.' And they made it up. They made friends. Afterwards she said to me: 'You know, I honestly think it was an unconscious malicious thing.' (Mary – 43)

Therapists who expressed some doubts that recovered memories of abuse are necessarily accurate commented on the unreliability of memory processes in general and the propensity of humans, both unintentionally and intentionally, to remember personal experiences in imprecise ways. These views covered a range of cognitive, psychological and psychodynamic perspectives on memory processes, recognizing that the brain as a biological and cognitive system can be prone to inventing, misperceiving and reconstructing views of past events subject to a range of influences and motivations:

I take what people say seriously but I don't, certainly not, take everything that people believe or believe what people say. I think partly, sometimes there's a sort of desperation for people to want to know whether they have been abused or whether there was abuse by mother or whatever. Desperately wanting to know that and to have that fact for whatever reason. And it's not there for whatever reason. And maybe to alleviate the distress of that not knowing and that uncertainty – the brain is quite capable of inventing beliefs that will work or something that will make that feeling OK. Or that might take the place of other feelings – struggling with towards parents – and labelling it abuse. (Mike – 62)

In considering the accuracy (or not) of recovered memories of abuse, there is one perspective which questions the validity and relevance of defining and attempting to establish literal 'truth'. Instead, the emphasis is placed upon alternative notions of 'personal' or 'narrative' truths'. This involves philosophical contemplation about the nature of truth and the disparate criteria used for 'proof' in different contexts – especially the difference between clinical, scientific and legal 'proof'. From this perspective, when it involves subjective experience of having been abused in whatever ways, then this is what constitutes the client's 'truth' and is the material to be explored therapeutically, irrespective of objective accuracy or symbolic content:

> *PD*: Is it possible to remember things in therapy that aren't true?
> *Sarah*: What do you mean by truth is what we come down to isn't it? We can go on just thinking about what's true. And what's literally true for one person is not literally true for another. (Sarah – 58)

On this basis the veracity question is seen as largely irrelevant:

> Does it matter what's literally true is what I'm coming to . . . If I've done my work right as I see it, the client will have some feeling that it really doesn't matter . . . What matters is how they themselves deal with it . . . I don't think truth or falsity in the ultimate sense are important. What is important is your perception of the event. (Sarah – 58)

'Personal truth' orientated therapists highlight the importance of working with each client's idiosyncratic experiences and construction of meaning for those experiences. I have argued in previous chapters in favour of this approach in contrast to therapists promoting and pushing their own preferred belief systems onto clients. However, in this area it is particularly important that therapists provide clients with the opportunity to reality test their experiences – especially in relation to recovered memories of child abuse. My concern about 'personal truth' (also known as 'narrative truth') notions is that therapists with this orientation seem reluctant to raise an eyebrow regardless of the content of the 'truth' which is being revealed. The therapist dutifully follows (or indeed leads) through childhood sexual abuse; into the territory of satanic/ritualistic abuse; multiple personalities; cult-programming and abduction by aliens. When therapists unquestioningly subscribe to, or inspire, clients' narrative construction of meanings, a real danger of co-constructed and mutually reinforcing delusions can emerge. In these situations professional responsibility to the client as a person, and social responsibility for the wider implications of the client's beliefs (for example, on families) can be neglected.

Robert gave an example of a response from a patient which had contributed toward a significant change in his perspective on this matter:

I used to think that it didn't actually matter. I remember once saying to a person who'd been abused – she was very concerned about whether it was true, whether it had really happened – and I rather naively said: 'Well, I think that the fact that you felt abused is all that matters.' And she absolutely flew at me and said: 'You stupid man, don't you understand? – it's of *great* importance to me to know whether what I remembered really happened or not – because I don't know what's real.' And she really taught me something.

So I moved on to pointing out that her insistence was actually an end game. Because there was no one who could any longer tell her whether her memory was accurate. And I suggested that we should work on the theory that *precisely* what she remembered had happened, and we would take that as the nearest to reality we would get. And she was OK with that. But it was my nonchalant assertion that it's – like it didn't matter – that was *very* offensive to her. And that was a real eye-opener to me. I realized I'd certainly misunderstood something central. (Robert – 07)

This experience highlights that without external corroboration it is often impossible to be sure one way or another about the veracity of recovered memories; and that learning to live with the uncertainty is likely to be part of the therapeutic challenge. In general therapists highlighted essentially the same criteria as clients as influencing their views regarding the accuracy of recovered memories: intuitive sense of knowing; vividness of imagery and intensity of emotional re-experiencing; and era appropriate contextual detail. This is likely to reflect that the same cultural influences have been assimilated by both groups and also that there is a lack of clear differentiation between the groups. Most therapists have been clients themselves and significant proportions of therapists report that they were abused as children.

It was notable that a number of the therapists seemed relieved to be able to explore dilemmas about belief in depth, as if there was a taboo around a discussion which could include any doubts about the accuracy of some clients' abuse memories. This was equally the case for therapists who had themselves been abused as children and those who had not, and therapists of both genders. Such discussions acknowledged the general unreliability of memory processes, the human propensity to reconstruct narrative memory and the suggestive potential of the high social profile of child abuse on vulnerable, confused and unhappy people.

It is possible that therapists who express doubt about the literal accuracy of recovered abuse memories may be considered, by some, to represent a continuing manifestation of a long social history of denial of child abuse. This would not be an accurate or fair characterization of any of the therapists in this study, who shared a deep concern about the reality of child abuse and the need to develop and improve therapeutic approaches and services to help clients effectively to overcome the consequences of abuse. However, this stance does not require that all 'recovered' memories of abuse are automatically believed and validated 'without question'. To do so can be naive, can fail to assist clients to develop their own reality testing abilities and can be potentially damaging to clients and their families.

With one exception, the therapists interviewed in this study did not fit the 'False Memory Syndrome' stereotype. They did not describe beliefs or practices which encouraged or routinely validated 'recovered' memories. Nor, at least according to their own accounts, did they appear to propel clients from their consulting rooms into the outside world hell-bent on confrontation, hunting for corroboration, severing family contacts, and initiating litigation. Moreover, when faced with the phenomena of recovered memories in clinical settings, many were concerned that therapy should include reality testing elements.

From this perspective, therapists can still respect clients' overall experiences of themselves and their histories, even if every recovered memory, image or symbol of abuse is not reinforced as being necessarily completely and literally accurate. While this may provide some reassurance that therapy wholesale is not driven by the search for 'repressed' memories, this does not allay concerns that dubious 'therapeutic' practice can influence the creation of inaccurate 'memories' of abuse.

11

Practice Implications

In this final chapter we will draw together some of the practice implications from the material in this book. It has been seen that clients' experiences have been very varied. Of the entire sample, 40% had wholly positive experiences of therapy, which pays tribute to the skills, thoughtfulness and sensitivity of many members of the therapeutic community and the potential for therapy to be helpful and efficacious.

However, it was equally common for clients to have experiences which were ineffective, unhelpful – or sometimes profoundly damaging. The striking nature of some of the unhelpful therapeutic practices described draws attention to the fundamental ethical principle of 'first do no harm'. Unfortunately, many of these experiences indicate that some therapists inadvertently are doing harm. To minimize the likelihood of therapy with adults abused as children being unhelpful or harmful, a number of practice points can be distilled from the experiences described in this book. These fall into two categories: those relating to the general context and process of therapy; and those which stem from the 'recovered memory' controversy.

General context and process of therapy

Many people are anxious about seeking therapeutic help. Often this is based on previous negative experiences of professional intervention. In recent years, these fears are likely to have been augmented by the bad press surrounding child protection and therapy which has arisen from the 'ritualistic abuse', 'false memory' and 'multiple personality' controversies. To minimize the impact of such deterrents to helpseeking, the therapeutic community could be more proactive in providing public information about effective and ethical therapeutic practice and required standards of care. Information is also needed to help potential clients through the difficult task of finding a suitable therapist.

In the early stages of therapy clients can feel unsure and bewildered about what to expect. When uncertain, many people tend to defer to the authority and presumed expertise and wisdom of the therapist. This can leave them highly vulnerable to unjustifiable therapeutic practices and inadequate standards of care. It can be very difficult for clients to discern whether a therapist is competent and suitable or not. Many clients would find it helpful and reassuring for therapists to routinely provide clear information (verbal or written) about what their approaches involve. Therapists should facilitate clients to feel free to choose not to proceed, to take time to consider, or look elsewhere.

The therapeutic environment and therapists' characteristics have a major impact on clients' experiences and expectations of therapy. Busy therapists should not forget the importance to clients of being responded to with human interest, warmth and respect – the 'human touch'. This seems self-evident, yet many experiences in this book illustrate that these characteristics somehow get lost.

Therapists working with adults who were abused as children should be well informed about theory and research relating to child abuse, trauma and therapeutic models. Care must be taken that therapeutic beliefs and style are not unduly influenced by anecdotal or prominent material which (notwithstanding its superficial attractiveness) does not have solid theoretical or research grounding. Theoretical foundations of practice must be coherent, explicit and located within justifiable parameters of safety and effectiveness as agreed by a substantial majority of the therapeutic and relevant scientific community. The disastrous effects of the absence of such checks is the major lesson which the therapy world must learn from the 'ritualistic abuse', 'recovered memory' and 'multiple personality' misadventures of the 1980s and 1990s.

Therapists should be vigilant not to work beyond their competence or emotional capacities. In particular, those who were themselves abused as children (many of whom make excellent therapists) have a particular responsibility to ensure that there is no inappropriate interplay between their own histories and the therapeutic approaches which they take with their clients. The therapists who were abused as children who participated in this study stressed this point particularly strongly.

Therapists should also consider carefully the impact of making self-disclosures to clients of personal material – especially regarding their own abuse. While within a well-functioning therapeutic relationship this can be experienced as profoundly helpful, there are also occasions when clients conceal their negative reactions to this practice and adapt defensively, thereby minimizing their potential for therapeutic change. In doing so, clients recognize that some 'unhealed' therapists introduce the topic of their own abuse without having satisfactorily resolved the impact of this on themselves. In consideration of their therapists' vulnerabilities negative reactions are concealed, resulting in an absence of feedback which reinforces therapists' self-disclosing behaviour.

Therapy should be tailored to the individual client's carefully assessed specific needs and preferences. 'One size fits all' therapies are oversimplistic, lazy and inappropriate. If the presenting problem involves a personal, family or social crisis, invariably the appropriate initial response will be on helping the client (most likely via a cognitive-behavioural focus) to stabilize their reactions to the situation. When this has been achieved, the client may feel that this is sufficient. There may then be no need to continue with therapy focused on the pain of abuse which was evoked during the crisis. On the other hand, there may well be precisely this need – as the client may feel that s/he remains susceptible to further crises unless the contributory factor of past abuse can be resolved. What is important is that this is a carefully considered decision and that neither the therapist nor the client automatically assumes that a long stretch of abuse-focused therapy must inevitably follow from help that is sought at points of crisis.

Clients need information about what different therapeutic approaches involve and to understand that there are many ways of tackling problems, abuse histories and working toward desired outcomes – not a single predetermined track. Given explanations of therapeutic options, with particular attention being paid to exploring what they want to achieve, clients can be engaged in making informed choices about how to proceed. Clients can benefit from information about the variety of therapeutic theories and styles so that they begin to make informed choices as to what feels comfortable and congruent for their own particular problems, personalities, interests and aspirations. This initial (and ongoing) exploratory and clarifying process is often liberating and therapeutic in itself. In this way, clients can be collaboratively involved in continually fine-tuning the style of their therapy. This demystifies the therapeutic process, creating a range of options which clients carefully consider, choose, experiment with or reject.

Accurate information may need to be provided which corrects misunderstandings about abuse. Great care must be taken that such information is theoretically sound (generally accepted within the mainstream therapeutic community) – and not a suggestive or distorting influence. For example, it can be useful for clients to be aware that the following statements are popular misconceptions:

- that extensive therapy is invariably necessary to 'recover' from abuse;
- that 'flashbacks' and 'recovered' memories of abuse are necessarily true;
- that hypnosis can 'prove' whether memories of abuse are true;
- that abused people will invariably abuse their own children;
- that an abuser will never change.

It is important that therapy is based on the principle and practice of regularly renewed fully informed consent and that any known risks of treatment approaches are carefully explained. Clients should be given

accurate information about any experimental and controversial therapeutic approaches so as to be able to make a fully informed choice about
whether or not to proceed. Not to inform clients of the controversial
nature of certain diagnoses and treatments (for example, MPD/DID
diagnoses and treatments) must be considered to be unethical practice.

Therapists should routinely review each client's sense of progress or
frustration in relation to specified goals and, when necessary, revise the
therapeutic style and contract accordingly. This includes being particularly alert to some clients' tendencies to inhibit the expression of dissatisfaction and to comply with therapists' methods and expectations.
Particular care should be taken in noting situations where there is a lack
of expected progress or significant deterioration and consideration
should be given to additional consultation or a second opinion.

Fully informed consent should routinely include information on how
to terminate therapy – without clients necessarily having to explain why.
As has been highlighted in this book, it is of concern that highly
dissatisfied clients can become marooned in unproductive or damaging
therapy without being able to communicate this to their therapists or to
leave. Regular reviews, which facilitate exploration of feelings of frustration and enable the therapy process to be fine-tuned (or ended), would
help prevent dissatisfied clients from remaining stuck in inappropriate
therapy.

Ways of approaching abuse experiences need to be carefully considered with each client. Being in the midst of a crisis is rarely an
effective time to focus on talking in detail about memories of abuse. To
do so can augment the destabilizing impact of intrusive recollections and
intensify or prolong the crisis.

Again, providing information can be helpful and reassuring. Information such as: not everybody necessarily needs to talk extensively about
the abuse details – although some people will need to do so. An
intermediate stage of 'talking about talking about the abuse' can be
very effective in facilitating consideration about expectations, fears and
fantasies about this aspect of therapy (including anxieties about the
therapist's reactions to the material). This enables the therapeutic style
to be carefully negotiated and agreed upon; for example, how much
encouraging to focus on abuse does the client want? This is a particularly
important issue for therapists and clients to work on collaboratively and
to review continually. There is a very fine line between an optimum
position and over-focusing or under-focusing on abuse – each of which
can generate negative consequences.

Clients often need to formulate their own views about continuing and
future relationships with abusers and significant others, as well as the
most meaningful ways of understanding why the abuse occurred and
their reactions to it. Therapists can help by neutrally facilitating exploration and the making of informed choices from carefully considered
options. It is important for therapists to avoid imposing their own

viewpoints and preferred outcomes, as clients may compliantly adapt to these (sometimes while silently disagreeing). Therapists must be theoretically and emotionally open to the range of potential (and sometimes surprising) resolution outcomes that clients will consider. These include (in no particular order of sequence or significance): confronting abusers; severing contact with abusers; recontacting abusers; maintaining ambivalent relationships with abusers; understanding abusers; forgiving abusers; and retracting allegations of abuse.

Implications for practice from the 'false'/'recovered' memory dispute

Certain forms of therapy during the 1980s and early 1990s were implicated in the generation of false beliefs and memories of childhood abuse (in clients who had no awareness of abuse at the time they sought therapy) on an unknown scale. The concept of 'False Memory Syndrome' describes the inculcation of inaccurate beliefs about abuse in suggestible people via powerful therapeutic influences (caricatured as 'Recovered Memory Therapy'). These include: repeated suggestion that extensive repression of traumatic childhood memories underlies a wide range of adult problems; use of various techniques of 'memory retrieval'; 'validation' of such 'memories' as being literally true; and encouragement of confrontation or severance of contact with alleged abusers. The existence of these non-justifiable and damaging practices has to be conceded (although the prevalence remains in dispute). High profile court cases have occurred in the USA (and more are pending), in which accused parents and ex-clients (so called 'retractors') are suing therapists and agencies for allegedly implanting beliefs of abuse, the veracity of which the clients have subsequently dismissed.

Apart from these continuing legal actions for compensation, the destructive era of polarization in the 'memory wars' is receding. Clinical and research knowledge has moved on – and it is vital that contemporary therapeutic practice eradicates the errors of the 1980s and 1990s. There is some evidence that this is happening: newly accused parent contacts with the 'False Memory' pressure groups in the USA, Canada, UK and New Zealand peaked in the mid-1990s and have declined consistently since. This welcome decrease is not to deny, minimize or ignore that the problems and consequences remain excruciatingly alive for individuals and families affected on both sides – those whose lives have been devastated by false denials and by false allegations of abuse.

The clinical and research community has responded to the False Memory Syndrome critique. Rapid progress has been made toward a more scientifically anchored and defensible common ground position regarding interpretation of memories of abuse, effective therapeutic practice and acceptable standards of care (Briere 1997; Courtois 1997;

Lindsay and Briere 1997). A gathering in France in 1996 (sponsored by NATO) brought together a large international group of researchers and experienced practitioners to debate these issues over an intensive period of ten days (Read and Lindsay 1997). As a very minor participant in this important event I was struck by the general acceptance of the need to move on from the destructive polarization paralysis. The resulting common ground position recognizes that:

1   Child abuse is a widespread phenomenon which causes significant harm.
2   Most adults who were abused as children have always been aware of all, or the most salient parts, of their abuse experiences.
3   A small proportion of adults abused as children report that there were periods in their lives when they had no conscious knowledge of their abuse – only to become aware of this in later life. Explanations for such periods of non-awareness remain uncertain and disputed.
4   False beliefs/memories/allegations of childhood abuse do occur. For example, inaccurate abuse 'memories' can be the product of delusional psychiatric states influenced by the topical high public profile of abuse. Another contributory factor is bad therapy with highly suggestible and vulnerable clients.
5   False beliefs/memories regarding abuse equally affects abusers as well as the abused. Actual abusers can have 'false memories' that they did not abuse. Genuine amnesia for abusing may stem from alcohol and drug use, or (more controversially) dissociative or fugue states. These are the so-called 'true liars' whose 'false memories' of not abusing are a genuine reflection of lack of conscious knowledge of their behaviour.
6   Some abusers (notwithstanding incontrovertible evidence) maintain inexorable stances of denial, including making counter-allegations such as that the abused person is suffering from 'False Memory Syndrome'. Such denial has been referred to, not entirely tongue in cheek, as 'Lying Perpetrator Syndrome'.

There are some specific practice implications which can be drawn from the 'Memory Wars' era and the emerging common ground:

1   Therapists should review assumptions that undisclosed or non-remembered childhood abuse lies behind presenting adult problems. It may – but adult problems also have many causes other than childhood abuse. Despite assertions in many high profile books – there is no collection of adult symptoms/problems which reliably indicates childhood abuse.
2   Therapists should be open minded when working with clients who experience 'recovered memories' of abuse. The content of such memories may be accurate, highly inaccurate, or mixtures of both. It

cannot be considered effective or ethical practice to introduce notions of certainty ('validation') regarding the literal accuracy of 'recovered' memories which have no source of external corroboration.

3 Therapists should review their attitudes about the literal accuracy of 'recovered' memories of abuse, especially those which relate to the very early years of life, or to extreme or bizarre instances. Therapists working in this area need to have some familiarity with relevant cognitive psychological research on normal and traumatic memory processes and the debates around this (Lindsay and Read 1994).

4 When memories of abuse do 'return', clients and therapists often believe that because the experience is so intense or vivid that this indicates a high level of veracity. This is not so – research indicates consistently that intensity and vividness of recall experience is as equally associated with 'memories' which turn out to be false as it is with those which turn out to be true.

5 When clients experience the 'recovery' of memories of abuse in therapy it is rarely helpful (or ethically justifiable) for therapists to facilitate intensification of clients' experience, for example, by promoting cathartic expression or regression. The most important therapeutic principle is of stabilization: helping the client to control and contain the experience, to maintain daily functioning, rather than to risk provoking non-coping or disintegration.

6 Certain therapeutic practices such as guided imagery, hypnotic regression and drug-assisted interviews are not valid, effective or good practice in relation to 'memory retrieval' and 'validation' of memories. These approaches are particularly vulnerable to the effects of direct and indirect suggestion in that clients may produce what they feel therapists are interested in.

7 Group therapists and self-help groups should consider the potential peer pressure impact on members to 'remember' abuse. Is this a conscious or unconscious group expectation? Do members have to produce abuse 'memories' to 'belong' to the group?

8 Therapists working with children where there is uncertainty or dispute regarding possible sexual abuse should be familiar with the research (and the controversies) surrounding the influence of suggestibility on children's reports (Ceci and Bruck 1993; Ney 1995).

The 'False Memory' era of therapy was predominantly an unintended consequence of the activities of therapists who were highly committed to raising the social profile of child abuse and helping those affected to deal with the effects of their experiences. The well-intentioned determination to 'deal with' child abuse at both a social and personal level produced seemingly coherent theories, practices and 'solutions' which were influentially promoted by charismatic leaders. These notions were uncritically adopted in good faith by significant numbers of practitioners who were largely unaware that they were unevaluated, theoretically flawed and contained the hidden potential to cause harm.

There are important lessons to be learned from the rise and fall of superficially attractive 'new solutions' to longstanding social and psychological problems. One particular lesson is that, while the focus may change, the underlying process can continue. For example, while the 'False Memory' era fades, a similar phenomenon appears to be occurring within minority sections of the therapeutic community in relation to uncritically accepted beliefs about Multiple Personality Disorder (also known as Dissociative Identity Disorder). Small groups of influential practitioners (predominantly in the USA) are convinced that this disorder is a commonplace consequence of severe ritualistic child abuse and that it is under-diagnosed on a large scale. Specific treatment approaches are utilized which result in the intensification of symptoms (acting out extensive elaborations of personality 'alters') and extensive family disruption (Bikel 1995).

There is, however, considerable evidence that MPD/DID is predominantly an iatrogenic (caused by social contagion and therapist influence) phenomenon (Kenny 1986; Mulhern 1994; Piper 1997; Spanos 1996). Moreover, the controversial extended treatment approaches are not validated and the clients as a whole do not seem to get better (Dale 1999). There are few coherent case studies involving follow-up of successful treatment and no independent outcome studies of this form of therapy. From 1998 some people who have undergone this form of therapy in the USA and Canada have brought successful lawsuits for malpractice and damages against their MPD/DID therapists (Grinfield 1997; Hanson 1998; Nissimov 1998).

Endnote

A major conclusion from this book is that therapy has the potential to facilitate considerable positive changes for adults who were abused as children – and also that poor therapy can cause significant harm. I have tried to keep a balance between these two findings. However, this is not easy as stylistically examples of bad practice and poor outcomes are more striking and memorable than accounts of good practice and positive outcomes. While wanting to alert a public and professional readership to what bad practice can involve, I do not want this book to be used as ammunition for those who wish to attack and undermine therapy as a whole. I hope that in highlighting areas of damaging practice I have not eclipsed the important (and sometimes profound) benefits which people (and their families) can derive from good practice therapy. My predominant message is that good therapy is likely to be very helpful – but that there are a lot of bad practice minefields to be avoided.

It is also important that warnings about bad therapeutic practice do not bring their own dangers. For example, while the 'False Memory Syndrome' critique has highlighted certain forms of unacceptable therapeutic practice, these criticisms are often overgeneralized to therapy as a whole. A negative consequence of this may be to discourage help seeking which would precipitate significant positive personal change for many people. Worse, by encouraging a culture shift which promotes public scepticism about the reality and impact of child abuse in general, there is a danger that the needs of contemporary children who are at risk, or who are being abused, may be increasingly ignored or disregarded.

Appendix

Interview Participants

Client group

Key
EA = Emotional Abuse
PA = Physical Abuse
SA = Sexual Abuse
NEG = Neglect

04 *Alice*

	Age 39, female
Stated ethnic origin	English
Stated occupation	Housewife
Types of abuse	PA/SA/EA
Number of abusers	3
Relationship of abusers	Mother/father/uncle
Age range of abuse	3–16 years
Time in abuse-related therapy	6 years
Number of therapists	4
Residual problems	Some

12 *Jamie*

	Age 49, male
Stated ethnic origin	White European
Stated occupation	Teacher
Types of abuse	SA
Number of abusers	1
Relationship of abuser	Uncle
Age range of abuse	8/9–16 years
Time in abuse-related therapy	25 years
Number of therapists	10
Residual problems	Some

13 *Ellen*

	Age 44, female
Stated ethnic origin	White European – Irish
Stated occupation	Social work trainer
Types of abuse	PA/SA/EA
Number of abusers	About 5
Relationship of abusers	Father/mother/lodgers/neighbour
Age range of abuse	5 years until adulthood
Time in abuse-related therapy	6 years overall

Number of therapists   8
Residual problems   Some

15 *Emily*   Age 28, female
Stated ethnic origin   British
Stated occupation   Graphic designer
Types of abuse   SA
Number of abusers   1
Relationship of abuser   Vicar of local church
Age range of abuse   7/8–12 years
Time in abuse-related therapy   2 years approx.
Number of therapists   2
Residual problems   Some

16 *Beth*   Age 32, female
Stated ethnic origin   White European
Stated occupation   Research scientist
Types of abuse   SA
Number of abusers   2
Relationship of abusers   2 brothers
Age range of abuse   10–15 years
Time in abuse-related therapy   4.5 years overall
Number of therapists   4
Residual problems   Some

17 *Carol*   Age 49, female
Stated ethnic origin   British (Jewish)
Stated occupation   Shop owner
Types of abuse   PA/SA/EA
    Other: 'Group Torture'
Number of abusers   7
Relationship of abusers   Mother/father/brother/grandmother/
    grandfather/uncle
Age range of abuse   9 months until 19 years
Time in abuse-related therapy   2.5 years
Number of therapists   3
Residual problems   Some

19 *Anna*   Age 46, female
Stated ethnic origin   White British
Stated occupation   Administrator
Types of abuse   PA/SA/EA
Number of abusers   2
Relationship of abusers   Mother/father
Age range of abuse   3/4–17 years
Time in abuse-related therapy   7 years
Number of therapists   2
Residual problems   Some

20 *Rose*   Age 53, female
  Stated ethnic origin   White European – British
  Stated occupation   Administrator
  Types of abuse   PA/SA/EA
  Number of abusers   2
  Relationship of abusers   Mother/uncle
  Age range of abuse   3 years approx. until 15–16 yrs
  Time in abuse-related therapy   18 months
  Number of therapists   2
  Residual problems   Some

21 *Anne*   Age 36, female
  Stated ethnic origin   White European
  Stated occupation   Mature student
  Types of abuse   PA/EA/NEG/?SA
  Number of abusers   2 'at least'
  Relationship of abusers   Mother/brother ('father colluded')
  Age range of abuse   'As soon as I was born' until age 15 ('I ran away')
  Time in abuse-related therapy   5 years
  Number of therapists   3
  Residual problems   Some

23 *Veronica*   Age 43, female
  Stated ethnic origin   Irish
  Stated occupation   (not given)
  Types of abuse   PA/SA/EA/NEG
                                   Other: Mental
  Number of abusers   '?'
  Relationship of abusers   Mother/half-brothers/half-sister
  Age range of abuse   ?3 years – ?41 years
  Time in abuse-related therapy   6 months plus overall
  Number of therapists   3
  Residual problems   Major

27 *Sue*   Age 38, female
  Stated ethnic origin   British
  Stated occupation   Lecturer
  Types of abuse   PA/EA
  Number of abusers   3
  Relationship of abusers   Mother/father/uncle
  Age range of abuse   3 years until 33 years ('they never really stopped!')
  Time in abuse-related therapy   5–6 years
  Number of therapists   6
  Residual problems   Major

30 *Sarah*   Age 43, female
  Stated ethnic origin   White British
  Stated occupation   Artist

Types of abuse	PA/EA
Number of abusers	3
Relationship of abusers	Mother/father/uncle
Age range of abuse	PA: 8–14 years
	EA: 2–14 yrs
Time in abuse-related therapy	3 years
Number of therapists	1
Residual problems	Some

31 *Mary*

	Age 55, female
Stated ethnic origin	British
Stated occupation	Creative writing tutor
Types of abuse	PA/EA/NEG
Number of abusers	1
Relationship of abuser	Mother
Age range of abuse	From birth until (recently): 'relationship always remained painful until Mother's death'
Time in abuse-related therapy	(not answered) – but evidently long-term
Number of therapists	3
Residual problems	Some

32 *Katie*

	Age 47, female
Stated ethnic origin	Caucasian
Stated occupation	Administrator
Types of abuse	SA/EA
Number of abusers	1 ('2 if include mother, who had inklings of what was going on')
Relationship of abusers	Father
Age range of abuse	11–17 years
Time in abuse-related therapy	14 sessions (individual), 12 sessions (couple)
Number of therapists	3 (2 individual, 1 couple)
Residual problems	Some

33 *Sonya*

	Age 36, female
Stated ethnic origin	White British
Stated occupation	Senior lecturer
Types of abuse	PA/SA/EA/NEG
Number of abusers	4
Relationship of abusers	Mother/grandmother/stepfather/husband when babysitting
Age range of abuse	Em: young child–16 years
	SA: 12–16 years
Time in abuse-related therapy	4 years
Number of therapists	5
Residual problems	Some

39 *Ragbag*

	Age 40, female
Stated ethnic origin	British
Stated occupation	Artist/teacher

Types of abuse	PA/SA/EA
Number of abusers	2 (at least)
Relationship of abusers	Father/uncle
Age range of abuse	2/3–13 years
Time in abuse-related therapy	9 months
Number of therapists	1
Residual problems	Major

40 *Lin*

	Age 44, female
Stated ethnic origin	English
Stated occupation	Student
Types of abuse	PA/EA/NEG
	Other: Financial exploitation
Number of abusers	2
Relationship of abusers	Mother/father
Age range of abuse	3 years until 40: 'When father died'
Time in abuse-related therapy	Residential treatment unit – timescale not clear
Number of therapists	2
Residual problems	Some

42 *Esme*

	Age 30, female
Stated ethnic origin	German/Russian
Stated occupation	Training officer
Types of abuse	PA/SA/EA/NEG
Number of abusers	9
Relationship of abusers	Mother/stepfather/stepfather's friends/ carer/2 attacks by acquaintance and stranger
Age range of abuse	3–20 years
Time in abuse-related therapy	8 years
Number of therapists	5
Residual problems	Major

45 *Eleanor*

	Age 32, female
Stated ethnic origin	English
Stated occupation	Hairdresser
Types of abuse	PA/SA/EA/NEG
Number of abusers	3
Relationship of abusers	Mother/stepfather/father
Age range of abuse	2–20 years
Time in abuse-related therapy	6 months overall
Number of therapists	1
Residual problems	Some

51 *Georgia*

	Age 41, female
Stated ethnic origin	European
Stated occupation	Mother/linguist/legal executive
Types of abuse	EA
Number of abusers	2
Relationship of abusers	Mother/father

Age range of abuse   Memories from age 6 – 'in some respects it still continues'
Time in abuse-related therapy   Nearly 3 years
Number of therapists   3 (1 was for couple therapy)
Residual problems   Some

53 *Mary*   Age 34, female
Stated ethnic origin   English
Stated occupation   WP operator
Types of abuse   PA/SA/EA/NEG
   Other: Spiritual
Number of abusers   4
Relationship of abusers   Mother/father/uncle/brother
Age range of abuse   8 years approx. until 15 (SA); 22 (EA)
Time in abuse-related therapy   3–20 years
Number of therapists   2
Residual problems   Major

54 *Sue*   Age 41, female
Stated ethnic origin   White
Stated occupation   Teacher: art/design
Types of abuse   PA/SA/EA
   Other: financial/moral
Number of abusers   1
Relationship of abuser   Mother
Age range of abuse   Always – until left home
Time in abuse-related therapy   3 years approx.
Number of therapists   2
Residual problems   Some

57 *Eva*   Age 28, female
Stated ethnic origin   Black British
Stated occupation   Voluntary sector employee
Types of abuse   SA
Number of abusers   1
Relationship of abuser   Son of foster parents
Age range of abuse   3/4 until ?7 years
Time in abuse-related therapy   2 years overall
Number of therapists   3
Residual problems   Hardly any/uncertain

55 *Mary*   Age 33, female
Stated ethnic origin   British
Stated occupation   Housewife/mother
Types of abuse   SA
Number of abusers   1
Relationship of abuser   Brother
Age range of abuse   10–14 years
Time in abuse-related therapy   3 months

| | Number of therapists | 2 |
| | Residual problems | Some |

63 *Grace* — Age 49, female

Stated ethnic origin	(not answered) – White British
Stated occupation	Aromatherapist/masseuse
Types of abuse	PA/SA/EA
Number of abusers	1
Relationship of abuser	Father
Age range of abuse	4 years approx. until 'I don't know'
Time in abuse-related therapy	'No time specific to abuse'
Number of therapists	5
Residual problems	Some

64 *Sophia* — Age 25, female

Stated ethnic origin	White
Stated occupation	Student (Psychology)
Types of abuse	SA/EA/?NEG
Number of abusers	3
Relationship of abusers	Mother/stepmother/babysitter
Age range of abuse	Baby–14 years
Time in abuse-related therapy	4 years
Number of therapists	4
Residual problems	Some

65 *Sally* — Age 39, female

Stated ethnic origin	White European
Stated occupation	Clerical assistant
Types of abuse	SA/EA
Number of abusers	2
Relationship of abusers	Father: EA/brother: SA
Age range of abuse	8 approx. until 15 years (SA); –22 years (EA)
Time in abuse-related therapy	3 years
Number of therapists	1
Residual problems	Some

67 Telephone interviewee — Details not obtained

68 *Claire* — Age 33, female

Stated ethnic origin	White British
Stated occupation	Care worker
Types of abuse	PA/SA/EA/NEG
Number of abusers	3
Relationship of abusers	Father/brother/boyfriend
Age range of abuse	6/18 months–14 years
Time in abuse-related therapy	10 months
Number of therapists	3
Residual problems	Major

69 Telephone interviewee — Details not obtained

Therapist abused as child group[1]

03 *Inga*
Age 59, female

Stated ethnic origin	British
Stated occupation	Therapist
Types of abuse	PA/EA/NEG/?SA
Number of abusers	★
Relationship of abusers	★
Age range of abuse	★
Time in abuse-related therapy	★
Number of therapists	★
Residual problems	★

06 *Paul*
Age 30, male

Stated ethnic origin	White UK
Stated occupation	Counsellor
Types of abuse	★
Number of abusers	★
Relationship of abusers	★
Age range of abuse	★
Time in abuse-related therapy	★
Number of therapists	★
Residual problems	★

07 *Robert*
Age 47, male

Stated ethnic origin	White English
Stated occupation	Psychiatrist/psychotherapist
Types of abuse	SA/EA/NEG
Number of abusers	★
Relationship of abusers	★
Age range of abuse	★
Time in abuse-related therapy	★
Number of therapists	★
Residual problems	★

09 *Abida*
Age 48, male

Stated ethnic origin	English
Stated occupation	Medical doctor, psychotherapist, hypnotherapist and healer
Types of abuse	SA
Number of abusers	2
Relationship of abusers	Mother/stepbrother
Age range of abuse	Earliest infancy until 13 (physical aspect) and 18 (emotional aspect)
Time in abuse-related therapy	8 years
Number of therapists	6
Residual problems	Some

10 *Sarah*

	Age 45, female
Stated ethnic origin	British
Stated occupation	Psychotherapist
Types of abuse	PA/SA/EA/NEG
	Other: 'Mental'
Number of abusers	2
Relationship of abusers	Father/mother
Age range of abuse	2–8/9 years
Time in abuse-related therapy	6 years
Number of therapists	4
Residual problems	Some

11 *Zoe*

	Age 38, female
Stated ethnic origin	British
Stated occupation	Psychotherapist
Types of abuse	SA/EA
Number of abusers	5
Relationship of abusers	Adopted mother/father/brother/brother's friends
Age range of abuse	2/3–12 years
Time in abuse-related therapy	7 years
Number of therapists	4
Residual problems	Hardly any

14 *Carol*

	Age 45, female
Stated ethnic origin	White British
Stated occupation	Holistic masseuse/counsellor/graphologist
Types of abuse	PA/SA/EA
Number of abusers	4
Relationship of abusers	Stranger (SA)/father (PA/EA)/mother (EA/Verbal)/friend of family (SA)
Age range of abuse	2–40 years
Time in abuse-related therapy	8 years
Number of therapists	5
Residual problems	Some

18 *Bea*

	Age 41, female
Stated ethnic origin	White European
Stated occupation	Counsellor/therapist
Types of abuse	SA/EA/NEG
Number of abusers	1
Relationship of abuser	Mother
Age range of abuse	<1–4 years (SA); EA and Neg: long-term
Time in abuse-related therapy	8 years
Number of therapists	2
Residual problems	Major

22 *Myrtle*   Age 43, female
  Stated ethnic origin   Caucasian
  Stated occupation   Occupational therapist
  Types of abuse   PA/SA/EA
  Number of abusers   2
  Relationship of abusers   Mother/father
  Age range of abuse   3–16 years
  Time in abuse-related therapy 1 year +
  Number of therapists   3
  Residual problems   Some

35 *Nor*   Age 40, male
  Stated ethnic origin   White European
  Stated occupation   Social worker
  Types of abuse   EA
  Number of abusers   ★
  Relationship of abusers   ★
  Age range of abuse   ★
  Time in abuse-related therapy ★
  Number of therapists   ★
  Residual problems   ★

36 *Jean*   Age 54, female
  Stated ethnic origin   Caucasian
  Stated occupation   Psychiatric nurse/counsellor
  Types of abuse   SA/NEG
  Number of abusers   2 +
  Relationship of abusers   Father/uncle/?aunt
  Age range of abuse $2\frac{1}{2}$–7 years approx.
  Time in abuse-related therapy 1 year
  Number of therapists   1
  Residual problems   Some

43 *Mary*   Age 54, female
  Stated ethnic origin   White British
  Stated occupation   Psychotherapist
  Types of abuse   SA/EA/NEG
  Number of abusers   1
  Relationship of abuser   Father
  Age range of abuse   7–12/13 years
  Time in abuse-related therapy Intermittently over 9 years
  Number of therapists   2
  Residual problems   Some

52 *Soraya*   Age 37, female
  Stated ethnic origin   Arab–German
  Stated occupation   Counsellor
  Types of abuse   SA
  Number of abusers   1

Relationship of abuser   Carer/childminder
Age range of abuse   4–6/7 years approx.
Time in abuse-related therapy   3 years
Number of therapists   1
Residual problems   Uncertain

56 All details omitted by request

58 *Sara*   Age 61, female
Stated ethnic origin   British
Stated occupation   Psychotherapist
Types of abuse   Other: 'enema'
Number of abusers   1
Relationship of abuser   Father
Age range of abuse   5–8 years
Time in abuse-related therapy   1 year
Number of therapists   1
Residual problems   Some

59 *Christopher*   Age 34, male
Stated ethnic origin   Caucasian
Stated occupation   Psychotherapist
Types of abuse   PA/SA/EA
Number of abusers   1
Relationship of abuser   Mother
Age range of abuse   3–11 years (SA), –16 years (PA)
Time in abuse-related therapy   6 years
Number of therapists   2
Residual problems   Some

62 *Mike*   Age 40, male
Stated ethnic origin   White European
Stated occupation   Counsellor/social worker
Types of abuse   SA/EA
Number of abusers   ★
Relationship of abusers   ★
Age range of abuse   ★
Time in abuse-related therapy   ★
Number of therapists   ★
Residual problems   ★

Therapist group

05 *Cliff*   Age 36, male
Stated ethnic origin   White
Stated occupation   Counsellor
Own abuse   No

08 *Dr S*   Age 43, male
   Stated ethnic origin   White British
   Stated occupation   Psychiatrist
   Own abuse   No

24 *Jane*   Age 47, female
   Stated ethnic origin   White British
   Stated occupation   Supervisor, counsellor, sex therapist
   Own abuse   No

34 *Catherine*   Age 49, female
   Stated ethnic origin   Caucasian
   Stated occupation   Doctor
   Own abuse   (not answered)

61 *Patricia*   Age 37, female
   Stated ethnic origin   White
   Stated occupation   Counsellor/psychotherapist
   Own abuse   No

66 *David*   Age 43, male
   Stated ethnic origin   White European
   Stated occupation   Senior lecturer (clinical) psychiatrist
   Own abuse   No

Note

1 As noted in Chapter 3, five therapists-abused-as-children were inadvertently given the therapist version of the questionnaire. Consequently certain information is missing for participants (03, 06, 07, 35, 62).

References

Alexander, P.C., Neimeyer, R.A. and Follette, V.M. (1991) 'Group therapy for women sexually abused as children – a controlled study and investigation of individual differences', *Journal of Interpersonal Violence*, 6 (2): 218–31.

Allen, L. (1990) 'A client's experience of failure', in D. Mearns and W. Dryden, *Experiences of Counselling in Action*. London: Sage.

Altheide, D.L. and Johnson, J.M. (1994) 'Criteria for assessing interpretive validity in qualitative research', in N.K. Denzin and Y.S. Lincoln, *Handbook of Qualitative Research*. Thousand Oaks: Sage.

American Psychiatric Association (APA) (1980) *Diagnostic and Statistical Manual of Mental Disorders* (DSM-111). Washington, DC: APA.

American Psychiatric Association (APA) (1987) *Diagnostic and Statistical Manual of Mental Disorders* (DSM-111-R). Washington, DC: APA.

American Psychiatric Association (APA) (1994) *Diagnostic and Statistical Manual of Mental Disorders* (DSM-1V). Washington, DC: APA.

Andrews, B. (1997) 'Forms of memory recovery among adults in therapy: preliminary results from an in-depth survey', in D. Read and S. Lindsay (eds), *Recollections of Trauma: Scientific Research and Clinical Practice*. New York: Plenum. pp. 455–60.

Andrews, B., Morton, J., Bekerian, D.A., Brewin, C.R., Davies, G.M. and Mollon, P. (1995) 'The recovery of memories in clinical practice: experiences and beliefs of British Psychological Society Practitioners', *The Psychologist*, 8 (5): 209–14.

Armsworth, M. (1989) 'Therapy of incest survivors: abuse or support?', *Child Abuse and Neglect*, 13 (4): 549–62.

Armsworth, M. (1990) 'A qualitative analysis of adult incest survivors' responses to sexual involvement with therapists', *Child Abuse and Neglect*, 14 (4): 541–54.

Baker, A. and Duncan, S. (1986) 'Prevalence of CSA in Great Britain', *Child Abuse and Neglect*, 9 (4): 457–69.

Barkham, M. and Shapiro, D.A. (1992) 'Response to Kline: "Problems of methodology in studies of psychotherapy" ', in W. Dryden and C. Feltham (eds), *Psychotherapy and its Discontents*. Buckingham: Open University Press.

Bartlett, F.C. (1932) *Remembering*. Cambridge: Cambridge University Press.

Bass, E. and Davis, L. (1988) *The Courage to Heal: A Guide for Women Survivors of Child Sexual Abuse*. New York: Harper and Row.

Bates, C.M. and Brodsky, A.M. (1989) *Sex in the Therapy Hour: A Case of Professional Incest*. New York: Guildford.

Beck, A.T. (1976) *Cognitive Therapy and Emotional Disorders*. New York: New American Library.

Becker, J.V., Skinner, G. and Cichonl, J. (1984) 'Time-limited therapy with sexually dysfunctional sexually assaulted women', *Journal of Social Work and Human Sexuality*, 3: 97–115.

Beitchman, J., Zucker, K., Hood, J., Dacosta, G., Akman, D. and Cassavia, E. (1992) 'A review of the long-term effects of child sexual abuse', *Child Abuse and Neglect*, 16: 101–18.

Bendiksen, M. (1996) 'Circumstances and the phenomonology of a recovered memory: a corroborated case study'. Poster presented at the NATO Advanced Study Institute on 'Recollections of Trauma: Scientific Research and Clinical Practice', Port de Bourgenay, France, 15–25 June.

Bentovim, A., Elton, A., Hildebrand, J., Tranter, M. and Vizard, E. (1988) *Child Sexual Abuse within the Family: Assessment and Treatment*. London: Wright.

Berger, P. and Luckman, T. (1966) *The Social Construction of Reality*. New York: Doubleday.

Bergin, A.E. (1971) 'The evaluation of therapeutic outcomes', in S.L. Garfield and A.E. Bergin (eds), *Handbook of Psychotherapy and Behaviour Change: An Empirical Analysis*. New York: Wiley.

Bergin, A.E. and Garfield, S.L. (eds) (1994) *Handbook of Psychotherapy and Behaviour Change*, 4th edn. Chichester: Wiley.

Bergin, A.E. and Lambert, M.J. (1978) 'The evaluation of therapeutic outcomes', in S.L. Garfield and A.E. Bergin (eds), *Handbook of Psychotherapy and Behaviour Change: An Empirical Analysis*, 2nd edn. New York: Wiley.

Beutler, L.E. and Hill, C.E. (1992) 'Process and outcome research in the treatment of adult victims of childhood sexual abuse: methodological issues', *Journal of Consulting and Clinical Psychology*, 60 (2): 204–12.

Beutler, L.E. and Sandowicz, M. (1994) 'The counseling relationship: what is it?', *The Counseling Psychologist*, 22: 98–103.

Beutler, L.E., Machado, P.P.P. and Neufeldt, S. A. (1994) 'Therapist variables', in A.E. Bergin and S.L. Garfield, *Handbook of Psychotherapy and Behaviour Change*, 4th edn. New York: Wiley.

Bikel, O. (1995) Divided memories. USA: *Frontline TV Documentary*. USA: Public Service Broadcast.

Blake-White, J. and Kline, C.M. (1985) 'Treating the dissociative process in adult victims of childhood abuse', *Social Casework*, 66: 394–402.

Blume, E.S. (1990) *Secret Survivors: Uncovering Incest and its Aftereffects in Women*. New York: Ballantine.

Bogdan, R. and Taylor, S.J. (1975) *Introduction to Qualitative Research Methods*. New York: Wiley.

Bolton, F.G. Jr., Morris, L.A. and MacEachron, A.E. (1989) *Males at Risk: The Other Side of Child Sexual Abuse*. Newbury Park: Sage.

Bonney, W.C., Randall, D.A. and Cleveland, J.D. (1986) 'An analysis of client-perceived curative factors in a therapy group of former incest victims', *Small Group Behaviour*, 17 (3): 303–21.

Bordin, E.S. (1979) 'The generalizability of the psychoanalytic concept of the working alliance', *Psychotherapy: Theory, Research, and Practice*, 16: 252–60.

Bott, D. (1990) 'Epistemology: the place of systems theory in an integrated model of counselling', *Counselling, Journal of the British Association for Counselling*, 1 (1): 23–5.

Bowers, K.S. and Farvolden, P. (1996) 'Revisiting a century-old Freudian slip – from suggestion disavowed to the truth repressed', *Psychological Bulletin*, 119: 355–80.

Bowlby, J. (1969) *Attachment and Loss*. London: Penguin.

Bowlby, J. (1988) *A Secure Base: Clinical Applications of Attachment Theory*. London: Routledge.

Bowman, C.G. and Mertz, E. (1996) 'A dangerous direction: legal intervention in sexual abuse survivor therapy', *Harvard Law Review*, 109 (3): 551–639.

Brannen, J. (1988) 'The study of sensitive subjects', *Sociological Review*, 36: 552–63.

Brannen, J. and Collard, J. (1982) *Marriages in Trouble: The Process of Seeking Help.* London: Tavistock.

Brewin, C. (1997) 'Clinical and experimental approaches to understanding repression', in D. Read and S. Lindsay (eds), *Recollections of Trauma: Scientific Research and Clinical Practice.* New York: Plenum. pp. 145–63.

Brewin, C. and Andrews, B. (1997) 'Reasoning about repression: inferences from clinical and experimental data', in M. Conway (ed.), *Recovered Memories and False Memories.* Oxford: Oxford University Press.

Briere, J. (1989) *Therapy for Adults Molested as Children: Beyond Survival.* New York: Springer.

Briere, J. (1992) *Child Abuse Trauma: A Theory and Treatment of the Lasting Effects.* London: Sage.

Briere, J. (1997) 'An integrated approach to treating adults abused as children with specific reference to self-reported recovered memories', in D. Read and S. Lindsay (eds), *Recollections of Trauma: Scientific Research and Clinical Practice.* New York: Plenum. pp. 25–41.

Briere, J. and Conte, J. (1993) 'Self-reported amnesia for abuse in adults molested as children', *Journal of Traumatic Stress*, 6 (1): 21–32.

Briere, J. and Runtz, M. (1988) 'Symptomatology associated with childhood sexual victimisation in a nonclinical adult sample', *Child Abuse and Neglect*, 12 (1): 51–9.

British Psychological Society (1995) *Recovered Memories: The Report of the Working Party of the BPS.* London: BPS.

Browne, A. and Finklehor, D. (1986) 'Impact of child sexual abuse: a review of the research', *Psychological Bulletin*, 99: 66–77.

Brunning, H. (1992) 'Auditing one's work: what do clients think about therapy?', *Clinical Psychology Forum*, 40: 7–10.

Buber, M. (1987) *I and Thou.* Edinburgh: T. and T. Clarke.

Bulmer, R.M. (1979) 'Concepts in the analysis of qualitative data', *Sociological Review*, 27 (4): 651–77.

Butler, S.F. and Strupp, H.H. (1986) 'Specific and nonspecific factors in psychotherapy: a problematic paradigm for psychotherapy research', *Psychotherapy*, 23: 30–40.

Cahill, C., Llewelyn, S.P. and Pearson, C. (1991a) 'Long-term effects of sexual abuse which occurred in childhood: a review', *British Journal of Clinical Psychology*, 30: 117–30.

Cahill, C., Llewelyn, S.P. and Pearson, C. (1991b) 'Treatment of sexual abuse which occurred in childhood: a review', *British Journal of Clinical Psychology*, 30: 1–12.

Cameron, C. (1996) 'Comparing amnesic and nonamnesic survivors of childhood sexual abuse: a longitudinal study', in K. Pezdek and W. Banks (eds), *The Recovered Memory/False Memory Debate.* New York: Academic Press.

Campbell, J. (1988) 'Inside lives: the quality of biography', in R. Sherman and R. Webb (eds), *Qualitative Research in Education: Focus and Methods.* Barcombe: Falmer.

Canter, S. (1989) 'Consumer research', *Clinical Psychology Forum*, 24: 29–31.

Carroll, L. (1993 [1865]) *Alice's Adventures in Wonderland.* London: Chancellor Press.

Carstensen, L., Gabrieli, J., Shepard, R., Levenson, R., Mason, M., Goodman, G., Bootzin, R., Ceci, S., Bronfrenbrenner, U., Edelstein, B., Schober, M., Bruck, M., Keane, T., Zimering, R., Oltmanns, T., Gotlib, I. and Ekman, P. (1993) 'Repressed objectivity', *APS Observer*, March: 23.

Casement, P. (1985) *On Learning From the Patient.* London: Routledge.

Cashdan, S. (1988) *Object Relations Therapy: Using the Relationship*. New York: Norton.

Caskey, N., Barker, C. and Elliot, R. (1984) 'Dual perspectives: clients' and therapists' perceptions of therapist responses', *British Journal of Clinical Psychology*, 23: 281–90.

Ceci, S.J. and Bruck, M. (1993) 'Suggestibility of the child witness: a historical review', *Psychological Bulletin*, 113: 403–39.

Ceci, S.J. and Loftus, E.F. (1994) ' "Memory work": a royal road to false memories?', *Applied Cognitive Psychology*, 8 (4): 351–64.

Clarkson, P. (1984) 'Voice of experience', *ITA News*, 8: 1.

Clarkson, P. (1993) *On Psychotherapy*. London: Whurr Publishers.

Clarkson, P. (1995) *The Therapeutic Relationship*. London: Whurr Publishers.

Clarkson, P. and Pokorny, M. (1994) *The Handbook of Psychotherapy*. London: Routledge.

Cohler, B.J. (1994) 'Memory recovery and the use of the past: a commentary on Lindsay and Read from psychoanalytic perspectives', *Applied Cognitive Psychology*, 8 (4): 365–78.

Conway, M. (1997) 'Past and present: Recovered memories and false memories', in M.A. Conway (ed.), *Recovered Memories and False Memories*. Oxford: Oxford University Press.

Cornell, W.F. and Olio, M.A. (1991) 'Integrating affect in treatment with adult survivors of physical and sexual abuse', *American Journal of Orthopsychiatry*, 61 (1): 59–69.

Courtois, C. (1988) *Healing the Incest Wound: Adult Survivors in Therapy*. New York: Norton.

Courtois, C.A. (1992) 'The memory retrieval process in incest survivor therapy', *Journal of Child Sexual Abuse*, 1: 15–32.

Courtois, C.A. (1995) 'Scientist-practitioners and the delayed memory controversy: scientific standards and the need for collaboration', *The Counselling Psychologist*, 23: 294–9.

Courtois, C.A. (1997) 'Informed clinical practice and the standard of care: proposed guidelines for treatment of adults who report delayed memories of childhood trauma', in D. Read and S. Lindsay (eds), *Recollections of Trauma: Scientific Research and Clinical Practice*. New York: Plenum. pp. 337–61.

Crews, F. (1995) The Memory Wars: Freud's Legacy in Dispute. NY: New York Review.

Cronbach, L.J. (1975) 'Beyond the two disciplines of scientific psychology', *American Psychologist*, 30: 116–27.

Cross, D.G., Sheehan, P.W. and Khan, J.A. (1982) 'Short and long term follow up of clients receiving insight-oriented therapy and behaviour therapy', *Journal of Consulting and Clinical Psychology*, 50: 103–12.

Dale, P. (1991) 'Dangerous families revisited', *Community Care*, 14 November.

Dale, P. (1993) *Counselling Adults Who Were Abused as Children*. Rugby: BAC.

Dale, P. (1998) 'Protection or prevention? An integrated approach to services for children and parents'. Plenary address: Kids First: Protecting Children – Problems and Solutions, Melbourne Convention Centre, Melbourne, Australia, 2–3 April.

Dale, P. (1999) 'Multiple personality disorder: a sceptical perspective', in M. Walker and A. Black, *Hidden Selves: An Exploration of Multiple Personality*. Buckingham: Open University Press.

Dale, P. and Allen, J. (1998) 'On memories of childhood abuse: a phenomenological study', *Child abuse and Neglect*, 22 (8): 799–812.

Dale, P. and Davies, M. (1985) 'A model of intervention in child abusing families: a wider systems view', *Child Abuse and Neglect*, 9 (4): 16–21.

Dale, P., Allen, J. and Measor, L. (1998) 'Counselling adults who were abused as children: clients' perceptions of efficacy, client-counsellor communication and dissatisfaction', *British Journal of Guidance and Counselling*, 26 (2): 141–57.

Dale, P., Davies, M., Morrison, T. and Waters, J. (1986a) *Dangerous Families: Assessment and Treatment of Child Abuse*. London: Tavistock/Routledge.

Dale, P. and Fellows, R. (1997) Independent child protection assessments: Incorporating a therapeutic focus from an integrated service context. Paper presented at: NSPCC Child Protection Assessment Conference, 25–26 September 1997.

Dale, P. and Fellows, R. (in press) Independent child protection assessments: Incorporating a therapeutic focus from an integrated service context. *Child Abuse Review*.

Dale, P., Waters, J., Davies, M., Roberts, W. and Morrison, T. (1986b) 'The towers of silence: creative and destructive issues for therapeutic teams dealing with sexual abuse', *Journal of Family Therapy*, 8 (1): 1–25.

Dalenberg, C. (1996) 'Accuracy, timing and circumstances of disclosure in therapy of recovered and continuous memories of abuse', *Journal of Psychiatry and Law*, 24 (2): 229–75.

Dalenberg, C. (1997) 'The prediction of accurate recollections of trauma', in D. Read and S. Lindsay (eds), *Recollections of Trauma: Scientific Research and Clinical Practice*. New York: Plenum. pp. 449–54.

Darlington, Y. (1993) 'The experience of childhood sexual abuse: perspectives of adult women who were sexually abused in childhood'. PhD dissertation, University of Queensland.

Davies, J.M. and Frawley, M.G. (1994) *Treating the Adult Survivor of Childhood Sexual Abuse: A Psychoanalytic Perspective*. New York: Basic Books.

Davies, D. and Robertson, N. (1996) 'A recovered memory of a traumatic event: a single case study'. Poster presented at the NATO Advanced Study Institute on Recollections of Trauma: Scientific Research and Clinical Practice, Port de Bourgenay, France, 15–25 June.

Davis, J., Elliot, R., Davis, M., Binns, M., Francis, V., Kelman, J. and Schroder, T. (1987) 'Development of a taxonomy of therapist difficulties: initial report', *British Journal of Medical Psychology*, 60: 109–19.

Demause, L. (1991) 'The universality of incest', *Journal of Psychohistory*, 19 (2): 123–64.

Denzin, N.K. and Lincoln, Y.S. (eds) (1994) *Handbook of Qualitative Research*. London: Sage.

Department of Health and Social Security (DHSS) (1988) *Report of the Inquiry into Child Abuse in Cleveland 1987 (Cm412), The Butler-Sloss Report*. London: HMSO.

De Young, M. (1981) 'Case reports: the sexual exploitation of incest victims by helping professionals', *Victimology*, 1 (4): 91–101.

Dinnage, R. (1988) *One to One: Experiences of Psychotherapy*. Harmondsworth: Penguin.

Dinsmore, C. (1991) *From Surviving to Thriving: Incest, Feminism, and Recovery*. New York: Albany.

Doe, J. (1991) 'How could this happen? Coping with a false accusation of incest and rape', *Issues in Child Abuse Accusations*, 3 (3): 154–65.

Dominelli, L. (1989) 'Betrayal of trust: a feminist analysis of power relationships in incest abuse and its relevance for social work practice', *British Journal of Social Work*, 19 (4): 291–307.

Dryden, W. (1985) *Therapists' Dilemmas*. London: Harper and Row.

Dryden, W. (ed.) (1992) *Hard-earned Lessons from Counselling in Action*. London: Sage.

Dryden, W. (ed.) (1993) *Questions and Answers on Counselling in Action*. London: Sage.

Dryden, W. and Feltham, C. (1992) *Psychotherapy and Its Discontents*. Buckingham: Open University Press.

Dunnette, M.D. (1966) 'Fads, fashions, and folderol in psychology', *American Psychologist*, 21: 343–52.

Egeland, B. (1988) 'Breaking the cycle of abuse: implications for prediction and intervention', in K. Browne, C. Davies and P. Stratton, *Early Prediction and Prevention of Child Abuse*. Chichester: Wiley.

Eich, E. (1995) 'Searching for mood-dependent memory', *Psychological Science*, 6: 67–75.

Eisner, E.O. (1981) 'On the differences between scientific and artistic approaches to qualitative research', *Educational Researcher*, 10 (4): 5–9.

Ellenson, G.S. (1986) 'Disturbances of perception in adult female incest survivors', *Social Casework*, 67: 149–59.

Elliot, D.M. (1997) 'Traumatic events: prevalence and delayed recall in the general population', *Journal of Consulting and Clinical Psychology*, 65: 811–20.

Elliot, D.M. and Briere, J. (1995) 'Posttraumatic stress associated with delayed recall of sexual abuse: a general population study', *Journal of Traumatic Stress*, 8: 629–47.

Elliot, M. (ed.) (1993) *Female Sexual Abuse of Children: The Ultimate Taboo*. London: Longman.

Elliot, R. (1979) 'How clients perceive helper behaviours', *Journal of Counselling Psychology*, 26: 285–94.

Elliot, R. (1983) 'That in your hands: a comprehensive process analysis of a significant event in psychotherapy', *Psychiatry*, 46: 113–29.

Elliot, R. and James, E. (1989) 'Varieties of client experience in psychotherapy: an analysis of the literature', *Clinical Psychology Review*, 9: 443–67.

Elliot, R. and Shapiro, D.A. (1988) 'Brief structured recall: a more efficient method for identifying and describing significant therapy events', *British Journal of Medical Psychology*, 61: 141–53.

Elliot, R. and Shapiro, D.A. (1992) 'Client and therapist as analysts of significant events', in S.G. Toukmanian and D.L. Rennie, *Psychotherapy Process Research: Paradigmatic and Narrative Approaches*. London: Sage.

Erikson, E.H. (1950) *Childhood and Society*. New York: Norton.

Etherington, K. (1995) *Adult Male Survivors of Childhood Sexual Abuse*. London: Pitman.

Everhart, R. (1977) 'Between stranger and friend: some consequences of long term fieldwork in schools', *American Educational Review*, 56 (3): 257–77.

Eysenck, H.J. (1952) 'The effects of psychotherapy: an evaluation', *Journal of Consulting Psychology*, 16: 319–24.

Eysenck, H.J. (1965) 'The effects of psychotherapy', *International Journal of Psychology*, 1: 97–178.

Eysenck, H.J. (1992) 'The outcome problem in psychotherapy', in W. Dryden and C. Feltham, *Psychotherapy and its Discontents*. Buckingham: Open University Press.

Feifel, H. and Eells, J. (1963) 'Patients and therapists assess the same psychotherapy', *Journal of Consulting Psychology*, 27 (4): 310–18.

Feinauer, L.L. (1989) 'Relationship of treatment to adjustment in women sexually abused as children', *American Journal of Family Therapy*, 17 (4): 326–34.

Feldman-Summers, S. and Pope, K.S. (1994) 'The experience of "forgetting" childhood abuse: a national survey of psychologists', *Journal of Consulting and Clinical Psychology*, 62 (3): 636–9.

Femina, D.D., Yeager, C.A. and Lewis, D.O. (1990) 'Child abuse: adolescent records vs. adult recall', *Child Abuse and Neglect*, 14: 227–31.

Finch, J. (1984) ' "It's great to have someone to talk to": the ethics and politics of interviewing women', in C. Bell and H. Roberts (eds), *Social Researching: Politics, Problems, Practice*. London: Routledge and Kegan Paul.

Finklehor, D. (1979) *Sexually Victimised Children*. New York: Free Press.

Finklehor, D. (1984) *Child Sexual Abuse: New Theory and Research*. New York: Free Press.

Finklehor, D. (ed.) (1986) *A Sourcebook On Child Sexual Abuse*. Beverly Hills: Sage.

Finklehor, D. and Russell, D. (1984) 'Women as perpetrators', in D. Finklehor (ed.), *Child Sexual Abuse: New Theory and Research*. New York: Free Press.

Fitts, W. (1985) *The Experience of Psychotherapy: What it's Like for Client and Therapist*. New Jersey: Van Nostrand.

Fortgang, S. (1992) 'An investigation into practice: adult incest victims and psychoanalytic psychotherapy', *Smith College Studies in Social Work*, 62 (3): 265–81.

Forward, S. (1990) *Toxic Parents: Overcoming the Legacy of Parental Abuse*. London: Bantam Press.

France, A. (1988) *Consuming Psychotherapy*. London: Free Association Books.

Frankl, V. (1946/1992) *Man's Search for Meaning*. London: Hodder and Stoughton.

Fransella, F. and Dalton, P. (1990) *Personal Construct Counselling in Action*. London: Sage.

Frederickson, R. (1992) *Repressed Memories: A Journey To Recovery From Sexual Abuse*. New York: Simon and Schuster.

Frenken, J. and Van Stolk, B. (1990) 'Incest victims: inadequate help by professionals', *Child Abuse and Neglect*, 14 (2): 253–63.

Freyd, J. (1993) 'Personal perspectives on the delayed memory debate', *Treating Abuse Today*, 3 (5): 13–20.

Freyd, J. (1996) *Betrayal Trauma: The Logic of Forgetting Childhood Abuse*. Cambridge, MA: Harvard University Press.

Freyd, P. (1992) *FMSF Newsletter*, February.

Friedlander, M.L., Thibodeau, J.R. and Ward, L.G. (1985) 'Discriminating the "good" from the "bad" therapy hour: a study of dyadic interaction', *Psychotherapy*, 22: 631–42.

Fuller, F. and Hill, C.E. (1985) 'Counselor and client perceptions of counselor intentions in relationship to outcome in a single counseling session', *Journal of Counseling Psychology*, 32: 329–38.

Furniss, T. (1983) 'Mutual influence and interlocking professional-family process in the treatment of child sexual abuse and incest', *Child Abuse and Neglect*, 7: 207–23.

Ganaway, G.K. (1989) 'Historical versus narrative truth: clarifying the role of exogenous trauma in the etiology of MPD and its variants', *Dissociation*, 2 (4): 205–20.

Gardner, F. (1990) 'Psychotherapy with adult survivors of child sexual abuse', *British Journal of Psychotherapy*, 6 (3): 285–94.

Garfield, S. (1992) 'Response to Eysenck: the outcome problem in psychotherapy', in W. Dryden and C. Feltham, *Psychotherapy and its Discontents*. Buckingham: Open University Press.

Garfield, S.L. and Bergin, A.E. (1978) *Handbook of Psychotherapy and Behaviour Change: An Empirical Analysis*, 2nd edn. New York: Wiley.

Garfield, S.L. and Bergin, A.E. (1986) *Handbook of Psychotherapy and Behaviour Change: An Empirical Analysis*, 3rd edn. New York: Wiley.

Garrett, T. and Davis, J. (1994) 'Epidemiology in the U.K.', in D. Jehu, *Patients as Victims: Sexual Abuse in Psychotherapy and Counselling*. Chichester: Wiley.

Gelinas, D. (1983) 'Family therapy: characteristic family constellation and basic therapeutic stance', in S. Sgroi, *Vulnerable Populations*, vol. 1. Lexington: Lexington Books.

Gelso, C.J. (1979) 'Research in counseling: methodological and professional issues', *The Counseling Psychologist*, 4 (3): 7–36.

Gelso, C.J. and Carter, J.A. (1985) 'The relationship in counseling and psychotherapy', *Counseling Psychologist*, 13 (2): 155–243.

Gelso, C.J., Betz, N.E., Friedlander, M.L., Helms, J.E., Hill, C.E., Patton, M.J., Super, D.E. and Wampold, B.E. (1988) 'Research in counseling psychology: prospects and recommendations', *The Counseling Psychologist*, 16: 385–406.

Giarretto, H. (1982a) 'A comprehensive child sexual abuse treatment programme', *Child Abuse and Neglect*, 6 (3): 263–78.

Giarretto, H. (1982b) *Integrated Treatment of Child Sexual Abuse: A Treatment and Training Manual*. Palo Alto: Science and Behaviour Books.

Gil, E. (1988) *Treatment of Adult Survivors of Childhood Abuse*. Walnut Creek: Launch Press.

Glaser, B.G. and Strauss, A.L. (1967) *The Discovery of Grounded Theory*. Chicago: Aldine.

Goldberg, D. and Huxley, P. (1992) *Common Mental Disorders: A Bio-Social Model*. London: Tavistock/Routledge.

Goldstein, E. and Farmer, K. (1992) *Confabulations: Creating False Memories; Destroying Families*. Boca Raton, FL: SIRS Books.

Goodman, G.S., Qin, J., Bottoms, B.L. and Shaver, P.R. (1995) *Characteristics and Sources of Allegations of Ritualistic Child Abuse. Final Report to the National Center of Child Abuse and Neglect*, cited in A.A. Scheflin and D. Brown (1996) 'Repressed memory or dissociative amnesia: what the science says', *Journal of Psychiatry & Law*, 24: 143–88.

Goodyear-Smith, F. (1993) *First Do No Harm: The Child Sexual Abuse Industry*. Auckland: Benton-Guy Publishing.

Greenberg, L.S. (1986) 'Change process research', *Journal of Consulting and Clinical Psychology*, 54: 4–15.

Greenberg, L.S. and Pinsof, W.M. (1986) *The Psychotherapeutic Process: A Research Handbook*. New York: Guilford Press.

Grierson, M. (1990) 'A client's experience of success', in D. Mearns and W. Dryden, *Experiences of Counselling in Action*. London: Sage.

Grinfield, M.J. (1997) 'Psychiatrists liable for millions in civil suits', *Psychiatric Times*, December.

Grosskurth, P. (1991) *The Secret Ring: Freud's Inner Circle and the Politics of Psychoanalysis*. Reading, MA: Addison-Wesley.

Guba, E.G. and Lincoln, Y.S. (1994) 'Competing paradigms in qualitative research', in N.K. Denzin and Y.S. Lincoln, *Handbook of Qualitative Research*. Thousand Oaks: Sage.

Guy, J.D. (1987) *The Personal Life of the Psychotherapist*. New York: Wiley.

Haaken, J. and Schlaps, A. (1991) 'Incest resolution therapy and the objectification of sexual abuse', *Psychotherapy*, 28 (1): 39–47.

Haller, O. and Alter-Reid, K. (1986) 'Secretiveness and guardedness: a comparison of two incest survivor samples', *American Journal of Psychotherapy*, 4: 554–63.

Hammersley, M. (1992) 'On feminist methodology', *Sociology*, 26: 187–206.

Hammersley, M. and Atkinson, P. (1983) *Ethnography: Principles in Practice*. London: Tavistock.

Hanson, C. (1998) 'Dangerous therapy', *Chicago Magazine*, May.

Heinemann, S.H. and Yudin, L.W. (1974) 'The consumer as evaluator: perceptions and satisfaction levels of former clients', *Journal of Community Psychology*, 2 (1): 21–3.

Heppner, P.P., Kivlighan, D.M. Jr. and Wampold, B.E. (1992) *Research Design in Counselling*. Belmont: Brooks/Cole.

Herman, J. (1981) *Father–Daughter Incest*. Cambridge, MA: Harvard University Press.

Herman, J. and Schatzow, E. (1987) 'Recovery and verification of memories of childhood sexual trauma', *Psychoanalytic Psychology* 4: 1–14.

Highlen, P.S. and Hill, C.E. (1984) 'Factors affecting client change in individual counseling: current status and theoretical speculations', in S.D. Brown and R.W. Lent (eds), *Handbook of Counseling Psychology*. New York: Wiley.

Hill, C.E. (1982) 'Counseling process research: philosophical and methodological dilemmas', *The Counseling Psychologist*, 10 (4): 7–20.

Hill, C.E. (1984) 'A personal account of the process of becoming a counseling process researcher', *The Counseling Psychologist*, 12 (3): 99–109.

Hill, C.E. (1989) *Therapist Techniques and Client Outcomes*. Newbury Park: Sage.

Hill, C.E. (1994) 'What is the therapeutic relationship? A reaction to Sexton and Whiston', *The Counseling Psychologist*, 22: 90–7.

Hobson, R. (1985) *Forms of Feeling: The Heart of Psychotherapy*. London: Routledge.

Hoffman, L. (1981) *Foundations of Family Therapy*. New York: Basic Books.

Holmes, D.S. (1990) 'The evidence for repression: an examination of sixty years of research', in J.L. Singer (ed.), *Repression and Dissociation: Implications for Personality Theory, Psychopathology and Health*. Chicago: University of Chicago Press. pp. 85–102.

Holmes, J. (1993) *John Bowlby and Attachment Theory*. London: Routledge.

Hooper, C. A. (1992) *Mothers Surviving Child Sexual Abuse*. London: Routledge.

Horowitz, M.J. (1986) *Stress Response Syndromes*, 2nd edn. Northvale, NJ: Jason Aronson.

Hoshmand, L.L.S.T. (1989) 'Alternate research paradigms: a review and teaching proposal', *The Counseling Psychologist*, 17: 3–79.

Howe, D. (1989) *The Consumers' View of Family Therapy*. Aldershot: Gower.

Howe, D. (1993) *On Being a Client: Understanding the Process of Counselling and Psychotherapy*. London: Sage.

Howe, D. (1994) 'Modernity, postmodernity and social work', *British Journal of Social Work*, 24: 513–32.

Howitt, D. (1995) *Paedophiles and Sexual Offences Against Children*. Chichester: Wiley.

Humphreys, C. (1990) 'Disclosure of child sexual assault: mothers in crisis'. Unpublished PhD thesis, University of New South Wales.

Hunt, J.C. (1989) *Psychoanalytic Aspects of Fieldwork*. Newbury Park: Sage.

Hunt, P. (1985) *Clients' Responses to Marriage Counselling*. Rugby: National Marriage Guidance Council.

Hunter, M. (ed.) (1990) *The Sexually Abused Male: Vol. 1. Prevalence, Impact, and Treatment*. Lexington, MA: Lexington.

Janesick, V.J. (1994) 'The dance of qualitative research design', in N.K. Denzin and Y.S. Lincoln, *Handbook of Qualitative Research*. Thousand Oaks: Sage.

Janet, P. (1889) *L'Automatisme Psychologique*. Paris: Alcan.

Janoff-Bulman, R. (1985) 'The aftermath of victimization: rebuilding shattered assumptions', in C.R. Figley (ed.), *Trauma and its Wake: The Study and Treatment of Post-Traumatic Stress Disorder*. New York: Brunner/Mazel.

Janoff-Bulman, R. (1989) 'Assumptive worlds and the stress of traumatic events: applications of the schema construct', *Social Cognition*, 7: 113–36.

Jehu, D. (1988) *Beyond Sexual Abuse: Therapy with Women Who Were Childhood Victims*. Chichester: Wiley.

Jehu, D. (1994) *Patients As Victims: Sexual Abuse in Psychotherapy and Counselling*. Chichester: Wiley.

Josephson, G.S. and Fong-Beyette, M.L. (1987) 'Factors assisting female clients' disclosure of incest during counseling', *Journal of Counseling and Development*, 65: 475–8.

Kaschak, E. (1978) 'Therapist and client: two views of the process and outcome of psychotherapy', *Professional Psychology*, 9: 271–7.

Kaufman, J. and Zigler, E. (1987) 'Do abused children become abusive parents?', *American Journal of Orthopsychiatry*, 57 (2): 186–92.

Kelly, G.A. (1955) *The Psychology of Personal Constructs*. New York: Norton.

Kempe, C.H., Silverman, F.N., Steele, B.F., Droegemueller, W. and Silver, H.K. (1962) 'The battered child syndrome', *Journal of Marriage and the Family*, 18: 17–24.

Kendall-Tackett, K.A., Williams, L.M. and Finklehor, D. (1993) 'Impact of sexual abuse on children: a review and synthesis of recent empirical studies', *Psychological Bulletin*, 113 (1): 164–80.

Kenny, M.G. (1986) *The Passion of Ansel Bourne: Multiple Personality in American Culture*. Washington, DC: Smithsonian Institution Press.

Kenny, M.G. (1995) 'The recovered memory controversy: an anthropologist's view', *Journal of Psychiatry and Law*, 23 (3): 437–60.

Kenny, M.G. (1997) 'Trauma, memory, and catharsis', in D. Read and S. Lindsay (eds), *Recollections of Trauma: Scientific Research and Clinical Practice*. New York: Plenum. pp. 475–81.

Kiesler, D.J. (1973) *The Process of Psychotherapy*. Chicago: Aldine.

Kihlstrom, J.F. (1994) 'False memory syndrome', *FMS Foundation Brochure*. Philadelphia: False Memory Syndrome Foundation. p. 2.

Kihlstrom, J.F. (in press) 'Exhumed memory', in S.J. Lynn and N.P. Spanos (eds), *Truth in Memory*. New York: Guilford Press.

Kinsey, A.C., Pomeroy, W.F., Martin, C.E. and Gebhard, P.H. (1953) *Sexual Behaviour in the Human Female*. Philadelphia, PA: W.B. Saunders.

Kirk, J. and Miller, M.L. (1986) *Reliability and Validity in Qualitative Research*. Newbury Park: Sage.

Kline, P. (1992) 'Problems of methodology in studies of psychotherapy', in W. Dryden and C. Feltham, *Psychotherapy and its Discontents*. Buckingham: Open University Press.

Kluft, R.P. (1995) 'The confirmation and disconfirmation of memories of abuse in DID patients: a naturalistic clinical study', *Dissociation: Progress in the Dissociative Disorders*, 8: 253–8.

Knafl, K.A. and Howard, M.J. (1984) 'Interpreting and reporting qualitative research', *Research in Nursing and Health*, 7: 17–24.

Kopelman, M.D. (1997) 'Anomalies of autobiographical memory: retrograde amnesia, confabulation, delusional memory, psychogenic amnesia, and false memories', in D. Read and S. Lindsay (eds), *Recollections of Trauma: Scientific Research and Clinical Practice*. New York: Plenum. pp. 273–97.

Krumboltz, J.D. and Mitchell, L.K. (1979) 'Relevant rigorous research', *Counselling Psychologist*, 8 (3): 50–2.

Laing, R.D. (1967) *The Politics of Experience and the Bird of Paradise*. London: Penguin.

Lambert, M.J. and Bergin, A.E. (1992) 'Achievements and limitations of psychotherapy research', in D.K. Freedheim (ed.), *History of Psychotherapy: A Century of Change*. Washington, DC: American Psychological Association.

Lambert, M.J., Shapiro, D.A. and Bergin, A.E. (1986) 'The effectiveness of psychotherapy', in S.L. Garfield and A.E. Bergin (eds), *Handbook of Psychotherapy and Behaviour Change*, 3rd edn. New York: Wiley.

Laslett, B. and Rapoport, R. (1975) 'Collaborative interviewing and interactive research', *Journal of Marriage and the Family*, 37: 968–77.

Lather, P. (1986) 'Research as praxis', *Harvard Educational Review*, 56 (3): 257–77.

Layder, D. (1982) 'Grounded theory: a constructive critique', *Journal for the Theory of Social Behaviour*, 12: 103–23.

Lee, R.M. (1993) *Doing Research on Sensitive Topics*. London: Sage.

Lietaer, G. (1992) 'Helping and hindering processes in client-centered/experiential psychotherapy', in S.G. Toukmanian and D.L. Rennie, *Psychotherapy Process Research: Paradigmatic and Narrative Approaches*. London: Sage.

Lietaer, G. and Neirinck, M. (1987) 'Non-helping and hindering processes in experiential psychotherapy: a content analysis of post-session comments', in W. Huber (ed.), *Progress in Psychotherapy Research*. Louvain-la-Neuve: Presses Universitaires de Louvain.

Lincoln, Y.S. and Denzin, N.K. (1994) 'The fifth moment', in N.K. Denzin and Y.S. Lincoln, *Handbook of Qualitative Research*. Thousand Oaks: Sage.

Lincoln, Y.S. and Guba, E.G. (1985) *Naturalistic Inquiry*. Beverly Hills, CA: Sage.

Lindberg, F.H. and Distad, L.J. (1985) 'Post-traumatic stress disorder in women who experienced childhood incest', *Child Abuse and Neglect*, 9: 329–34.

Lindsay, D.S. and Briere, J. (1997) 'The controversy regarding recovered memories of childhood sexual abuse: pitfalls, bridges, and future directions', *Journal of Interpersonal Violence*, 12: 631–47.

Lindsay, D.S. and Read, J.D. (1994) 'Psychotherapy and memories of childhood sexual abuse: a cognitive perspective', *Applied Cognitive Psychology*, 8 (4): 281–338.

Lindsay, D.S. and Read, J.D. (1995) ' "Memory work" and recovered memories of childhood sexual abuse: scientific evidence and public, professional, and personal issues', *Psychology, Public Policy, and Law*, 1 (4): 846–908.

Lipkin, S. (1948) 'The client evaluates nondirective psychotherapy', *Journal of Consulting Psychology*, 12: 137–46.

Lishman, J. (1978) 'A clash in perspective? A study of worker and client perceptions of social work', *British Journal of Social Work*, 8 (3): 301–11.

Llewelyn, S. (1988) 'Psychological therapy as viewed by clients and therapists', *British Journal of Clinical Psychology*, 27: 223–37.

Llewelyn, S.P. and Hume, W.I. (1979) 'The patient's view of therapy', *British Journal of Medical Psychology*, 52: 29–35.

Loftus, E.F. (1993) 'The reality of repressed memories', *American Psychologist*, 48 (5): 518–37.

Loftus, E.F., Garry, M. and Feldman, J. (1994a) 'Forgetting sexual trauma: what does it mean when 38% forget?', *Journal of Consulting and Clinical Psychology*, 62: 1177–81.

Loftus, E.F., Polonsky, S. and Fullilove, M.T. (1994b) 'Memories of childhood sexual abuse: remembering and repressing', *Psychology of Women Quarterly*, 18: 67–84.

Lomas, P. (1987) *The Limits of Interpretation: What's Wrong With Psychoanalysis?* London: Pelican.

Lomas, P. (1994) *Cultivating Intuition: An Introduction To Psychotherapy*. Harmondsworth: Penguin.

Luborsky, L. and Spence, D. (1978) 'Quantitative research on psychoanalytic therapy', in S.L. Garfield and A.E. Bergin (eds), *Handbook of Psychotherapy and Behaviour Change*, 2nd edn. New York: Wiley.

Luborsky, L., Singer, B. and Luborsky, L. (1975) 'Comparative studies of psychotherapies: is it true that "everyone has won and all must have prizes"?', *Archives of General Psychiatry*, 32: 995–1008.

McCann, I.L. and Pearlman, L.A. (1990) *Psychological Trauma and the Adult Survivor: Theory, Therapy, and Transformation*. New York: Brunner/Mazel.

McCracken, G. (1988) *The Long Interview*. Newbury Park: Sage.

McElroy, L.P. and McElroy, R.A. (1991) 'Countertransference issues in the treatment of incest families', *Psychotherapy*, 28 (1): 48–54.

McGuire, W. (ed.) (1991) *The Freud/Jung Letters: The Correspondence Between Sigmund Freud and C.G. Jung*. London: Penguin.

McLeod, J. (1990) 'The client's experience of counselling and psychotherapy: a review of the research literature', in D. Mearns and W. Dryden (eds), *Experiences of Counselling in Action*. London: Sage.

McLeod, J. (1994) *Doing Counselling Research*. London: Sage.

MacLeod. M. and Saraga, E. (eds) (1988) *Child Sexual Abuse: Towards a Feminist Professional Practice*. London: PNL Press.

Mahrer, A.R. (1985) *Psychotherapeutic Change*. New York: Norton.

Mair, M. (1989) *Between Psychology and Psychotherapy: A Poetics of Experience*. London: Routledge.

Mair, K. (1992) 'The myth of therapist expertise', in W. Dryden and C. Feltham (eds), *Psychotherapy and its Discontents*. Buckingham: Open University Press.

Maltz, W. and Holman, B. (1987) *Incest and Sexuality: A Guide to Understanding and Healing*. Lexington: Lexington Books.

Maluccio, A.N. (1979) *Learning From Clients: Interpersonal Helping as Viewed by Clients and Social Workers*. New York: Free Press.

Masson, J. (1985) *The Assault on Truth*. Harmondsworth: Penguin.

Masson, J. (1988) *Against Therapy*. London: Fontana.

Masson, J. (1992) 'The tyranny of psychotherapy', in W. Dryden and C. Feltham, *Psychotherapy and its Discontents*. Buckingham: Open University Press.

Mayer, A. (1992) *Women Sex Offenders: Treatment and Dynamics*. Holmes Beach, FL: Learning Publications.

Mayer, J.E. and Timms, N. (1970) *The Client Speaks: Working Class Impressions of Casework*. London: Routledge and Kegan Paul.

Mearns, D. (1990) 'The counsellor's experience of failure', in D. Mearns and W. Dryden (eds), *Experiences of Counselling in Action*. London: Sage.

Mearns, D. and Dryden, W. (eds) (1990) *Experiences of Counselling in Action*. London: Sage.

Mearns, D. and McLeod, J. (1984) 'A person-centred approach to research', in R.F. Levant and J.M. Shlien, *Client Centred Therapy and the Person-Centred Approach*. New York: Praeger.

Meiselman, K.C. (1990) *Resolving the Trauma of Incest: Reintegration Therapy With Survivors*. San Francisco: Jossey Bass.

Mendel, M.P. (1995) *The Male Survivor: The Impact of Sexual Abuse*. Thousand Oaks: Sage.

Merrington, D. and Corden, J. (1981) 'Families' impressions of family therapy', *Journal of Family Therapy*, 3: 243–61.

Miles, M.B. and Huberman, A.M. (1984) *Qualitative Data Analysis: A Sourcebook of New Methods*. Newbury Park: Sage.

Miller, A. (1983) *For Your Own Good: The Roots of Violence in Child Rearing*. London: Faber and Faber.

Mostyn, B. (1985) 'The content analysis of qualitative research data: a dynamic approach', in M. Brenner, M. Brown and A.D. Carter (eds), *The Research Interview*. London: Academic Press.

Moustakas, C. (1990) *Heuristic Research: Design, Methodology, and Applications*. Newbury Park: Sage.

Mulhern, S. (1994) 'Satanism, ritual abuse and multiple personality: a socio-historical perspective', *International Journal of Clinical and Experimental Hypnosis*, 62 (4): 265–88.

Mulhern, S. (1997) 'Commentary on the logical status of case histories', in D. Read and S. Lindsay (eds), *Recollections of Trauma: Scientific Research and Clinical Practice*. New York: Plenum. pp. 126–42.

Neimeyer, G. and Resnikoff, A. (1982) 'Major contribution: qualitative strategies in counseling research', *Counseling Psychologist*, 10 (4): 75–85.

Neisser, U. (1988) 'The ecological approach to perception and memory', *New Trends in Experimental and Clinical Psychiatry*, 4 (3): 153–66.

Neisser, U. (1993) 'Memory with a grain of salt', invited address USA: False Memory Syndrome Foundation Conference.

Ney, T. (ed.) (1995) *True and False Allegations of Child Sexual Abuse: Assessment and Case Management*. New York: Brunner/Mazel.

Nin, A. (1993) *Incest: A Journal of Love: The Unexpurgated Diary of Anais Nin, 1932–1934*. London: Peter Owen.

Nissimov, R. (1998) 'Woman sues over false memories', *Houston Chronicle*, 20 April.

Noblitt, R. and Perskin, P. (1995) *Cult and Ritual Abuse: Its History, Anthropology, and Recent Discovery in Contemporary America*. Westport, CT: Praeger.

Oakley, A. (1981) 'Interviewing women: a contradiction in terms', in H. Roberts (ed.), *Doing Feminist Research*. London: Routledge.

O'Carroll, R.E. (1997) 'Commentary on relevance of neuroendocrine alterations in PTSD to memory-related impairments of trauma survivors', in D. Read and S. Lindsay (eds), *Recollections of Trauma: Scientific Research and Clinical Practice*. New York: Plenum. pp. 243–50.

Ochberg, F.M. (1991) 'Post-traumatic therapy', *Psychotherapy*, 28 (1): 5–15.

Ofshe, R. (1989) 'Coerced confessions: the logic of seemingly irrational action', *Cultic Studies Journal*, 6 (1): 1–15.

Ofshe, R. and Watters, E. (1994) *Making Monsters: False Memories, Psychotherapy, and Sexual Hysteria*. New York: Scribner's.

Olafson, E., Corwin, D.L. and Summit, R.C. (1993) 'Modern history of child sexual abuse awareness: cycles of discovery and suppression', *Child Abuse and Neglect*, 17: 7–24.

Oldfield, S. (1983) *The Counselling Relationship: A Study of the Client's Experience*. London: Routledge and Kegan Paul.

Olio, K.A. (1989) 'Memory retrieval in the treatment of adult survivors of sexual abuse', *Transactional Analysis Journal*, 19 (2): 93–100.

Oliver, J.E. (1993) 'Intergenerational transmission of child abuse: rates, research, and clinical implications', *American Journal of Psychiatry*, 150 (9): 1315–24.

Orlinsky, D.E. and Howard, K.I. (1977) 'The therapists experience of psychotherapy', in A.S. Gurman and A.M. Razin, *Effective Psychotherapy: A Handbook of Research*. Oxford: Pergamon Press.

Orlinsky, D.E. and Howard, K.I. (1986) 'Process and outcome in psychotherapy', in S.L. Garfield and A.E. Bergin, *Handbook of Psychotherapy and Behaviour Change: An Empirical Analysis*, 3rd edn. New York: Wiley.

Orlinsky, D.E., Grawe, K. and Parks, B.K. (1994) 'Process and outcome in psychotherapy – noch einmal' in A.E. Bergin and S.L. Garfield, *Handbook of Psychotherapy and Behaviour Change*, 4th edn. New York: Wiley.

Park, J. (1992) *Shrinks: The Analysts Analysed*. London: Bloomsbury.

Parkes, P. (1990) *Rescuing the 'Inner Child': Therapy for Adults Sexually Abused as Children*. London: Souvenir Press.

Parloff, M.B., Waskow, I.E. and Wolfe, B.E. (1978) 'Research on therapist variables in relation to process and outcome', in S.L. Garfield and A.E. Bergin, *Handbook of Psychotherapy and Behaviour Change*, 2nd edn. New York: Wiley. pp. 232–82.

Parton, C. (1990) 'Women, gender oppression and child abuse', in The Violence Against Children Study Group, *Taking Child Abuse Seriously*. London: Unwin Hyman.

Parton, N. (1985) *The Politics of Child Abuse*. London: Macmillan.

Patton, M.J. (1991) 'The qualitative approach to research on college students: some methodological considerations', *Journal of College Student Development*, 32: 389–96.

Patton, M.Q. (1990) *Qualitative Evaluation and Research Methods*, 2nd edn. Newbury Park: Sage.

Pendergrast, M. (1995) *Victims of Memory: Sex Abuse Accusations and Shattered Lives*. Vermont: Upper Access.

Persons, R.W., Persons, M.K. and Newmark, I. (1974) 'Perceived helpful therapists' characteristics, client improvements and sex of therapist and client', *Psychotherapy: Theory, Research and Practice*, 11: 63–5.

Peters, S.D., Wyatt, G.E. and Finklehor, D. (1986) 'Prevalence', in D. Finklehor (ed.), *A Sourcebook on Child Sexual Abuse*. Beverly Hills, CA: Sage. pp. 15–59.

Pezdek, K. and Banks, W.P. (eds) (1996) *The Recovered Memory/False Memory Debate*. San Diego: Academic Press.

Piper, A. Jr. (1997) *Hoax and Reality: The Bizarre World of Multiple Personality Disorder*. Northvale, NJ: Jason Aronson.

Polusny, M.A. and Follette, V.M. (1996) 'Remembering childhood sexual abuse: a national survey of psychologists' clinical practices, beliefs, and personal experiences', *Professional Psychology: Research and Practice*, 27 (1): 41–52.

Poole, D.A., Lindsay, D.S., Memon, A. and Bull, R. (1995) 'Psychotherapy and the recovery of memories of childhood sexual abuse: U.S. and British practitioners' opinions, practices, and experiences', *Journal of Consulting and Clinical Psychology*, 63 (3): 426–37.

Pope, K.S. (1996) 'Memory, abuse, and science: questioning claims about the false memory syndrome epidemic', *American Psychologist*, 51 (9): 957–74.

Pope, K. and Bouhoutsos, J. (1986) *Sexual Intimacy Between Therapists and Patients*. New York: Praeger.

Pope, K.S. and Brown, L.S. (1996) *Recovered Memories of Abuse: Assessment, Therapy, Forensics*. Washington, DC: American Psychological Association.

Pope. H.G. and Hudson, J.I. (1995) 'Can memories of childhood sexual abuse be repressed?', *Psychological Medicine*, 25: 121–6.

Pope, K.S. and Tabachnick, B.G. (1995) 'Recovered memories of abuse among therapy patients: a national survey', *Ethics and Behaviour*, 5 (3): 237–48.

Pope, K.S., Tabachnick, B.G. and Keith-Soiegal, P. (1987) 'Ethics of practice: the beliefs and behaviours of psychologists as therapists', *American Psychologist*, 42: 993–1006.

Powell, R.A. and Boer, D.P. (1994) 'Did Freud mislead patients to confabulate memories of abuse?' *Psychological Reports*, 74: 1283–98.

Read, J.D. and Lindsay, D.S. (1997) *Recollections of Trauma: Scientific Research and Clinical Practice*. New York: Plenum Press.

Reder, P., Duncan, S. and Gray, M. (1993) *Beyond Blame: Child Abuse Tragedies Revisited*. London: Routledge.

Rennie, D.L. (1992) 'Qualitative analysis of the client's experience of psychotherapy: the unfolding of reflexivity', in S.G. Toukmanian and D.L. Rennie, *Psychotherapy Process Research: Paradigmatic and Narrative Approaches*. London: Sage.

Rennie, D.L. (1994a) 'Clients' deference in psychotherapy', *Journal of Counselling Psychology*, 41 (4): 427–37.

Rennie, D.L. (1994b) 'Human science and counselling psychology: closing the gap between research and practice', *Counselling Psychology Quarterly*, 7 (3): 235–50.

Rennie, D.L. and Toukmanian, S.G. (1992) 'Explanation in psychotherapy process research', in S.G. Toukmanian and D.L. Rennie, *Psychotherapy Process Research: Paradigmatic and Narrative Approaches*. London: Sage.

Rennie, D.L., Phillips, J.R. and Quarto, G.K. (1988) 'Grounded theory: a promising approach to conceptualisation in psychology?', *Canadian Psychology/Psychologie Canadienne*, 29: 139–50.

Renzetti, C.M. and Lee, R.M. (1993) *Researching Sensitive Topics*. Newbury Park, CA: Sage.

Rice, L.N. (1992) 'From naturalistic observation of psychotherapy process to micro theories of change', in S.G. Toukmanian and D.L. Rennie, *Psychotherapy Process Research: Paradigmatic and Narrative Approaches*. London: Sage.

Riley, J. (1990) *Getting the Most From Your Data: A Handbook of Practical Ideas on How to Analyse Qualitative Data*. Bristol: Technical and Educational Services.

Rippere, V. and Williams, R. (1985) *Wounded Healers: Mental Health Workers' Experiences of Depression*. Chichester: Wiley.

Robbins, S. (1995) 'Wading through the muddy waters of recovered memories', *Journal of Contemporary Human Services*, 76 (8): 478–89.

Roe, C.M. and Schwartz, M.F. (1996) 'Characteristics of previously forgotten memories of sexual abuse: a descriptive study', *The Journal of Psychiatry and Law*, 24 (2): 189–206.

Rogers, C.R. (1957) 'The necessary and sufficient conditions of therapeutic personality change', *Journal of Consulting Psychology*, 21: 95–103.

Rose, D.S. (1991) 'A model for psychodynamic psychotherapy with the rape victim', *Psychotherapy*, 28 (1): 85–95.

Ross, C. (1989) *Multiple Personality Disorder: Diagnosis, Clinical Features and Treatment*. New York: Wiley.

Rowan, J. (1983) *The Reality Game*. London: Routledge.

Rowan, J. (1992) 'Response to Mair, K.: "The myth of therapist expertise" ', in W. Dryden and C. Feltham (eds), *Psychotherapy and its Discontents*. Buckingham: Open University Press.

Royal College of Psychiatrists (1997) 'Reported recovered memories of child sexual abuse: recommendations for good practice and implications for training, continuing professional development and research', *Pyschiatric Bulletin*, 21: 663–5.

Russell, D.E.H. (1983) 'The incidence and prevalence of intrafamilial and extra-familial sexual abuse of female children', *Child Abuse and Neglect*, 7: 133–46.

Russell, D.E.H. (1986) *The Secret Trauma: Incest in the Lives of Girls and Women*. New York: Basic Books.

Russell, J. (1993) *Out of Bounds: Sexual Exploitation in Counselling and Therapy*. London: Sage.

Rutter, P. (1991) *Sex in the Forbidden Zone*. London: Mandala Books.

Ryan, V.L. and Gizynski, M.N. (1971) 'Behaviour therapy in retrospect: patients' feelings about their behaviour therapies', *Journal of Consulting and Clinical Psychology*, 37: 581–8.

Sainsbury, E. (1975) *Social Work with Families: Perceptions of Social Casework Among Clients of a Family Service Unit*. London: Routledge.

Sainsbury, E. (1987) 'Client studies: their contribution and limitations in influencing social work practice', *British Journal of Social Work*, 17: 635–44.

Sainsbury, E., Nixon, S. and Phillips, D. (1982) *Social Work in Focus*. London: Routledge.

Salter, A. (1995) *Transforming Trauma: A Guide to Understanding and Treating Adult Survivors of Child Sexual Abuse*. Thousand Oaks: Sage.

Sandelowski, M. (1986) 'The problem of rigor in qualitative research', *Advances in Nursing Science*, 8 (3): 27–37.

Sanderson, C. (1990) *Counselling Adult Survivors of Child Sexual Abuse*. London: Jessica Kingsley.

Sanford, L. (1991) *Strong at the Broken Places: Overcoming the Trauma of Childhood Abuse*. London: Virago.

Scheflin, A.A. and Brown, D. (1996) 'Repressed memory or dissociative amnesia: what the science says', *Journal of Psychiatry and Law*, 24: 143–88.

Schein, E.H. (1987) *The Clinical Perspective in Fieldwork*. Newbury Park: Sage.

Schofield, W. (1964) *Psychotherapy: The Purchase of Friendship*. New Jersey: Prentice Hall.

Schooler, J.W. (1994) 'Seeking the core: the issues and evidence surrounding recovered accounts of sexual trauma', *Consciousness and Cognition*, 3: 452–69.

Schooler, J.W., Bendiksen, M. and Ambadar, Z. (1997) 'Taking the middle line: can we accommodate both fabricated and recovered memories of sexual abuse?', in M.A. Conway (ed.), *Recovered Memories and False Memories*. Oxford: Oxford University Press. pp. 251–92.

Sexton, T.L. and Whiston, S.C. (1994) 'The status of the counseling relationship: an empirical review, theoretical implications, and research directions', *Counseling Psychologist*, 22: 6–78.

Sgroi, S.M. (1982) *Handbook of Clinical Intervention in Child Sexual Abuse*. Lexington: Lexington Books.

Shaffir, W.B. and Stebbins, R.A. (eds) (1991) *Experiencing Fieldwork: An Inside View of Qualitative Research*. Newbury Park: Sage.

Shapiro, D.A. and Firth, J. (1987) 'Prescriptive vs. exploratory psychotherapy: outcomes of the Sheffield Psychotherapy Project', *British Journal of Psychiatry*, 151: 790–9.

Shapiro, D.A. and Shapiro, D. (1982) 'Meta-analysis of comparative therapy outcome studies: a replication and refinement', *Psychological Bulletin*, 92: 581–604.

Shaw, I. (1984) 'Literature review: consumer evaluations of the personal social services', *British Journal of Social Work*, 14 (3): 277–84.

Sheingold, K. and Tenney, Y.J. (1982) 'Memory for a salient childhood event', in U. Neisser (ed.), *Memory Observed: Remembering in Natural Contexts*. San Francisco: Freeman. pp. 201–12.

Silver, R.L., Boon, C. and Stones, M.H. (1983) 'Searching for meaning in misfortune: making sense of incest', *Journal of Social Issues*, 39: 81–102.

Sloane, R.B., Staples, F.R., Whipple, K. and Cristol, A.H. (1977) 'Patients' attitudes toward behaviour therapy and psychotherapy', *American Journal of Psychiatry*, 134: 134–7.

Smith, M.L., Glass, G.V. and Miller, T.L. (1980) *The Benefits of Psychotherapy*. Baltimore: Johns Hopkins University Press.

Spanos, N.P. (1996) *Multiple Identities and False Memories*. Washington, DC: American Psychological Association.

Speed, B. (1991) 'Reality exists OK? An argument against constructionism and social constructionism', *Journal of Family Therapy*, 13: 395–410.

Spence, D.P. (1984) *Narrative Truth and Historical Truth*. New York: Norton.

Spiegel, H. (1974) 'The grade 5 syndrome: the highly hypnotizable person', *International Journal of Clinical and Experimental Hypnosis*, 22: 303–19.

Spinelli, E. (1989) *The Interpreted World: An Introduction to Phenomenological Psychology*. London: Sage.

Spinelli, E. (1994) *Demystifying Therapy*. London: Constable.

Spradley, J. (1989) *The Ethnographic Interview*. New York: Holt, Rinehart and Winston.

Spring, J. (1987) *Cry Hard and Swim: The Story of an Incest Survivor*. London: Virago.

Steele, B. and Pollack, C. (1968) 'A psychiatric study of parents who abuse infants and small children', in R. Helfer and C.H. Kempe (eds), *The Battered Child Syndrome*. Chicago: University of Chicago Press.

Stiles, W.B. (1988) 'Psychotherapy process-outcome correlations may be misleading', *Psychotherapy*, 25: 27–35.

Stiles, W.B. (1993) 'Quality control in qualitative research', *Clinical Psychology Review*, 13: 593–618.

Stiles, W.B. (1995) 'In what sense does outcome depend on process?', *Changes*, 13 (3): 219–24.

Storr, A. (1979) *The Art of Psychotherapy*. London: Secker and Warburg.

Strauss, A. and Corbin, J. (1990) *Basics of Qualitative Research: Grounded Theory Procedures and Techniques*. Newbury Park: Sage.

Stricker, G. and Fisher, M. (eds) (1990) *Self-Disclosure in the Therapeutic Relationship*. New York: Plenum Press.

Strupp, H., Fox, R.E. and Lessler, K. (1969) *Patients View Their Psychotherapy*. Baltimore: Johns Hopkins University Press.

Strupp, H., Wallach, M. and Wogan, M. (1964) 'Psychotherapy experience in retrospect: questionnaire survey of former patients and their therapists', *Psychological Monographs: General and Applied*, 78 (11): 1–45.

Summit, R.C. (1988) 'Hidden victims, hidden pain: society's avoidance of child sexual abuse', in G.E. Wyatt and G.J. Powell (eds), *Lasting Effects of Child Sexual Abuse*. Newbury Park: Sage.

Terr, L.C. (1991) 'Childhood traumas: an outline and overview', *American Journal of Psychiatry*, 148: 10–20.

Terr, L.C. (1994) *Unchained Memories: True Stories of Traumatic Memories, Lost and Found*. New York: Basic Books.

Tesch, R. (1990) *Qualitative Research: Analysis Types and Software Tools*. Basingstoke: Falmer.

Timms, N. and Blampied, A. (1985) *Intervention in Marriage: The Experience of Counsellors and Their Clients*. University of Sheffield: Joint Unit for Social Services Research.

Thompson, B.J. and Hill, C.E. (1991) 'Therapist perceptions of client reactions', *Journal of Counseling and Development*, 69: 261–5.

Truax, C.B. and Carkhuff, R.R. (1967) *Toward Effective Counseling and Psychotherapy: Training and Practice*. Chicago: Aldine.

Tucci, J. (1995) 'Dangerous Families and beyond: an interview with Peter Dale', *Children Australia*, 20 (2): 32–5.

Tulving, E. and Thompson, D.M. (1973) 'Encoding specificity and retrieval processes in episodic memory: overview and exploratory study', *Journal of Traumatic Stress*, 8: 505–25.

Tyson, K.B. (1992) 'A new approach to relevant scientific research for practitioners: the heuristic paradigm', *Journal of Social Work*, 37 (6): 541–56.

Tzeng, O.C.S., Jackson, J.W. and Karlson, H.C. (1991) *Theories of Child Abuse and Neglect*. New York: Praeger.

Ussher, J.M. and Dewberry, C. (1995) 'The nature and long-term effects of childhood sexual abuse: a survey of adult women survivors in Britain', *British Journal of Clinical Psychology*, 34 (2): 177–92.

van der Kolk, B.A. (1994) 'The body keeps the score: memory and the evolving psychobiology of post-traumatic stress', *Harvard Review of Psychiatry*, 1: 253–65.

van der Kolk, B.A. and Fisler, R. (1995) 'Dissociation and the fragmentary nature of traumatic memories: overview and exploratory study', *Journal of Traumatic Stress*, 8: 505–25.

van der Kolk, B.A. and van der Hart, O. (1991) 'The intrusive past: the flexibility of memory and the engraving of trauma', *American Imago*, 48: 425–54.

van Deurzen-Smith, E. (1988) *Existential Counselling in Action*. London: Sage.

van Deurzen-Smith, E. (1996) 'An existential framework', in S. Palmer, S. Dainow and P. Milner (eds), *Counselling: The BAC Counselling Reader*. London: Sage.

Wakefield, H. and Underwager, R. (1992) 'Recovered memories of alleged sexual abuse: lawsuits against parents', *Behavioural Sciences and the Law*, 10: 483–507.

Walker, M. (1992) *Surviving Secrets*. Milton Keynes: Open University Press.

Wassil-Grimm, C. (1995) *Diagnosis for Disaster: The Devastating Truth about False*

Memory Syndrome and its Impact on Accusers and Families. Woodstock, NY: Overlook.

Webster, R. (1995) *Why Freud Was Wrong: Sin, Science and Psychoanalysis.* London: HarperCollins.

Weinberg, K. (1955) *Incest Behaviour.* New York: Citadel Press.

Weiskrantz, L. (1995) 'Comments on the report of the working party of the British Psychological Society on "recovered memories" ', *The Therapist,* Winter: 5–8.

Welldon, E.V. (1988) *Mother, Madonna, Whore: The Idealization and Denigration of Motherhood.* London: Free Association Books.

Werman, D.S., Agle, D., McDaniel, E. and Schoof, K.G. (1976) 'Survey of psychiatric treatment effectiveness in a medical student clinic', *American Journal of Psychotherapy,* 30 (2): 294–302.

Westcott, H. (1993) *Abuse of Children and Adults with Disabilities.* London: NSPCC.

White, M. and Epston, D. (1989) *Literate Means to Therapeutic Ends.* Adelaide: Dulwich Centre Publications.

Widom, C.S. and Shepard, R.L. (1996) 'Accuracy of adult recollections of childhood victimization: Part 1. Childhood physical abuse', *Psychological Assessment,* 8 (4): 412–21.

Williams, L.M. (1994) 'Recall of childhood trauma: a prospective study of women's memories of child sexual abuse', *Journal of Consulting and Clinical Psychology,* 62 (6): 1167–76.

Winnicott, D. (1965) *The Maturational Process and the Facilitating Environment.* London: Hogarth.

Wiseman, H. (1992) 'Conceptually-based interpersonal process recall (IPR) of change events: what clients tell us about our micro theory of change', in S.G. Toukmanian and D.L. Rennie, *Psychotherapy Process Research: Paradigmatic and Narrative Approaches.* London: Sage.

Wolff, L. (1988) *Postcards from the End of the World: Child Abuse in Freud's Vienna.* New York: Athenaum.

Woods, S.C. and Dean, K.S. (1984) *Final Report: Sexual Abuse of Males Research Project.* Washington, DC: National Centre on Child Abuse and Neglect.

Yalom, I.D. (1989) *Love's Executioner and Other Tales of Psychotherapy.* Harmondsworth: Penguin.

Yapko, M. (1993) 'Suggestibility and repressed memories of abuse: a survey of psychotherapist's beliefs', *American Journal of Clinical Hypnosis,* 36 (3): 163–71.

Yehuda, R. and Harvey, P. (1997) 'Relevance of neuroendocrine alterations in PTSD to memory-related impairments of trauma survivors', in D. Read and S. Lindsay (eds), *Recollections of Trauma: Scientific Research and Clinical Practice.* New York: Plenum. pp. 221–42.

Index